DEVELOPING WORD RECOGNITION

The Essential Library of PreK–2 Literacy

Sharon Walpole and Michael C. McKenna, *Series Editors*

www.guilford.com/PK2

Supporting the literacy development of our youngest students plays a crucial role in predicting later academic achievement. Grounded in research and theory, this series provides a core collection of practical, accessible resources for every teacher, administrator, and staff developer in the early grades. Books in the series contain a wealth of lesson plans, case examples, assessment guidelines, and links to the Common Core State Standards. Issues specific to each grade—and the essential teaching and learning connections between grades—are discussed. Reproducible materials in each volume are available online for purchasers to download and print in a convenient 8½″ × 11″ size.

**Reading Intervention in the Primary Grades:
A Common-Sense Guide to RTI**
Heidi Anne E. Mesmer, Eric Mesmer, and Jennifer Jones

Developing Word Recognition
Latisha Hayes and Kevin Flanigan

Developing Vocabulary and Oral Language in Young Children
Rebecca D. Silverman and Anna G. Meyer

Developing Word Recognition

Latisha Hayes
Kevin Flanigan

Series Editors' Note by
Sharon Walpole and Michael C. McKenna

THE GUILFORD PRESS
New York   London

© 2014 The Guilford Press
A Division of Guilford Publications, Inc.
72 Spring Street, New York, NY 10012
www.guilford.com

Printed in the United States of America

This book is printed on acid-free paper.

Last digit is print number: 9 8 7 6 5 4 3 2 1

Library of Congress Cataloging-in-Publication Data

Hayes, Latisha.
  Developing word recognition / Latisha Hayes, Kevin Flanigan.
    pages cm.—(The essential library of PreK-2 literacy)
  Includes bibliographical references and index.
  ISBN 978-1-4625-1415-1 (paperback)—ISBN 978-1-4625-1577-6 (cloth)
  1. Word recognition. I. Flanigan, Kevin. II. Title.
  LB1050.44.H39 2014
  372.46'2—dc23

                                            2014010774

To Patrick, Preston, and Bella
—L. H.

To Karin, Jack, Grace, and Clare
—K. F.

About the Authors

Latisha Hayes, PhD, is Clinical Assistant Professor in the Department of Curriculum, Instruction, and Special Education at the University of Virginia, where she teaches courses on the diagnosis and remediation of reading difficulties. She also works with preservice and inservice teachers at the McGuffey Reading Center, which provides students across the grades with diagnostic and tutoring services. As a special educator and reading specialist, Dr. Hayes has taught students with reading disabilities in the primary through middle grades. Her interests have focused on supporting struggling readers through university-based programs and partnerships.

Kevin Flanigan, PhD, is Professor in the Literacy Department at West Chester University of Pennsylvania (WCU). He works in the WCU Reading Center along with master's students to assess and teach children who struggle to read and write. A former middle-grades classroom teacher and reading specialist/coach, Dr. Flanigan researches and writes about developmental word knowledge and struggling readers.

Series Editors' Note

While the specifics of the debate about how to ensure children's success in school change over time, one idea seems to endure: Ensuring children's academic success is essential to the health of our society. The question, of course, is how. An old metaphor likens literacy to a house. In order to be strong and safe, it must be built on a solid foundation. Our youngest students, including children most at risk, rely on their teachers to provide entry into their own literacy structures so that they can set and realize their goals.

It is no coincidence that the Common Core State Standards (CCSS, 2010) use the term *foundational* to describe the basic skills that are the cornerstones of strong literacy. Without these basic skills, there would be no house to enter. It is the task of teachers in schools to ensure that these building blocks are in place—day by day and grade by grade.

The foundational skills of word recognition, and phonics in particular, are targeted in the CCSS and are the focus of this book. Remember that foundational skills are a means to an end; we build these skills so that children can do the complex reading and writing that are necessary to expand their knowledge. Because the CCSS set aggressive goals from the first years of schooling through high school, it is now more important than ever that teachers develop a sophisticated understanding of how research on word knowledge development should direct instructional decisions. This teacher knowledge is necessary to support early readers who should leave the early primary grades with the skills and dispositions that they will need for success with texts of increasing variety and complexity.

What is unique about this book is the authors' stance that decoding and spelling skills stand at opposite ends of a word knowledge zone in terms of complexity, with decoding skills establishing a "front end" and spelling skills a "back end." Their common-sense (and evidence-rich) approach makes it possible for teachers to keep sight of both decoding and spelling, without sacrificing any attention to real reading and writing. In fact, real reading and writing are required in their approach. They direct teachers to be organized and strategic, guaranteeing that children will read, write, and manipulate words and transfer their word knowledge to context.

Latisha Hayes and Kevin Flanigan are the ideal authors for this book. Both are wordsmiths. More than that, though, both are advocates for children. They make development transparent and instruction accountable. You will discover that they know young children well. They take the time to contextualize word learning experiences in activities and games that mask their laser focus on essential skills building. They recognize the power of children's interactions and the magic of an engaged classroom. Last, they anticipate the diversity that every early primary teacher will face on the first day of school. Differentiation is the way they do business.

This is a book you will revisit. As you see these foundational concepts at work with students, your understanding will deepen. You will get to know and trust these authors by putting them to the test in your classroom. We hope that you will read this book with your colleagues, comparing your informal assessment data, sharing the work of creating materials and lesson plans, and engaging in frank discussions of the extent to which your instructional choices result in strong development for your children. We think you'll find that this book will make a difference. We suspect it will cause you to see yourself not only as a teacher but as an architect, helping children build a foundation solid enough to ensure that their literacy structures will have many windows that open onto the world.

SHARON WALPOLE, PhD
MICHAEL C. MCKENNA, PhD

Preface

The ability to recognize words quickly and accurately is essential to reading. Children who can process words efficiently can devote more attention to the meaning of a story. Children who cannot process words efficiently and must laboriously sound out words will have few attentional resources left to focus on a story's meaning. The most effective literacy teachers differentiate instruction according to their students' needs. This book provides you with assessment tools to help you pinpoint where to begin instruction and implement activities to help your students develop their word recognition skills. Essentially, we have provided you with an "instructional road map."

In Chapter 1, we introduce the foundational word knowledge concepts that lay the groundwork for the rest of this book and that will be discussed again and again as you continue reading. Most important, these concepts serve as the overarching strands that tie the remaining chapters together. The core concepts include (1) teaching developmentally; (2) doing word work at both ends of the word knowledge zone; (3) directly and explicitly teaching high-utility patterns appropriate for each stage of development; (4) using a "toolkit approach" in which the activities you choose match your instructional purposes and your students' needs; and (5) contextualizing word knowledge instruction within the framework of a balanced, comprehensive approach to literacy instruction. In each of the successive chapters, we explain what these concepts look like in the real world of your classroom and at each stage of development.

After reading Chapter 1, the next step is to administer the Tiered Spelling Inventory in Chapter 2 to your children. This chapter leads you through the process of scoring and analyzing the results of this assessment with your students. Importantly, this chapter also helps you determine the different stages of your children's word knowledge development and directs you to the relevant stage chapters for instruction. In other words, Chapter 2 serves as a "switching station," guiding you to the chapters most relevant to the needs of your students.

Chapters 3–8 are the *stage* chapters, with two chapters devoted to each developmental stage: emergent, beginner, and transitional. In the first chapter for each stage, we describe the reading and writing/spelling characteristics of children at that level and identify the key features of study—including phonics, spelling patterns, and decoding strategies—for that stage. This chapter also provides guidelines for a comprehensive literacy "diet" as well as ideas for scheduling word knowledge instruction. At the end of these introductory stage chapters, we include ways to monitor your children's progress within each stage and alert you to when your students are ready to move to the next stage. In the second chapter for each stage, our *toolkit* chapters, we outline effective activities and strategies specifically targeted for the knowledge and skills students need to learn at that stage of development.

A companion website (*www.guilford.com/hayes4-forms*) that accompanies this book provides two useful appendices. Appendix A contains the reproducible assessment materials you will need for both student recording and scoring, as described in Chapter 2. Appendix B contains the Toolkit Activities corresponding to each of the stage chapters. All materials in these appendices can be downloaded and printed as 8½″ × 11″ forms and handouts for use in your classroom.

Acknowledgments

We begin by thanking Series Editors Sharon Walpole and Michael C. McKenna for inviting us to write this book and for their invaluable guidance and feedback throughout the process. Much appreciation also goes to Craig Thomas, Mary Beth Anderson, and Louise Farkas at The Guilford Press. We would also like to thank our teachers, students, and colleagues who have taught us so much, with special thanks to Mary Abouzeid, Donald Bear, Kristin Gehsmann, Laurie Nelson Gill, Tom Gill, Lori Helman, Marcia Invernizzi, Francine Johnston, Darrell Morris, and Shane Templeton. Last, this book is inspired by the children we work with every day in our reading centers.

Contents

1. An Introduction to Word Recognition: What You Need   1
to Know about How Words Work

Guiding Questions   1
Why Focus on Word Recognition?   2
The Language of Language: Defining Our Terms   4
What Does It Mean to "Know" a Word?   5
The Reading Mind as a Pattern Detector   7
Word Knowledge Development and Instruction: One Size Doesn't Fit All   8
The Word Knowledge Instructional Zone:
    Negotiating the Spelling–Reading Slant   13
The Balanced Literacy "Diet": A Comprehensive Approach
    to Literacy Instruction   15
The Word Knowledge Instructional Toolkit   16
Transferring Word Knowledge to Context: The Missing Link in Word
    Study Instruction   19
Literacy Standards in the Common Core   20
Conclusion   24

2. Assessing Word Knowledge: A Comprehensive Look   25
at the Word Knowledge Zone

Guiding Questions   25
A Look at Word Knowledge through Spelling   26
The Emergent Tier   30
The Beginner Tier   37
The Transitional Tier   42
Interpreting the TSI: Three Ways   43

Ways to Monitor Your Students' Progress 47
Conclusion 54

3. The Emergent Reader and Writer: 56
Building Foundational Skills That Facilitate Word Learning

Guiding Questions 56
Characteristics of Emergent Readers and Writers 58
Common Core Alignment 67
Emergent Readers and Writers: A Balanced Literacy Diet 67
Emergent Milestones 69
Daily and Weekly Schedules 69
When Will Your Students Be Ready to Move to the Next Stage? 72
Conclusion 75

4. The Emergent Reader's Toolkit: 76
Activities and Student Strategies

Guiding Questions 76
Word Knowledge Toolkit Part I: Reading Words 77
Word Knowledge Toolkit Part II: Writing Words 83
Word Knowledge Toolkit Part III: Manipulating Words 92
Word Knowledge Toolkit Part IV: Transferring Word Knowledge
    to Context 100
Conclusion 103

5. The Beginning Reader and Writer: 104
Building a Bank of Known Words

Guiding Questions 104
Characteristics of Beginning Readers and Writers 107
Beginning Readers' Word Knowledge Development:
    Common Features of Study 112
Common Core Alignment 121
Beginning Readers and Writers: A Balanced Literacy Diet 122
Beginner Milestones 123
Daily and Weekly Schedules 123
When Will Your Students Be Ready to Move to the Next Stage? 126
Conclusion 129

6. The Beginning Reader's Toolkit: 130
Activities and Student Strategies

Guiding Questions 130
Word Knowledge Toolkit Part I: Reading Words 132
Word Knowledge Toolkit Part II: Writing Words 150
Word Knowledge Toolkit Part III: Manipulating Words 161

Word Knowledge Toolkit Part IV: Transferring Word Knowledge
   to Context   169
Conclusion   175

7. The Transitional Reader and Writer: Building Automatic Word Knowledge for Fluency

Guiding Questions   176
Characteristics of Transitional Readers and Writers   178
Transitional Readers' Word Knowledge Development: Common Features
   of Study   182
Common Core Alignment   187
Transitional Readers and Writers: A Balanced Literacy Diet   188
Transitional Milestones   189
Daily and Weekly Schedules   190
When Will Your Students Be Ready to Move to the Next Stage?   192
Conclusion   195

8. The Transitional Reader's Toolkit: Activities and Student Strategies

Guiding Questions   196
Word Knowledge Toolkit Part I: Reading Words   198
Word Knowledge Toolkit Part II: Writing Words   209
Word Knowledge Toolkit Part III: Manipulating Words   212
Word Knowledge Toolkit Part IV: Transferring Word Knowledge
   to Context   216
Focus on Decoding: Word Knowledge Instruction at the Front End
   of the Zone   219
Conclusion   221

References

223

Index

228

CHAPTER 1

. . . .

An Introduction to Word Recognition

WHAT YOU NEED TO KNOW ABOUT HOW WORDS WORK

GUIDING QUESTIONS

....

- How does word recognition influence reading comprehension?
- How can skilled readers recognize words so quickly, even unfamiliar words they may never have seen before?
- Why is a "one-size-fits-all" approach to word knowledge instruction not effective?
- How can a developmental model of word knowledge serve as your instructional "road map" when teaching your students phonics, spelling, and word recognition?
- What is the "spelling–reading slant" and how does it play into your instructional practices?
- How is an "instructional toolkit" approach different from an "activity bank" approach?

Take a moment and think of something that you are skilled at, something that you have done so often that you don't have to really think about it anymore. It could be shooting a basketball, playing the violin, cooking a favorite recipe, backpacking, painting, speaking another language, or simply tying your shoes. Now, take a step back in time and try to remember what it was like *before* you had gained this level of skill, what it was like as you were first learning. To illustrate this point, consider the following experience of a man remembering what it was like just learning to play soccer as a child.

"During my first soccer practice with the 'Red Raiders,' two things quickly became apparent to me: (1) basic soccer skills that the professionals made look so easy on television, like controlling and dribbling the ball, were in reality *not* that easy, and (2) most of the other players on my team, those who had been playing since first grade, were a lot more skilled than me. Fortunately for me, our coaches taught us where we were, focusing on the foundational skills for the more novice players like me, while targeting advanced skills for the more experienced players.

"During my first couple of seasons playing soccer, I spent most of my time focusing on learning the basic skills and trying to use what I learned in actual games. In that first season, I remember having to focus so intently on simply controlling the ball at my feet during games that I could not look up to see where the other players on the field were around me. Because of this, I always played with my head down. This meant that I was unable to see the 'bigger picture' of the game around me in order to make accurate passes and good decisions. No matter how hard I tried to follow my coach's instructions to 'play with my head up,' I just couldn't. Simply put, I was not able to do two things at once: (1) control the ball with my feet, while at the same time (2) look around me to decide who to pass it to next. Simultaneously performing these two skills was impossible for me, because the first skill was a stepping stone for the second skill.

"However, I remember when things gradually started to click for me. Controlling the ball with my feet became more and more effortless and eventually automatic for me; I really didn't have to think about it anymore, I could just do it. This meant that I could finally play with my head up, enabling me to see the 'bigger picture' of the game. These foundational skills allowed me to move on to more advanced skills like 'give and go' passes. As I could see my own improvement, I was motivated to play and learn even more."

Why Focus on Word Recognition?

How does learning soccer, or learning any sport or skill, relate to word recognition and reading? Just like in soccer, where a solid foundation in certain skills, like ball control, is necessary to progress as a player, there are certain foundational literacy skills in which children must gain some level of proficiency if they are to continue to move forward as readers and writers. One of these foundational skills, word recognition, is the focus of this book.

Why is word recognition so important? First, the ability to accurately and automatically recognize words, even without semantic context, is a hallmark of skilled readers (Stanovich, 2000). Second, word recognition is a linchpin skill that enables access to and processing of written language and influences reading comprehension (Perfetti, 2007). Third, and more specifically, word recognition is necessary (but not sufficient) for comprehension—the ultimate goal of reading. Children who can process words efficiently are better able to focus on the meaning of the text. Children who cannot process words efficiently, who must laboriously sound out words letter by letter and sound by sound, will have few attentional resources left to focus on the meaning of the word, sentence, paragraph, or story. Similar to a developing soccer player's inability to keep his head up until he mastered basic ball control, these children will have a difficult time seeing the "big picture"—comprehending the meaning of the text—while reading.

Figure 1.1 compares this resource trade-off between word recognition and comprehension for Kara, a skilled reader, and Sylvia, a struggling reader. According to cognitive psychologists, we only have a limited amount of cognitive resources, or "mental energy," to consciously spend on any one task at a time. During reading, recognizing words and comprehending text compete for these limited cognitive resources (LaBerge & Samuels, 1974).

For the sake of illustration, assume both Kara and Sylvia have 10 units of "mental energy" to spend on *either* word recognition *or* comprehension. Kara, the skilled second-grade reader, can read words accurately and quickly. Therefore, she only has to spend one unit of her "mental energy" on word recognition, freeing up her remaining resources—nine units—to spend on comprehending what she is reading. In contrast, Sylvia, a second-grade reader who struggles with word recognition, uses up the majority of her "mental energy"—nine units—decoding the words, leaving only one unit to spend on making meaning. All other factors

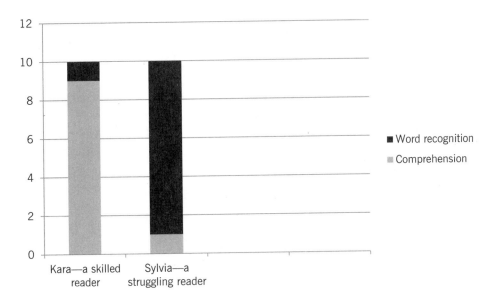

FIGURE 1.1. The word recognition/comprehension trade-off.

being equal, such as background knowledge and motivation, Sylvia will likely have a much more difficult time comprehending the same text. Put simply, children who can accurately and automatically recognize words will have greater cognitive resources available to make meaning while reading (Cunningham, Nathan, & Schmidt Raher, 2011; Duke & Carlisle, 2011).

The Language of Language: Defining Our Terms

Before we move on, we would like to discuss and define some foundational terms we will use throughout the rest of this book to talk about the language of word recognition. Remember that you can be skilled at word recognition (you are reading this book!) without knowing any of the cognitive language associated with it. Figure 1.2 illustrates how many of these terms fit together. Our "umbrella term" in this figure is *word recognition*, which we define as the ability to accurately identify printed words. Basically, we think of two different ways that readers can identify words: automatically or by decoding. Words that readers can recognize automatically are *sight words*, because the reader knows them by sight, without needing to resort to any conscious attempt to figure them out. As you can imagine, the more sight words a reader has, the fewer cognitive resources she must use on word recognition, freeing up her remaining cognitive capacity to make meaning.

If readers cannot recognize a word by sight, they must *decode* that word, meaning they must attempt to use their knowledge of the spelling system, our alphabetic "code," to identify the word. We think of two basic avenues for decoding words: by analogy or by word parts. Readers who decode words by analogy use

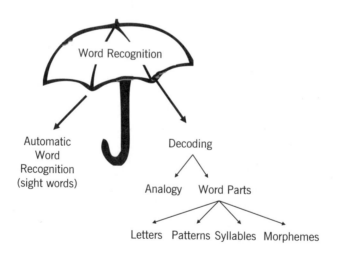

FIGURE 1.2. The word recognition umbrella.

their knowledge of a similarly spelled and/or sounded word to help them decode that word. For example, a child who cannot immediately identify the word *boast* could think of another word she already knows that is similarly spelled and/or sounded, like *roast* or *toast*, to help figure out the word.

A second way to decode an unknown word is by breaking a word down by familiar *word parts*. These word parts include *letters, common spelling patterns, syllables,* and *morphemes* (see Figure 1.3 for definitions and examples of these terms). For example, a beginning reader who cannot immediately recognize the word *mat* could sound out this word, letter–sound by letter–sound, as in *m-a-t*. A more advanced reader could break apart the unfamiliar word *explode* by breaking the word down into two syllables *ex* and *plode* (the reader may or may not know that the *ex* syllable is also a morphemic, or meaning unit, meaning "out," but simply being able to identify this syllable is enough information to help decode this word). The second syllable, *plode*, includes the familiar vowel–consonant–*e* spelling pattern, providing further information to the advanced reader.

What Does It Mean to "Know" a Word?

When, as skilled readers, we "read" a word, what exactly happens in our minds? How are we able to recognize words, even words we don't frequently encounter like *cynical* and *barbarous,* so quickly and accurately? What types of information do skilled readers know about words? What should we teach children to help them develop the deeply rooted, flexible word knowledge that equips them to (1) quickly and effortlessly recognize sight words and (2) efficiently decode unfamiliar words?

Definition	Examples
Letter—one of the 26 symbols used in the English alphabet to represent speech sounds.	*B, E, L, O, R, T, s, m, a, g*
Spelling pattern—a sequence of letters that consistently represents a sound.	*OU* in *cloud, mouth,* and *sound*
Syllable—a unit of sound anchored on a vowel that may or may not be preceded or followed by a consonant or consonants.	*Cat, I, stay* and *at* are one-syllable words *Thicken* has two syllables—*thick + en*
Morpheme—a unit of meaning represented in the spelling of words.	The *-ed* in *jumped* indicates the past tense The root *spect* (meaning "look") in words like *spectacles, spectator,* and *inspector*

FIGURE 1.3. The language of language: Defining our terms.

Three Essential Components of Knowing a Word: Phonological, Orthographic, and Semantic

When teaching children about words, we keep in mind three essential, interrelated aspects of word knowledge: (1) the phonological, or sound, representation of the word; (2) the orthographic, or visual, representation of the word; and (3) the semantic, or meaning, representation of the word. Figure 1.4 illustrates how the mind might store and represent these three different types of information about the word *stain*.

The phonological information for the word *stain* includes the four different phonemes that, when combined together, produce the oral form of the word *stain*—/s/-/t/-/ā/-/n/. The orthographic information for this word consists of the visual representation or image of the exact sequence of letters or letter patterns—S-T-A-I-N—that, when combined, form the spelling of the word *stain*. Importantly, a skilled reader would store this orthographic image in common spelling patterns, or "chunks," as in *ST-AIN*. Finally, the semantic information would include the definition of the word *stain* (a discoloration or spot) and how it might be used in a variety of contexts (such as the more figurative definition of *stain* as a "blemish" on one's reputation).

The stronger each of these three word knowledge sources are, and the stronger the connections among them, the more efficient and flexible a child's overall word knowledge will be. In this book, we pay particular attention to discussing how to teach the first two components of word knowledge: the phonological and the orthographic. However, we also incorporate the meaning aspects of word knowledge—vocabulary—throughout a number of the activities in the stage chapters (Chapters 3–8). We also encourage you, as the teacher, to discuss the meanings of words with children, particularly word meanings that children might be unsure of, even when the focus of an activity might be the spelling or sound of a word.

FIGURE 1.4. Three components of the word *stain*.

The Reading Mind as a Pattern Detector

We have used the following activity with teachers to illustrate how skilled readers and writers process words when we read and spell (Flanigan et al., 2011). Take no more than a second to read the following nonsense word, cover it up, and then try and spell it without looking back:

FLACKERNUSTER

Next, try the same exact procedure with a second nonsense word—read the word in about a second, cover it up, and then try to spell it without looking back:

TLKRNCEUFSREA

How well could you read and spell the two words? Which word was easier to read and spell? Which was more difficult? You probably found the second word much more difficult to read and spell than the first, even though (1) both words are unfamiliar to you and (2) *both words contain the exact same 13 letters* (go ahead and check if you don't believe us!).

What accounts for the difference in difficulty between the two words? This psycholinguistic experiment illustrates an important insight into how our minds process written words. First, *our mind is not a camera.* We do not take "pictures" of words that we store in our lexicon—our mental library of words—so that we can retrieve them when needed later while reading or writing. If this were the case, you would have been able to read and spell both words equally well because both words consist of the exact same letters.

So, why did you have an easier time reading and spelling the first word, even though you had never seen it before? It is because you could process the first word into a few *familiar spelling patterns*, or chunks, as illustrated below:

FL-ACK-ER-NUST-ER

You already knew the *fl*-consonant blend from words like *flight, fly, Florida,* and *fleece.* You already knew the *-ack* short vowel family from words like *back, sack, stack,* and *lack.* You know the *-ust* short vowel family from words like *must, just, dust,* and *bust.* And, you know the *-er* suffix from words like *bigger, stronger, mother,* and *father.* For this word, you didn't have to memorize 13 distinct letters; your reading mind only needed to process five chunks, or word parts, that you already knew quite well.

This ability to chunk words results in a much lighter cognitive load. For a skilled reader such as yourself, it makes all the difference in the world because it allows you to decode words you may never have encountered before; you don't need to know the entire word, you just need to know the patterns that make up the word.

So, what does all this mean for teaching children about words? Because our reading mind is a *pattern* detector, not a camera, it makes very good sense to directly and explicitly teach children the common, high-utility *patterns* found in our language. For kindergartners at the beginning of the year, this may include listening for words that begin with the same sound, or onset, such as the initial consonant /b/ sound in *ball, boy*, and *bat*. For first-grade children in the fall, this might include looking and listening for short vowel word patterns like the *-ig* in *dig, pig*, and *big*. Finally, for second graders, this might include focusing on long vowel patterns like the *oa* in long *o* words such as *soap, boat*, and *moat*.

This focus on directly teaching common spelling patterns to children also makes sense in light of the research on eye movements during skilled reading. Contrary to folk wisdom, when skilled readers read connected text, they do not skip many words, nor do they read based only on partial cues (e.g., only attending to the *dev* in *development*). In fact, quite the opposite is true. We know that skilled readers (1) fixate on nearly every single word while reading connected text and (2) process nearly every single letter of the words they fixate on (see Adams, 1990, for a summary of the eye movement research in reading). If skilled readers process words and letter patterns so completely and thoroughly, it makes sense to directly teach developing readers how to accurately and efficiently process letters, letter patterns, and words.

So, instead of trying to teach our children every single word they might some-day encounter, one word at a time, we can teach them the common, high-utility patterns that underlie the majority of words they will read and spell. For example, when we teach our children the long-*i* vowel–consonant–*e* pattern in words like *five, mine*, and *ripe*, we will also be teaching them how to apply this knowledge when encountering unfamiliar words that we might not directly teach, like *whine, prime*, and *pastime*. See Figure 1.5 for an example of 10 words (there are many, many more) that follow the long-*i* vowel–consonant–*e* pattern. When we teach this way, we like to say that when you learn one word, you actually learn 10 words, 20 words, or even more (Templeton, 2007). This approach to word knowledge instruction is powerful and efficient because we are teaching children (1) about *specific words* and, just as important, (2) about *how words work*.

Word Knowledge Development and Instruction: One Size Doesn't Fit All

Imagine that you have decided to learn to play the piano and have signed up to take weekly lessons from a local piano teacher. You walk into the studio for your first lesson, and your teacher immediately hands you an intermediate-level piano book.

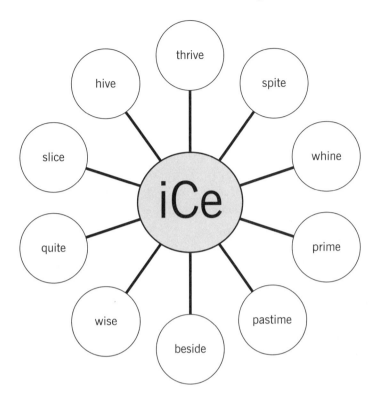

FIGURE 1.5. Ten words that follow the long-*i* vowel–consonant–*e* pattern.

Without bothering to find out what you already know about playing the piano or about music in general, your teacher proceeds to give you an intermediate-level lesson.

If you were a novice piano player, you would quickly become overwhelmed and frustrated. If you were really motivated, you might try and tread water for as long as possible, but your lack of foundational knowledge in music and technical skill would eventually come to light. You probably would not learn very much, if anything, during the lesson and might even walk out, give up, and probably not return for a second lesson. On the other hand, if you were an advanced player, you would quickly become bored and annoyed with the knowledge that you are not learning anything (just as the novice player, but for a different reason) and would probably also not return if things did not change very quickly.

Effective piano teachers do not base their instruction simply on your age or a predetermined starting point, such as "the intermediate level," because that is where most of their students are. Rather, any good piano teacher first finds out what *you* already know and what *you* can already do. He or she might ask about your background in music and how many years of lessons you have had.

Importantly, the teacher would also ask you to play some pieces of music to help gauge your ability level. Based on this initial assessment, she would determine where to begin your instruction, with an eye toward continually modifying and tailoring this instruction based on *your* speed of development and *your* specific needs.

Remember, though, that a piano teacher is teaching only one musician at a time. A band instructor gets a group of musicians, all at different levels, and must find ways to teach all of them. He likely has a goal in mind (a particular piece to perform on a date already set in the school's master calendar). The instructor uses that performance goal to strategize and to decide how to pace and group the musicians so that all will master what is required (and some will far exceed the requirements of that piece).

We know that the most effective literacy teachers differentiate instruction based on their children's needs, just like effective piano teachers and band instructors do. We want to avoid lessons in which all students are receiving the same word knowledge instruction, all learning the same letter of the alphabet, or the same "phonics rule" simply because they all happen to be kindergartners or first graders sitting next to one another in the same classroom, regardless of their word knowledge abilities.

Figure 1.6 illustrates what this one-size instruction might look like in a first-grade classroom, where the advanced readers, the "on-grade-level" readers, and the readers who are struggling are all being taught the same phonics feature: short vowels. If we do not adhere to this "one-size-fits-all" instructional mentality when teaching music, sports, or in other areas of education and learning, why would we do it when teaching word recognition, when as educators we know all too well of the great variability of skills within a single classroom? For example, short vowel instruction in the latter half of first grade would likely only benefit the struggling readers, leaving the others bored and neglecting their word recognition needs.

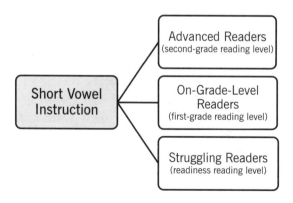

FIGURE 1.6. "One-size-fits-all" word knowledge instruction in first grade.

A Developmental Model of Word Knowledge:
A Teacher's Instructional Road Map

Just like the effective piano teacher described above, effective literacy teachers can pinpoint where to begin instruction for different children. Of course, you can't pinpoint where to *begin* instruction unless you know where students are coming *from* and where they are *going*—what they already know and what they need to learn next. For this, you need an "instructional road map." Fortunately, based on over four decades of research, we have such an instructional road map for word knowledge development. During this time, researchers have articulated and elaborated on a developmental model of word knowledge that describes the skills progression that defines word knowledge development.

As the title of this book indicates, the ability to recognize words is a developmental skill. This skill is based on a child's underlying, abstract knowledge about how words work, which *develops* over time. We first learned about children's developing word knowledge at the University of Virginia, where we were incredibly fortunate to study and work in the McGuffey Reading Center. Much of our thinking about children's development and effective instruction has been shaped by our time and experiences there, and by the groundbreaking work in children's spelling and word knowledge done by Edmund Henderson and his colleagues at the University of Virginia. This line of research, known as the Virginia studies, culminated in a comprehensive model of developmental word knowledge that serves as a foundation for much of our work in this book (Bear, Invernizzi, Templeton, & Johnston, 2012; Henderson, 1990; Templeton & Bear, 1992; Templeton & Morris, 2000).

Based on the Virginia studies described above, and on other important stage models of development in the field of literacy (Chall, 1983; Ehri, 1997; Frith, 1985), we have organized word knowledge development in the primary grades into three stages for this book: emergent, beginner, and transitional. Chapters 3–8 of this book focus on word knowledge instruction for each of these stages.

How can this developmental model actually help you as a primary grades teacher? Many of the teachers we work with are familiar with the basic concepts and literacy skills that children should learn about words such as rhyme, phonemic awareness, alphabet knowledge, phonics, and acquiring a basic sight vocabulary. However, we are often asked questions such as:

"When should I teach what skill?"
"Should I teach some sight words in kindergarten?"
"When should I stop teaching sight words?"
"How much phonemic awareness is enough?"
"Should I teach the sounds first, and then the letters? Or should I teach them together?"
"What should I do for the struggling reader? For my more advanced writers?"

These questions, focused on the timing and pacing of instruction and on differentiation, are critical questions for teachers to ask. How do we answer these questions? This is where the explanatory power of a developmental model of word knowledge comes into play.

A Developmental Model of Word Knowledge for Grades K–2

Figure 1.7 summarizes the developmental model of word knowledge that we use for teaching our own teacher education students and that we used to organize this book. For each of the three stages of development—emergent, beginner, and transitional—we have listed the key developmental skills. Of course, Chapters 3–8 explore these stages in more depth. As you look over this model, note that the *developmental model is organized by stage, not grade.* The developmental model reflects the reality in your classroom: that you will have students in a range of skill levels. All first graders are not the same; some struggling first graders might be emergent readers, first graders on grade level might be at the beginner stage, and more advanced first graders might be at the transitional stage.

Stage	Developmental Skills
Emergent (Chapters 3 and 4)	• Alphabet knowledge (including letter recognition and sounds) • Phonological awareness: 　o Rhyme and alliteration 　o Syllable awareness 　o Partial phoneme awareness • Concept of word in text • Decoding focus: Beginning sounds
Beginner (Chapters 5 and 6)	• Full phoneme awareness • Automatic recognition of high-frequency words • Features of focus: 　o Consonant blends and digraphs 　o Short vowels • Decoding focus: Letter-by-letter strategy (beginning, middle, and end)
Transitional (Chapters 7 and 8)	• Automatic word recognition leading to fluent reading • Features of focus: 　o Vowel patterns (long, abstract, *r*-controlled) 　o Consonant patterns • Decoding focus: Pattern or chunking strategy (including syllable and morpheme)

FIGURE 1.7. A developmental model of word knowledge for grades K–2.

The Developmental Model as an Instructional Road Map

We use the developmental model illustrated above as our instructional road map. When you determine a child's stage, you know what skills to teach. Because these skills are developmental, your children need to gain proficiency in skills that are foundational for learning at the next stage. For example, children cannot acquire a large bank of sight words (a beginning reader focus) if they have limited alphabet knowledge (an emergent reader focus). As we describe the developmental model throughout the rest of this book, we focus on the following three components of instruction:

- *What* to teach (what developmental skills to teach).
- *When* to teach (knowing when a child is best ready to profit from instruction in a certain skill—this will depend on the child's stage of development).
- *How* to teach (the most effective instructional strategies and methods).

The "what" to teach and the "how" to teach—the word knowledge features and instructional strategies—are covered in depth in each of the stage chapters (Chapters 3–8). However, how do we know "when" to best focus on a certain concept or skill, such as phonemic awareness, or sight-word instruction? In Chapter 2, we explain in detail how you can administer and analyze a Tiered Spelling Inventory (TSI) to help you determine what stage of development each of your students is in. When you determine what stage a child or group of children in your classroom is in, you can turn to that particular chapter in this book for instructional strategies that target the skills associated with learners at that level of development. When approached this way, word knowledge instruction changes from a "one-size-fits-all" model to a tailored approach that can result in precise and powerful differentiated instruction for your students.

The Word Knowledge Instructional Zone: Negotiating the Spelling–Reading Slant

Why would we include a spelling assessment in a book about word recognition development? The spelling–reading slant is another important concept that underlies effective word knowledge instruction (Frith, 1980; Helman, Bear, Templeton, Invernizzi, & Johnston, 2012). The spelling–reading slant posits that, in general, *spelling is harder than reading*. Or, put another way, *in general, children will be able to read words that they cannot yet spell*. For example, a second grader reading *A Perfect Time for Pandas* (Osborne, 2012), one of the *Magic Tree House* series books, would be able to read words like *different, weird, wrapped*, and *moment*, but might have difficulty spelling them accurately.

Figure 1.8 illustrates how this spelling–reading slant plays out instruction-ally. Notice how a child's spelling and reading ability defines the two ends of a *word knowledge instructional zone.* Spelling is the most rigorous measure of a child's word knowledge, providing a "window" into that child's knowledge about words (Henderson, 1990). Because spelling is more difficult than reading, spell-ing spotlights the "back end" of the word knowledge instructional zone. Reading spotlights the "front end" of the instructional zone.

Throughout the stage chapters, we include activities that, importantly, target both ends of this zone. Some activities will be focused on the "spelling end" of the zone, shoring up word knowledge features and patterns that students are "using, but confusing," but have not yet mastered (Bear et al., 2012). Other activities will be focused on the "reading end" of the zone, challenging children to grapple with word knowledge features and patterns that are at the very instructional edge of their conceptual grasp, providing an accelerated component to children's word work.

It is important to recognize that work on the spelling end of the zone is not only for spelling, and that work on the reading end of the zone is not only for reading. Working on both children's reading and spelling skills is important to developing their overall knowledge about how words work. It is through this type of balanced approach to word knowledge instruction that we can support our stu-dents' consolidation of certain foundational skills while continuing to move them forward in their literacy development.

Finally, there is a developmental component to the spelling–reading slant: The difference between children's reading ability and spelling ability tends to grow as their literacy skills progress over time. As Figure 1.9 illustrates, for children at the emergent stage, their reading and spelling ability are usually very closely tied together. As children move through the beginner stage and into the transitional

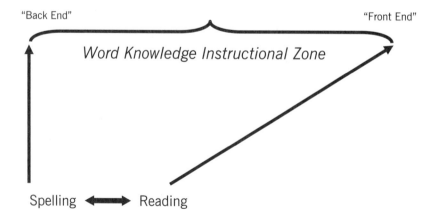

FIGURE 1.8. Word knowledge instructional zone.

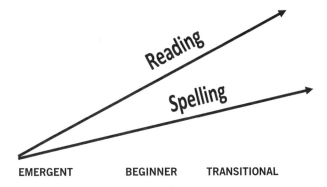

FIGURE 1.9. The relationship between children's reading and spelling growth over time.

stage, their ability to read and decode words begins to outpace their ability to spell words. You will see this difference in our stage chapters, as we place an increased focus on differential instruction for reading and spelling as children progress in their development.

The Balanced Literacy "Diet": A Comprehensive Approach to Literacy Instruction

The ultimate goal of word knowledge instruction is to help children become better readers and writers. Word study is one essential component of a balanced literacy "diet." This metaphor of the diet was another important guiding instructional principle we learned during our own education at the University of Virginia. Just as a balanced nutritional diet consists of the proper proportions of fruits, vegetables, whole grains, and lean proteins, a balanced literacy diet consists of balanced proportions of reading, writing, word study, and exposure to rich oral and written language. Figure 1.10 illustrates this four-part instructional framework, with the arrows indicating how each of these four components interacts with the others: growth in one area will promote growth in the other areas.

We believe that children should spend most of the instructional time during their literacy block (1) reading for meaning in appropriate and engaging texts at their independent or instructional reading level and (2) writing for real purposes. In addition, children should (3) be exposed to rich oral and written language at a level higher than they can read themselves, at the very cutting edge of their listening comprehension level. This rich language can be in the form of interactive read-alouds from fairytales, poems, stories, and engaging informational texts. Read-alouds offer many benefits, including introducing students to more sophisticated academic vocabulary and story language, exposing them to different genres and topics, and motivating them to read.

FIGURE 1.10. A balanced literacy diet.

Of course, the focus of this book is the fourth component of a balanced approach to literacy: word knowledge. While the amount of time we spend on word knowledge instruction is usually smaller than the other areas of the diet (approximately 15 minutes per day), it is just as critical. In each of the stage chapters in this book, we refer to the balanced literacy diet as an instructional framework for literacy. Throughout these stage chapters we also include Figure 1.10, but with slightly different proportions of recommended time for each component of the literacy diet depending on the particular needs of children at each stage. In summary, we want you to take away two important points from this section:

1. Children need high-quality instruction in word knowledge to support their development as readers and writers.
2. Word knowledge instruction alone isn't enough; children also need to spend large amounts of time reading, writing, and experiencing rich language as part of a comprehensive, balanced approach to literacy instruction.

The Word Knowledge Instructional Toolkit

According to dictionary.com (2013), a toolkit is a "set of tools designed to be used together or for a particular purpose." As this definition reveals, each tool in a toolkit has a particular purpose: A saw is used for cutting, a hammer for driving home a nail. As teachers, our instructional strategies and activities are some of our most important tools. Just as a carpenter would not use a hammer to cut a two-by-four, as teachers we shouldn't use an instructional strategy for the wrong purpose. For example, we would not use a speed sort (an activity discussed in Chapter 8 that targets automaticity for transitional readers and writers) with a beginning reader who is still acquiring a basic sight-word vocabulary and is focusing on accuracy. In other words, our strategies and activities should match our instructional purposes and the needs of our children. We believe that teachers' ability to choose the right tool for the right job develops over time and marks teacher effectiveness. In this book, we get you started on building your toolkit and understanding its potential.

In each of the stage chapters we include an instructional toolkit tailored to the needs of children at that particular stage of development. To help you choose the appropriate strategies for your students and their instructional goals at each stage, we include the instructional purpose of each activity to help you decide which strategy to use to best target your children's specific needs. In addition, each toolkit is divided into four categories of activities that children should be engaged in over the course of a typical week: (1) reading words, (2) writing words, (3) manipulating words, and (4) transferring words to contextual reading and writing. Figure 1.11 illustrates the organization of our four-part word knowledge instructional toolkit that you will see again in each of the upcoming toolkit chapters for each stage (Chapter 4: Emergent Toolkit, Chapter 6: Beginner Toolkit, Chapter 8: Transitional Toolkit). Under each of the four categories in this figure, we identify the specific instructional word knowledge goals that each category of activity supports.

Reading Words	Writing Words	Manipulating Words	Transferring Words
GOALS	**GOALS**	**GOALS**	**GOALS**
Acquire:	*Acquire:*	*Acquire the ability to process words by:*	*Acquire the ability to process words by:*
1. Accurate, automatic bank of sight words	1. Accurate, automatic store of spelling words	1. Breaking words into parts	1. Applying word knowledge into contextual reading and writing in both supported and, eventually, independent contexts
2. Working knowledge of common, high-utility spelling and phonics patterns while reading	2. Working knowledge of high-utility spelling and phonics patterns while writing	2. Building words from their parts	
3. Decoding strategies	3. Spelling strategies		

FIGURE 1.11. The four-part instructional Word Knowledge Toolkit.

Reading Words

First and most obvious, if we want students to be able to accurately and efficiently recognize words, we need to provide them with a lot of practice reading words. Practice reading words will support children's (1) acquisition of a core set of automatic sight words and (2) ability to apply their word knowledge to unfamiliar words. While this may seem obvious, we are sometimes surprised by activities and worksheets where students don't get a lot of "bang for their buck"—where students don't get a lot of practice reading words. One of our criteria for choosing activities is their "practice-to-time" ratio. We have specifically chosen activities for the toolkits that provide a lot of practice in a relatively short amount of time. For example, in many of the activities, students are reading a word every 8–10 seconds, providing 40–60 practice "repetitions" per 10 minutes of instructional time. This result is in stark contrast to some phonics worksheets in which we have seen a child take 15 minutes to work with five words—a practice-to-time ratio of only one word every 3 minutes!

Writing Words

Practice reading words is not enough. Students also need practice writing words. Some might question the inclusion of activities that support writing and spelling in a book on word recognition. However, there is a strong correlation between reading and spelling. According to researcher Linnea Ehri (2000), spelling and reading are flip sides of the same instructional coin. Moreover, the Common Core State Standards (CCSS, 2010) lists the phonics and word recognition features at each grade level in terms of the benchmark spelling patterns. Indeed, the act of spelling words reinforces a child's knowledge of phonics and spelling patterns through a different avenue—encoding as opposed to decoding. This is like "cross training" in sports, where an athlete might swim one day, run another day, lift weights a third day, and practice yoga a fourth day. By including different types of workouts in a comprehensive fitness program, the athlete's overall fitness and health is improved. In the same way, the different types of activities in the instructional toolkit support the overall development of a child's word knowledge.

Manipulating Words

In addition to reading and writing words, children need practice manipulating word parts, the third part of our instructional toolkit. As children progress through the stages, these word parts will include phonemes, individual letters, spelling patterns, syllables, and eventually frequently occurring prefixes and suffixes. The manipulating words category includes two opposite but mutually supportive processes: (1) breaking whole words into parts and (2) building words from their parts, or "breaking words down" and "building words up" in our instructional shorthand.

Transferring Words

Finally, children need to be explicitly taught, supported, and coached in transferring word knowledge into contextual reading and writing—the ultimate goal of word knowledge instruction. Unfortunately, we have found that teaching for transfer is often the "missing link" in word knowledge instruction, as children are sometimes expected to apply phonics and spelling skills immediately and independently without being given sufficient opportunity, instruction, or support in how to do it. In the next section, we discuss why application is so difficult and introduce some guiding principles for teaching transfer that will set up the activities in the stage chapters to follow.

Transferring Word Knowledge to Context: The Missing Link in Word Study Instruction

We are often told by teachers, "My students get 100% correct on the weekly spelling tests, but they can't seem to transfer this spelling knowledge to their actual writing." Or, "My students are able to successfully read the words and patterns during a word study activity, but they aren't able to decode words with those exact same patterns during guided reading." It's no surprise that this is such a common concern, because the transfer of any new skill to independent practice is one of the most difficult and time-consuming parts of the learning process. Because transfer of word knowledge is our ultimate goal, let's spend some time discussing it. The following are four ideas to keep in mind about transfer to independent practice:

1. *Transfer to independent practice takes time, a lot of time.* Remember learning how to properly perform a jump shot in basketball, an arabesque in ballet, or learning your scales on the clarinet? How long did it take from the time you were first introduced to the skill until you could perform it accurately and automatically, without thinking, in a game or performance? A couple of seasons? A year or two? Literacy skills are no different in this regard. In our experience, it takes the *average* learner 1½–2 years to progress through the transitional stage. Do not be disheartened if your students are not consistently applying a new phonics skill the week after you introduce it—this is completely normal. And, just like your basketball coach or your ballet teacher, you will periodically need to cycle back and reteach certain skills that have not been mastered. This is part of the learning process and takes time.

2. *Transfer to independent practice takes practice, a lot of practice.* Time alone will not do it. It is also critical how we spend our instructional time on a daily basis. Research points to the large amounts of time our students should be actually reading and writing. If you feel your students aren't transferring their

skills to context, ask yourself the following question: "How much time do my students actually spend reading and writing in context every day, week, and month?" If we aren't giving them enough time to practice their skills in context, how will our students ever master these skills in context? To put some numbers on it, we ask ourselves the following questions:

> "Are my students actually reading (not doing worksheets or listening to the teacher talk) appropriate, engaging texts, and having rich discussions about these texts, for 90 minutes every day in school? 7½ hours every week?" (Allington, 2011)

> "Are my students actually writing (not doing worksheets) for real purposes for at least 30 minutes each day in school? 2½ hours per week?"

3. *Transfer to independent practice takes skilled coaching.* For most students, transferring a skill requires the assistance of someone who can skillfully guide them during the throes of actually trying out that skill in context—a coach. Remember the first time you tried out that jump shot in a scrimmage or that arabesque in a practice performance? It felt a lot different than doing it in isolation. Why? Because you were trying to put it into context and connect it to other parts of your game or performance. However, your coach was there to provide you those important tips and suggestions about how to integrate this new skill into the ongoing game. This skilled coaching during guided practice is essential to eventual independent practice.

4. *Transfer to independent practice requires* **student** *ownership of independent word learning strategies.* Part and parcel with the coaching process is our ultimate goal—independent strategy use by the students. We want our students to become reflective word learners who are equipped with a toolkit of strategies that they can independently use on their own when their coach is not next to them— while they are independently reading and writing.

To help you support your students' transfer of word knowledge, in each stage chapter you will find (1) activities that will provide your students with a lot of opportunities to apply their growing word knowledge skills in context and (2) word knowledge strategies you can teach your children so that they can successfully recognize and decode new words they encounter when reading independently.

Literacy Standards in the Common Core

How does a developmental model of word knowledge as outlined in this chapter fit with the grade-specific expectations and standards of your district or state? Because it has been so widely adopted by so many states, we focus our discussion in this section on the specific word recognition, phonics, and spelling standards found in the CCSS; however, the larger points in this section also apply to district and state standards in general.

The CCSS is a set of Mathematics and English/Language Arts standards that, as of this writing, 45 states and the District of Columbia have adopted. The introduction to the CCSS places its standards in the context of real classrooms, stating: "No set of grade-specific standards can fully reflect the great variety in abilities, needs, learning rates, and achievement levels of students in any given classroom" (CCSS, 2010, p. 6). We believe it is important to note that the CCSS explicitly acknowledges the great variability in knowledge and skills of the children you work with every day in your classroom. The introduction to the "Reading: Foundational Skills" section of the CCSS goes on to address the instructional implications of this great variability, stating:

> These standards are directed toward fostering students' understanding and working knowledge of concepts of print, the alphabetic principle, and other basic conventions of the English writing system. These foundational skills are not an end in and of themselves; rather, they are necessary and important components of an effective, comprehensive reading program designed to develop proficient readers with the capacity to comprehend texts across a range of types and disciplines. Instruction should be differentiated: good readers will need much less practice with these concepts than struggling readers will. The point is to teach students what they need to learn and not what they already know—to discern when particular children or activities warrant more or less attention. (p. 15)

Right at the outset of the section covering phonics and word recognition skills, the CCSS explicitly states that instruction should be *differentiated*, acknowledging the importance of teaching students *what they need to learn*. Therefore, a developmentally grounded, learner-centered approach like the one we describe in this text is in line with the intent of the CCSS (Gehsmann & Templeton, 2011/2012). Figure 1.12 identifies the foundational CCSS skills targeted at each stage of development.

For many students, the standards in the CCSS will align with their developmental levels. However, there will be discrepancies for more advanced students and for those who are struggling with literacy skills. For our more advanced students, we should not waste valuable instructional time teaching them what they already know, but should instead teach them what they are ready to learn next. For our students who are struggling with literacy skills, we will target their areas of need at their appropriate level of word knowledge and provide them the additional time and attention necessary to accelerate their development. When we teach developmentally appropriate words and skills to children who struggle, they are much more likely to (1) make gains in word knowledge and (2) maintain these gains over time than if we taught them at a level that is beyond their conceptual grasp (Morris, Blanton, Blanton, Nowacek, & Perney, 1995). We can help these students

	Print Concepts	Phonological Awareness	Phonics and Word Recognition	Spelling
Emergent	• Follow words from left to right, top to bottom, and page by page • Recognize that spoken words are represented in written language by specific sequences of letters • Understand that words are separated by spaces in print • Recognize and name all upper- and lowercase letters of the alphabet	• Recognize and produce rhyming words • Count, pronounce, blend, and segment syllables in spoken words • Blend and segment onsets and rimes of single-syllable spoken words • Add or substitute individual sounds (phonemes) in simple, one-syllable words to make new words	• Begin to demonstrate a basic knowledge of some one-to-one letter–sound correspondences	• Write a letter or letters for most consonant sounds (phonemes) • Spell simple words phonetically, drawing on knowledge of sound–letter relationships
Beginner		• Isolate and produce the initial, medial vowel, and final sounds (phonemes) in three-phoneme (consonant–vowel–consonant [CVC]) words • Distinguish long from short vowel sounds in spoken single-syllable words • Orally produce single-syllable words by blending sounds (phonemes), including consonant blends • Add or substitute individual sounds (phonemes) in simple, one-syllable words to make new words	• Read common high-frequency words by sight • Demonstrate a solid one-to-one letter–sound correspondence • Know the spelling–sound correspondences for common consonant digraphs • Decode regularly spelled one-syllable words • Read words with inflectional endings • Recognize and read grade-appropriate irregularly spelled words	• Spell simple words phonetically, drawing on knowledge of sound–letter relationships • Conventional spelling for words with common spelling patterns

Transitional			
	• Segment spoken single-syllable words into their complete sequence of individual sounds (phonemes)	• Know final -e and common vowel team conventions for representing long vowel sounds • Use knowledge that every syllable must have a vowel sound to determine the number of syllables in a printed word • Decode two-syllable words following basic patterns by breaking the words into syllables • Read words with inflectional endings • Distinguish long and short vowels when reading regularly spelled one-syllable words • Know spelling–sound correspondences for additional common vowel terms • Decode regularly spelled two-syllable words with long vowels • Decode words with common prefixes and suffixes	• Generalize learned spelling patterns when writing words

FIGURE 1.12. CCSS foundational skills.

make progress toward the grade-level expectations more quickly and efficiently if we teach them where they are; put simply, "A step back is a step forward" when we teach in a developmentally responsive way (Bear et al., 2012).

In Chapters 3, 5, and 7 we identify how we target the specific word knowledge skills listed in the CCSS. For example, after the "Common Features of Study" section in Chapter 5, we list the CCSS word knowledge skills that are targeted in that stage of development. In addition, the activities in the chapter provide opportunities to practice these CCSS target skills.

Conclusion

Word recognition development is a crucial piece of the language arts curriculum of the primary grades. Quick and accurate word recognition is not only a hallmark of skilled readers, but it also influences reading comprehension. When a word is not automatically recognized, we decode and look for patterns. Our "reading mind" is a pattern detector; therefore, teaching common, high-utility patterns found in our language is an essential component of word recognition development. However, one size instruction does not fit all. We need an "instructional road map" to help us match our instruction to our students' developmental needs. To this end, in Chapter 2 we offer an assessment for you to identify your starting point on the "map," and the chapters that follow address needs of word knowledge within stages of development rather than grade levels. Every stage is presented with an "instructional toolkit" that will guide you through a series of activities that provide your students with ample opportunities to read, write, and manipulate words. Ultimately, the main goal is for your students to transfer these skills while reading and writing—your final destination on the "instructional road map."

CHAPTER 2

• • • • • • • • • • •

Assessing Word Knowledge

A COMPREHENSIVE LOOK
AT THE WORD KNOWLEDGE ZONE

GUIDING QUESTIONS

• How do you assess your students' word knowledge development?

• Which instructional activities are most appropriate for your students?

• How can you assess your students' response to your instruction and provide a record of their progress over the course of the year?

• How can you look for evidence of maintenance and transfer of your students' word knowledge?

This chapter describes how to assess and interpret results in order to plan your word knowledge instruction. The assessment described in this chapter is designed to offer flexibility and efficiency for emergent, beginner, and transitional reading instruction. Since these readers can be found in any of the primary grades, we offer a Tiered Spelling Inventory (TSI) that can be navigated based on the performance of your students. We first guide you through the administration of the spelling inventory as well as how to score it. Then we explain how to use the scores to guide you in this book *and* in your instruction. The end of the chapter offers guidance on using the inventory and other measures to monitor your students' progress over the course of the school year.

Your classroom is a busy place with great demands put on classroom time. Often, teachers are put in push–pull situations. You want to provide ample time for instruction but are expected to administer a variety of assessments that can take large amounts of your instructional time. These assessments are important—assessment-driven instruction is critical to providing an appropriate educational program for your students (Bear et al., 2012; Ganske, 2014; Invernizzi, Meier, & Juel, 1996; Johnston, Invernizzi, Juel, & Lewis-Wagner, 2009; Morris, 2005; Walpole & McKenna, 2007). However, assessments can take extraordinary amounts of time, pulling you from valuable instructional time. You need assessments that are both valuable and efficient. You need assessments that give you the most information about your students with the least amount of administration time. With this in mind, we often turn to group-administered assessments but know that sometimes the best information comes from individually administered assessments. Before beginning your instruction, you must first find out what your students know about words and how they work.

The TSI described in this chapter will enable you to turn to the appropriate chapters in this book and pinpoint instructional activities that will boost your students' word knowledge. The TSI evaluates your students' word knowledge through tasks probing spelling. As discussed in Chapter 1, spelling and reading are closely intertwined. Many studies have shown that scores on qualitative spelling inventories are consistently related to, and predict with great accuracy, the reading achievement of school-age children (Bear, Templeton, & Warner, 1991; Bear, Truex, & Barone, 1989; Edwards, 2003; Ehri, 2000; Ellis & Cataldo, 1992; Morris, Nelson, & Perney, 1986). Moreover, spelling assessments have long been considered a door into student word knowledge (Bear et al., 2012; Henderson, 1990). The TSI is a developmental spelling assessment that allows you to target your instruction to your students' developmental needs.

A Look at Word Knowledge through Spelling

Developmental spelling assessments, such as the TSI, are made up of lists of words that represent a variety of orthographic features at increasing levels of difficulty. The words are chosen to assess your students' knowledge of these features as they relate to different stages of word knowledge. These stages correlate to the reading stages that are covered in Chapters 3–8.

- Chapters 3 and 4 focus on the emergent reader.
- Chapters 5 and 6 address the needs of the beginning reader.
- Chapters 7 and 8 concentrate on the transitional reader.

This chapter outlines the TSI and provides you with three versions, or forms, that can be used across the school year. Figure 2.1 presents each form and the corresponding reader stage chapters.

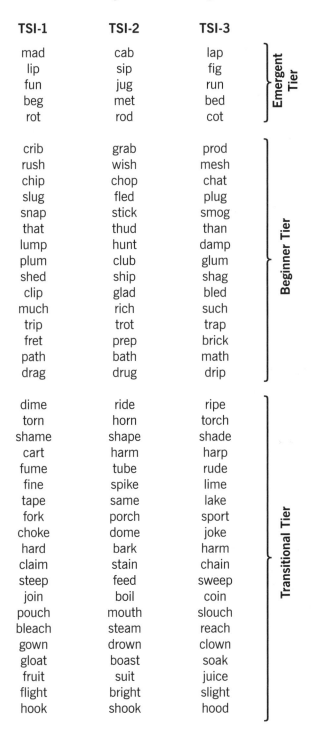

TSI-1	TSI-2	TSI-3	
mad	cab	lap	Emergent Tier
lip	sip	fig	
fun	jug	run	
beg	met	bed	
rot	rod	cot	
crib	grab	prod	Beginner Tier
rush	wish	mesh	
chip	chop	chat	
slug	fled	plug	
snap	stick	smog	
that	thud	than	
lump	hunt	damp	
plum	club	glum	
shed	ship	shag	
clip	glad	bled	
much	rich	such	
trip	trot	trap	
fret	prep	brick	
path	bath	math	
drag	drug	drip	
dime	ride	ripe	Transitional Tier
torn	horn	torch	
shame	shape	shade	
cart	harm	harp	
fume	tube	rude	
fine	spike	lime	
tape	same	lake	
fork	porch	sport	
choke	dome	joke	
hard	bark	harm	
claim	stain	chain	
steep	feed	sweep	
join	boil	coin	
pouch	mouth	slouch	
bleach	steam	reach	
gown	drown	clown	
gloat	boast	soak	
fruit	suit	juice	
flight	bright	slight	
hook	shook	hood	

FIGURE 2.1. Tiered Spelling Inventory (TSI).

What Is the TSI?

The TSI is a qualitative spelling inventory similar to other assessments readily available such as those from *Words Their Way* (Bear et al., 2012), *The Howard Street Tutoring Manual* (Morris, 2005), *Word Journeys* (Ganske, 2014), and the *Phonological Awareness Literacy Screening* (Invernizzi et al., 1996). (*Note*: If you already use one of these inventories, you do not need to administer the TSI and can move to chapters in this book using those results.) The TSI is designed to provide you with the most information about your students and their word knowledge. It is built to allow you to administer it in tiers, building to the full list, to maximize the information you gain about your students and utilize the time allotted for the assessment. It is divided into three tiers:

- Emergent Tier. The emergent tier consists of the first 5 words. These words were chosen to capture features mastered early in a child's literacy career, the kindergarten year. The following features are included:
  o Consonant sounds—the initial /f/ in *fit* and the final /g/ in *beg*.
  o Short vowel sounds—the /ă/ in *cat* and the /ŏ/ in *pot*.
- Beginner Tier. The following 15 words make up the beginning reader tier. These words continue to explore short vowels and bring in digraphs and blends. Short vowels are generally learned by the end of kindergarten and into the beginning of first grade, and consonant digraphs and blends are mastered by the spring of the first grade year:
  o Short vowels—the /ă/ in *glad*, the /ĕ/ in *shed*, and the /ŭ/ in *plug*.
  o Consonant digraphs—the /sh/ in *ship*, the /ch/ in *chop*, and the /th/ in *that*.
  o Consonant blends—the *s*-blend in *snap*, the *l*-blend in *clip*, the *r*-blend in *brag*, and the preconsonantal nasal in *lump*.
- Transitional Tier. The next 20 words on the inventory make up the transitional tier. These words explore features often mastered by the end of first grade or within the second-grade year. By the end of first grade, you should see your students using the vowel–consonant–*e* pattern. As your students move through their second grade year, they should gradually master *r*-controlled vowels and vowel teams. You will notice that these words include vowel patterns.
  o Vowel–consonant–*e* pattern—the *a*–consonant–*e* in *shake*.
  o R-controlled vowel pattern—the *ar* in *harp* and the *or* in *short*.
  o Vowel teams including:
    ▪ Other long vowel patterns— the *oa* in *gloat* and the *ee* in *steep*.
    ▪ Abstract vowel patterns—the *ou* in *pouch* and the *oi* in *join*.

The TSI is scored for both total correct and correct use of the target features. Total correct scores will guide you to the appropriate chapters in this book for instructional guidelines and activities. While the feature scores will help you make decisions about word knowledge patterns you will target for instruction. Both scores are useful for exploring growth across the course of a semester and/or year. Guidelines for all three purposes are provided later in the chapter.

The printable forms in online Appendix A: Assessments (see *www.guilford. com/hayes4-forms*) can be used for both student recording and your scoring. Fold the paper to reveal only the blank numbered lines for the students to record their spellings. The other side will be used for your scoring. Have a copy of the alphabet available (see the Alphabet Chart in online Appendix A) for a reference in the event a student is unsure of how to write a letter. It is important to provide this chart for all students in kindergarten; the alphabet strip may be useful for students in later grades if they still have confusions about letter formation.

Some students may be very comfortable attempting to spell words, especially as they move up in the grades. However, some students will be unfamiliar with connecting sounds to letters to form words. Others may be hesitant because they can segment some of the sounds but cannot find the letter–sound connections. As with all assessments, anecdotal notes are crucial in understanding and interpreting student performance. You will have the quantitative data from the scoring, but you may also be greatly assisted by information about student behaviors while attempting the spelling tasks.

How Do You Know Where to Start Assessing?

The TSI provides guidelines of starting points by grade level but also allows for flexibility. We can predict students to be at certain points in their development on the basis of grade levels, and our starting points for the TSI follow this lead. However, we also acknowledge that some students may be behind and some students may be advanced. Therefore, the TSI allows you flexibility. The tiers let you make adjustments based on your students' performance.

- Kindergarten. Administer the first 5 words, using the Emergent Tier.
- First grade. Administer words 1 through 20, moving to the Beginner Tier.
- Second grade. Administer words 1 through 40, finishing with the Transitional Tier.

Your students' performance on the tiers will determine whether they should be given additional tiers. For example, a kindergarten teacher may choose to start all kindergartners with the Emergent Tier. Some students may have scores on the Emergent Tier TSI indicating they have moved out of an emergent stage of reading and writing. These students will need to move to the Beginner Tier for additional assessment. Figure 2.2 outlines how to navigate the tiers of the TSI. We also provide guidelines throughout the chapter as we detail each tier.

	What does the score mean?	What are my next steps?
Emergent Tier	Correct score 0 = *little or no letter–sound correspondence and segmentation ability; emerging skills with letter–sound correspondence*	*Stop* testing
	Correct score 1 to 5 points = *possibly movement to the beginner stage of word knowledge*	*Continue* with the Beginner Tier
Beginner Tier	Correct score 0 to 5 points = *some knowledge of letter–sound correspondence and segmentation ability*	*Score* only first five words using Emergent Tier guidelines
	Correct score 6 to 17 points = *building solid letter–sound correspondence*	*Stop* testing
	Correct score 18 to 20 points = *including blends and short vowels*	*Continue* with the Transitional Tier
Transitional Tier	Correct score 21 to 25 points = *beginning knowledge of vowel patterns*	*Finish* Transitional Tier

FIGURE 2.2. Score interpretation and next steps.

The Emergent Tier

Students, especially in kindergarten, will come to the table with a variety of strengths based on their previous experiences. You will administer the TSI in kindergarten to small groups of children rather than the entire class. This approach will allow you to not only monitor the students to ensure they understand the task but also observe and take notes about their performance. It will also help you to ensure that the kindergartners do not consider this a cooperative task—they are not especially used to "doing their own work."

Anecdotal notes can help you make better decisions about your students' strengths and needs. For example, you will have kindergartners with scores of 0 on the TSI. These notes provide additional information to further unpack that score, because a score of 0 by itself does not provide you with enough information for emergent readers. Students can obtain a score of 0 for a multitude of reasons. Figure 2.3 details example scenarios of why this might happen as students spell the word *mad*.

Just scanning these few examples provides you with information about how these students are different. The student who leaves each space blank, while unsure of what the task actually involves, is quite different from the student who can segment sounds but has had little experience with letter sounds and letter formation. Considering the student responses with your anecdotal notes/observations provides you with important information about these students. These students will most likely respond to instruction at different paces possible with varying degrees of success.

Student Spellings	Descriptions
_____	• Leave each space blank with no connection to sounds. *These children are unfamiliar with connecting speech to print and, therefore, are unsure how to proceed.*
lllo	• Make scribbles. *These children are unfamiliar with forming letters, segmenting sounds, and connecting sounds to letters.*
X〔σ	• Use letter-like forms. *These children know they need some sort of "symbol" but may be unfamiliar with segmenting sounds and connecting sounds to letters.*
ASBSM4N	• Use random symbols. *These children are familiar with forming letters but may not be familiar with segmenting sounds and connecting to letters.*
_____	• Leave each space blank but isolate sounds. *These children can segment sounds but are unfamiliar with either letter formation, the letter representations for the sounds, or both.*

FIGURE 2.3. Emergent Tier TSI score of 0.

Before you begin the TSI, you should model spelling a word. To do this, you will think aloud while "sounding out" the word *sat* and writing it out where your students can clearly see how you are connecting letters to sounds. Make sure you are writing large enough for the group to see and that the paper is oriented for them to see your word right side up. The following is offered as you think aloud:

"We are going to write some words. I'm going to write a word first. The word I'm going to write is *sat*: *sssssssssssssaaaaaat*. I need to write down the first sound I hear. The word starts with *sssssssssssssssssss*. That's the letter *S*. [Point to *S* on your alphabet strip to demonstrate using the strip and reinforce the letter–sound connection. Then write *S*.] Let's listen for the sound I hear next: *sssssssssssssaaaaaaaaaaa*. Now I hear *aaaaaaaaaaa*. That's the letter *A*. [Again, point out the *A* on the strip and write *A*.] What do we hear at the end? *Sssssssssssssaaaaaaaaat*. [Emphasize the ending *T*.] I'm going to end this word with the letter *T*. [Point to the *T* on the strip and write *T*.] This spells the word *sat*. [Run your finger under the word as you say it.] Now that we've written *sat*, I'm going to call out some words for you to spell. Just do the best you can and think about the sounds you hear in the word. Then write the letters you need for the sounds. You can use your alphabet strip to help you."

You are ready to begin the TSI. For the Emergent Tier, you will administer the first 5 words. A printable form specific to the Emergent Tier is provided in online Appendix A: Assessments for students only doing the first 5 words. These words are consonant–vowel–consonant words, surveying all short vowels and a variety of consonant sounds. Pronounce the words as clearly as you can and naturally. *However, do not stretch the words or emphasize sounds.* This was done in the think-aloud to introduce the TSI but is not to be done during the assessment. In the introduction's think-aloud, you are doing the heavy lifting—you are doing the segmentation and letter–sound connection. The Emergent Tier of the TSI seeks to provide information about your students' ability to segment sounds in words and apply letter–sound connections. If you elongate words or emphasize sounds, then we do not have an adequate measure of the students' skills and knowledge.

As students spell words, you can prompt them and provide a generic level of support. Limit your prompts to questions like:

"What else do you hear?"
"Do you hear any more sounds?"

If a student asks if a word is spelled correctly, simple say, "You are doing a good job listening for sounds." If students ask for help, respond by letting them know that you want them to do their best. Be sure to monitor their writing so that you can inquire if you are unsure of any of the letters.

How Do You Score the Emergent Tier?

After eliciting the spelling responses, you are ready to score the sample. The following describes scoring the Emergent Tier of the TSI (first 5 words) only. These emergent tier words will be scored in two ways yielding two scores:

1. Correct score—correct word spellings.
2. Feature scores—correct features or close approximations.

If you only administer the first 5 words, a student's highest possible correct score is 5. It is equally important to calculate the feature scores. The Emergent Tier explores (1) initial sounds, (2) final sounds, and (3) medial short vowels. Both upper- and lowercase letters will be accepted and reversals will not count as errors. The sounds do not need to be correct; they can also be close approximations. Students early in their understandings of letters and sounds often confuse similar sounds, such as the nasal consonant sounds /m/ and /n/. See Figure 2.4 for common close approximations. Since these close approximations are common with young students, we allow these to count positively in our scoring. This practice will enable us to also acknowledge a student's ability to segment sounds, which is an equally important observation to make at this stage.

Score the TSI by checking the appropriate boxes for each of the sounds the child was able to represent correctly or provide a close approximation of the letter-to-sound correspondence. You will score by item, looking for features and correct

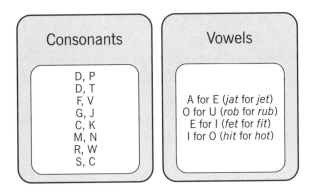

FIGURE 2.4. Common close approximations.

word spelling. For example, the first word, *mad*, gives you two options for the first /m/: (1) the correct representation—*M* and (2) the close approximation—*N*. Circle the letter if it is represented, either *M* or *N*. Now move to the medial vowel sound. In this case, only *A* is accepted. Circle the letter if it is represented. Moving to the final sound, you will see two options: *D* and *T*. Circle the letter used by the student. Last, if the word is spelled correctly, make a check in the final box titled "Correct." See Figure 2.5 for a student's spelling of the word *mad* and how it was scored.

After scoring each word, you will tally up your scores. Go down each column and note the number of circled features and the number of correctly spelled words. Then sum the total number of features and correct scores. This score will be the score we will use later to guide us and will be placed in the bottom left cell titled "Total Score." See Figure 2.6 for a scored spelling inventory sample. This student has an emerging understanding of letter sounds and can segment initial and final

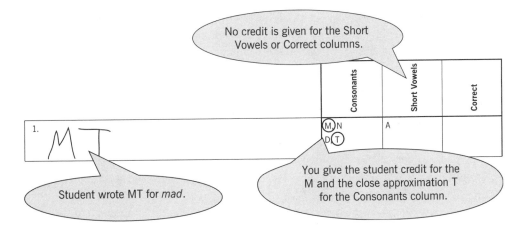

FIGURE 2.5. Scoring *mad*.

Emergent TSI—Form 1

Date: _January_

Name: _____

	Consonants	Short Vowels	Correct
DEVIN			
1. MT	(M),N D,T	A	
2. L–	(L) P,D	I, E	
3. VM	F,(V) N,(M)	U, O	
4. B⊃	(B),P (G)	E, A	
5. T	R (T)D	O, U	
	8 /10	0 /5	0 /5
	Total Score	8 /20	

FIGURE 2.6. Scored sample: Emergent Tier.

sounds in consonant–vowel–consonant words. Notice how the student wrote in blanks for LIP on number 2 and ROT on number 5. The student could segment those sounds but did not know the letter–sound connection, so the student chose to put a "marker" for the sound. The student's sample yielded a correct score of 0 but had a total score of 8.

Once you have your scored samples, you can use the guidelines in Figure 2.7 to make decisions about the next step in the assessment. You will either stop or continue on with 15 more words (from the Beginner Tier).

When Should You *Stop* Testing?

Students who score between 1 and 5 points for the total score do not need to go any further in the TSI. There is no need to move forward if the student has not demonstrated an established knowledge of how letters and sounds work to make words. Students who have no responses, make scribbles, or write in letter-like forms or random symbols obviously are not demonstrating sufficient evidence of letter–sound connections. Some students will show a beginning knowledge using salient sounds or initial sounds. When students use salient sounds, they will pay attention to parts of the word that resonate with them. For example, students may pop their lips like the *p* in *tap* or "hold on to" sounds like the continuous consonant sound /mmmmmm/ in *mat*. Those students who pay attention to salient sounds will represent initial or final sounds but no vowels. Other students may be more advanced and are, therefore, more deliberate in their thinking about sounds in words. These students will more consistently segment the initial sound. They will provide you with a one-letter answer for the first 5 words. See Figure 2.8 for examples of student spelling samples showing when you should stop the spelling task. Notice each of these samples has a correct score of 0 and a total score between 0 and 5.

Students with a correct score of 0 and scores of 0 or 1 on the feature scores will need an assessment of their general alphabet knowledge. You can use any informal letter-naming assessment you have. One suggestion is that you first assess

	Child Responses for *Fun*
When should I *stop* testing? Correct score 0	• No response • Scribbles (ℓℓℓ) • Letter-like forms (Κℚ) • Random symbols (BDLSM65D) • Salient sounds (N) • Initial sounds only (F or V)
When should I *continue* testing? Correct score 1 to 5	• Initial and final sounds (FN or VN) • Initial, final, and medial sounds (FON or FUN)

FIGURE 2.7. Emergent Tier: When do I stop? When should I continue?

Name:		Consonants	Short Vowels	Correct	*Total score less than 5— stop testing*
1. mad	M	Ⓜ N D, T	A		• Total score of 4; 4 feature points and no points for correct spellings. • Student represented initial sounds with no other sounds provided. • All letter–sound connections were either correct or reasonable misrepresentations except for number 5, the word *rot*. • Student may not have known the letter for /r/ and, therefore, randomly assigned a letter.
2. lip	J	Ⓛ P, D	I, E		
3. fun	V	F, Ⓥ N, M	U, O		
4. beg	B	Ⓑ P G			
5. rot	V	R T, D	O, U		
		4 /10	0 /5	0 /5	
		Total Score 4 /20			

Name:		Consonants	Short Vowels	Correct	*Score less than 5—stop testing*
1. mad	MLJ	Ⓜ N D, T	A		• Total score of 1; 1 feature point and no points for correct spellings. • Student represented /m/ in *mad* but no other sounds were represented. • Student appears to be randomly writing symbols (letters and the number 3) for most words.
2. lip	NV	L P, D	I, E		
3. fun	L3	F, V N, M	U, O		
4. beg	JD	B, P G			
5. rot	N3	R T, D	O, U		
		1 /10	0 /5	0 /5	
		Total Score 1 /20			

FIGURE 2.8. Emergent TSI examples.

their recognition of lowercase letters. If your student knows fewer than 12 of the lowercase letters, then get a measure of their uppercase letter recognition. We also suggest using uppercase letters for a letter–sound measure. Uppercase letters are preferred since young students generally have a better grasp of uppercase relative to lowercase. Additionally, we suggest you target short vowel sounds for the vowels, as well as the hard consonant sounds for G and C. Armed with this information, you will be better advised on the letter sounds to target using the activities available in Chapter 4.

When Should You *Continue* Testing?

Your students may demonstrate more knowledge about how letters and sounds make up words. Students who have developed the "alphabetic principle" will represent more sounds in words. When children make the connection between letters and sounds, they have started to grasp the alphabetic principle. Students will also need a working knowledge of letter sounds and formation of letters, as well as some skill in segmenting sounds in spoken words. These are the skills your students will need in order for your continuation of the inventory to be beneficial. Students who use initial and final sounds without medial vowels (e.g., MD for *mad* or LP for *lip*) are demonstrating some ability to segment sounds with letter–sound connections but are not able to segment words fully. Students scoring a 0 for the correct score on the Emergent Tier should not continue with the TSI.

Students who score between 1 and 5 points for the correct score should continue testing with the next 15 words. These students included medial sounds even if they were incorrect (e.g., FON for *fun* or BAG for *beg*) but would have at least one word spelled correctly. However, you might occasionally notice a student spelling one word correctly, getting a correct score of 1, but no letter sounds were represented in other words. This might happen with a child who has visually memorized a certain word but has not developed letter–sound connections. These students need not continue testing. More often, a score of 1 or higher will indicate connections between letters and sounds. With correct scores of 1 or higher, you will want additional information about their word knowledge and will need to administer the next 15 words, which are introduced in the Beginner Tier, described next. These words will give you more information about digraphs (*sh, th, ch*) and consonant blends (*l-, s-,* and *r-*blends), as well as more instances to observe their short vowel knowledge.

The Beginner Tier

Students in first and second grades will most likely begin with the first 20 words on the TSI, starting with the first 5 discussed above in the Emergent Tier. However, if you have information about a certain student who is still an emergent reader, then you could use the guidelines for administering and scoring the first 5 words only. For those students who can begin with the first 20, give them the printable form for the Beginner Tier of the TSI found in online Appendix A: Assessments. Direct them to fold the inventory; the side with the numbered blanks is for them to record their answers and the other side is for your scoring. Then provide them with an explanation similar to the following not only to give them directions but also to help them feel comfortable:

> "I am going to ask you to spell some words. Some of the words may be easy and others may be harder. Do the best you can with each word. Your work will let me know how I can help you better with your reading and spelling."

Now you are ready to begin calling out the words on the Beginner Tier of the TSI. You can call out the words to small groups or to your entire class. Pronounce each word naturally without segmenting the sounds. Say each word twice. You can choose to use the word in a sentence or short phrase if you feel it is necessary. For example, with *shop* you could:

> Use a sentence: "My mom went to the store to *shop* for a new dress."
> Use a phrase: "*shop* at a store."

Regardless, the only reason to use a sentence or phrase is because you feel you need to provide some context for the word. If not, simply say the words twice. Monitor your students' responses to make sure they are recording the words and you can clarify any questionable letters. Help your students keep up with the words by saying the numbers prior to calling out words.

You can also monitor the room to make notes about your students' behaviors. Note students who are writing quickly. These students may not require "think time" because they already know the correct spelling. However, the flipside is equally important to note. Other students may need to sound out each word or consider sounds along with letter choices. After you have finished calling out all of the words, you may want to give your students a second opportunity with the words. You can do this simply by calling out the words one more time, leaving a bit of time between words. To ensure students are utilizing this second look, have them point to each word while you say it. If you have already administered the first five words, you can start on number 6 of the Beginner Tier. Again, the first 5 words are from the Emergent Tier. Moving to the remaining 15 words, notice the inclusion of consonant blends and digraphs.

Now you have 20 words; we will show you how to score them. This set of words will *not* be scored in the exact manner as the first 5 words administered to emergent readers, in which we assigned points for reasonable substitutions. At this point in the assessment, students must represent the target feature correctly to obtain points.

How Do You Score the Beginner Tier?

You will score the sample by obtaining feature scores and a correct score. First, check the appropriate boxes according to the sounds the child was able to represent correctly. Unlike the guidelines for the emergent readers, you will *not* give credit for close approximations. If the word is spelled correctly, make a check next to the word. After scoring each word, tally your scores. Go down each column and note the number of correct features (feature scores) and correctly spelled words (correct score). See Figure 2.9 for a sample scored spelling inventory.

Notice in this sample, the student demonstrates a good understanding of consonant sounds as we can first see by that feature score of 25 out of 25. Moving to the next feature, short vowels, we can see that the student is doing well but has become confused. The feature score of 15 out of 20 illustrates this point, but we can also see more specifically a confusion of short *e*, *a*, and *i* (e.g., CHREP for *trip* and SHAD for *shed*). As we consider the consonant blends and digraph feature, we see the student also has some confusion with a score of 10 out of 15. A closer look at the spelling errors reveals affricate errors with CHREP for the *tr* blend in *trip* and JRAG for the *dr* blend in *drag*. Each of these spelling features will be described in detail in Chapter 5. Last, this student received a correct score of 14.

You can use the guidelines in Figure 2.10 to make decisions about the next step in the assessment. You will either stop or continue on with 20 more words. Figure 2.10 outlines the procedure for stopping or continuing with testing using the correct word scores. Looking at our sample in Figure 2.9, we can see the teacher should *stop* testing with this student whose correct score is 14. This assessment already reveals a starting place for instruction, so it is unnecessary to gather more data.

When Should You *Stop* Testing?

Students who score between 0 to 5 correct score points do not need to go any further in the inventory. If a student scored 5 correct score points or lower, look closely at the sample. Make note of whether or not the student consistently used initial and final sounds, as well as medial vowels. If the student did not include medial vowels, you may want to step back and only consider the first 5 words, using the Emergent Tier guidelines.

Also, stop testing for those students scoring between 1 and 17 total correct words. Even though these students are making letter–sound connections, you will have enough information from the Beginner Tier to move forward with

Beginner TSI—Form 1

Date: _September_

Name: Lexie	Consonant	Short Vowel	Digraph and Blend
1. Mad	Ⓜ Ⓓ	Ⓐ	
2. lil	Ⓛ Ⓟ	Ⓘ	
3. fun	Ⓕ Ⓝ	Ⓤ	
4. bag	Ⓑ Ⓖ	E A	
5. rot	Ⓡ Ⓣ	Ⓞ	
6. crib	Ⓑ	Ⓘ	ⒸⓇ
7. rush	Ⓡ	Ⓤ	ⓈⒽ
8. Chip	Ⓟ	Ⓘ	ⒸⒽ
9. SLuG	Ⓖ	Ⓤ	ⓈⓁ
10. Sap	Ⓟ	Ⓐ	SN S
11. that	Ⓣ	Ⓐ	ⓉⒽ
12. LoP	Ⓛ	U O	MP P
13. PLuG	Ⓖ	Ⓤ	ⓅⓁ

(continued)

FIGURE 2.9. Scored sample: Beginner Tier.

Beginner TSI—Form 1 *(continued)*

14. *Shad*	Ⓓ	E A	ⓈⒽ
15. *CLiP*	Ⓟ	Ⓘ	Ⓒ Ⓛ
16. *much*	Ⓜ	Ⓤ	Ⓒ Ⓗ
17. *chrep*	Ⓟ	I E	TR CHR
18. *Fat*	Ⓣ	E A	FR F
19. *Path*	Ⓟ	Ⓐ	ⓉⒽ
20. *JraG*	Ⓖ	Ⓐ	DR JR
	25 /25	*15* /20	*10* /15
	Correct Score	*14* /20	

FIGURE 2.9. *(continued)*

your instruction. For these students, your feature scores will help you define your instructional goals.

When Should You *Continue* Testing?

Students scoring 18 correct score or higher should most likely continue testing with the next 20 words. These students accurately spelled many short vowel sounds, as well as consonant blends and digraphs. You will want additional information about their word knowledge, particularly vowel patterns. The next 20 words on the Transitional Tier will give you more information about long vowels (e.g., *dime*

	Correct score 0 = *some knowledge of letter–sound correspondence and segmentation ability*	Score only first 5 words using Emergent Tier guidelines
Beginner Tier	Correct score 1 to 17 points = *building solid letter–sound correspondence*	*Stop* testing
	Correct score 18 to 20 points = *including blends and short vowels*	*Continue* with the Transitional Tier

FIGURE 2.10. Beginner Tier: When should I stop? When should I continue?

and *steep*), *r*-controlled vowels (e.g., *hard* and *torn*), and abstract vowels (e.g., *gown* and *join*).

The Transitional Tier

You may have previous data indicating your students have strong scores on the Beginner Tier of the TSI or another spelling inventory with similar "beginning" features (e.g., short vowels). In either case, strong performance on previous assessments with these features means you do not need to administer the Beginner Tier first. In this case, you should bypass the Beginner Tier and only administer the 20 words from the Transitional Tier. This option demonstrates the flexibility of the TSI; you only need to administer the tier(s) that are warranted.

You will follow the guidelines of the Beginner Tier with the next 20 words of the Transitional Tier. You can administer the TSI to small groups or to your entire class. Pronounce each word naturally without elongating the sounds and use the word in a sentence or short phrase if you feel it is necessary. If not, simply say the words twice. Help your students keep up with the words by saying the numbers prior to calling out words.

You should monitor the room to inquire about questionable letters and make notes about your students' behaviors. Some of your students will write quickly, while others will require some time to think through the sounds and patterns in unknown words. These notes will be helpful to consider. For example, some students who are quick in writing may or may not be accurate in their spellings. If students are quick and inaccurate, then you will need to pay particular attention to helping the student be a more strategic speller. After you have finished calling out all of the words, you can give your students a second opportunity with the words. Simply call out the words one more time, leaving a bit of time between words.

If you notice students are not using vowel patterns on the first 10 words in the Transitional Tier, then you can consider stopping, as noted in Figure 2.11. For example, a student who spells *shame* as SHAM, *cart* as CRT, or *choke* as CHOCK

Transitional Tier	Correct score of 0 on first 10 words = *lacking long vowel patterns*	*Stop* testing and move to the Beginner Tier
	Correct score 1 to 4 points = *building knowledge of vowel patterns*	Consider revisiting the Beginner Tier
	Correct score 5 points or higher = *good initial knowledge of vowel patterns*	*Finish Transitional Tier*

FIGURE 2.11. Transitional Tier: When should I stop testing? When do I finish the Tier?

is not demonstrating knowledge of long or *r*-controlled vowel patterns. Therefore, moving to the second 10 words is not necessary. If, however, you feel some students might feel "singled out" if they do not continue while others do, then finish the entire set of 20 words. Students who are not representing vowel patterns in the first 10 words are probably in the Beginner Tier. If you do stop after 10 words, you will need to administer the Beginner Tier if you have not already done so. You will use the score results from that tier to guide your instruction. In this case, there is no need to use the limited information from the Transitional Tier for instructional purposes.

How Do You Score the Transitional Tier?

The Transitional Tier is scored similarly to the Beginner Tier. Words are scored by spelling feature and by correct spelling, giving you a correct score and feature scores. As you look at the additional words and features, notice the attention to vowel patterns. With this tier comes vowel–consonant–*e* as in *tape* and *fine*, *r*-controlled vowels as in *fork* and *hard*, and vowel teams as in *bleach*, *pouch*, and *join*. Each of these spelling features is explained in detail in Chapter 7. Also notice, the highest correct score a student can receive is 20. Even if you have already administered the Beginner Tier, the correct scores from each tier are considered separately rather than building from one tier to the next.

Figure 2.11 also provides guidance for students scoring between 1 to 4 on the correct score of 5 or more. Students scoring 1 to 4 are demonstrating a beginning, yet limited, knowledge of vowel patterns. While they may be ready to work within the transitional stage, it would be prudent to explore their performance on the Beginner Tier to ensure those features are mastered. Those students scoring 5 or higher should continue on to finish the Transitional Tier.

See the sample in Figure 2.12 as an example of scoring in the Transitional Tier. This student demonstrates some initial understanding of vowel patterns, such as the vowel–consonant–*e* pattern. This particular feature yields a score of 4 out of 6. Looking at the student's spellings, we can also see this pattern when the student is trying to spell words with unfamiliar vowel teams (e.g., CLAME for *claim* and GLOTE for *gloat*). We can also see the student is beginning to represent *r*-controlled vowel patterns in words like *hard* and *fork*. The student's correct score of 10 also indicates some beginning understanding of the features in this tier.

Interpreting the TSI: Three Ways

Now that you have scored the assessments, you will want to use the scores to assist your grouping and instructional decisions. You can maintain records of your

Transitional TSI—Form 1

Date: *January*

Name: *David*	Digraph and Blend	Vowel–Consonant-*e*	Vowel-*r*	Vowel Team
1. dime		(I–E)		
2. torn			(OR)	
3. shame	(SH)	(A–E)		
4. card			(AR)	
5. gub		U–E		
6. fire		(I–E)		
7. tape		(A–E)		
8. fork			(OR)	
9. chock	(CH)	O–E / OCK		
10. hard			(AR)	
11. clame	(CL)			AI / A–E
12. steap	(ST)			EE / EA
13. joyeen				OI / OY

(continued)

FIGURE 2.12. Scored sample: Transitional Tier.

Transitional TSI—Form 1 *(page 2 of 2)*

14. *pach*	(CH)			OU / A
15. *bleech*	(BL) (CH)			EA / EE
16. *gane*				OW / A
17. *glote*	(GL)			OA / O–E
18. *froot*	(FR)			UI / OO
19. *flight*	(FL)			(IGH)
20. *stood*				(OO)
	10/25	4/6	4/4	2/10
	Correct Score 10/20			

FIGURE 2.12 *(continued)*

students using the TSI class record. See the class record in Figure 2.13. Notice how the teacher recorded the students' scores from lowest to highest correct score. This practice allows you to more easily identify students with similar needs. We will use the assessment in three ways: (1) the correct score will guide you to the appropriate chapter and related instructional activities for children at that stage, (2) the feature scores will help you make decisions about the specific spelling features to target within each stage, and (3) both scores will allow you to gauge your students' overall progress across the year.

Looking across your class and their correct scores, you can use the guidelines in Figure 2.14 to help you determine the appropriate chapters for instructional guidelines and activities.

As you transition to the instructional chapters, you will want to consider the feature scores you calculated. These feature scores will help you make decisions about the spelling features to target as you work at the "back end" of the word knowledge zone. Generally, we suggest targeting features where your students make two or more errors within a given feature. For example, a feature score of 13 out of 15 or lower on the consonant blend and digraph feature from the Beginner Tier warrants a closer look and should be considered as a target feature for instruction.

The feature scores obtained on the Emergent Tier can also be used to guide your specific letter–sound instruction. We have chosen words for this tier to provide you

Beginner Class Record

Student Name	Initial/Final	TSI			IDI					Total Score
		Short Vowels	Blends/Digraphs	Correct Score	Short Vowels	Blends/Digraphs	R-Controlled Vowels	Vowel-Consonant-e	Vowel Teams	
Preston	25	20	15	20	10	10	8	9	7	64
Roderick	25	20	15	20	10	10	7	10	5	62
Taniqua	25	18	13	18	10	10	6	6	2	52
Min Wha	25	17	13	17	10	10	0	5	1	43
Maria	25	17	13	17	10	10	0	5	1	43
Joshua	25	16	13	15	9	9	0	6	0	39
Lexie	25	15	10	14	6	7	0	1	0	28
Demetrius	25	15	10	14	7	7	0	0	1	29
Lamont	25	13	9	12	6	6	0	1	0	25
Ché	25	13	8	12	6	6	0	0	0	24
Rosie	25	12	8	12	7	5	0	1	0	25
Trey	25	12	8	12	5	7	0	0	0	24
Tessa	25	13	7	11	6	5	0	0	0	22
Elijah	25	12	6	10	5	7	0	1	0	23
Finn	24	12	3	8	5	6	0	0	0	20
Josephine	24	11	3	8	6	5	0	0	0	19
Cordrick	22	11	2	7	6	5	1	0	0	19
Beo Yu	20	11	1	6	5	4	0	0	0	15
Lucy	20	10	0	5	5	2	0	0	0	12
Uniqua	19	11	0	5	6	1	0	0	0	12
Diego	17	4	0	2	5	0	0	0	0	7
Dylan	14	2	0	1	6	0	0	0	0	7
William	12	3	0	1	4	0	0	0	0	5
Umberto	15	0	0	0	5	0	0	0	0	5
Isabella	7	0	0	0	0	0	0	0	0	0

FIGURE 2.13. TSI class record.

TSI Scores	Focus Chapters
• Emergent Tier TSI correct score of 0 • Beginner Tier TSI correct score of 0	→ Go to Chapters 3 and 4 for instructional activities for emergent readers
• Emergent Tier TSI scores 1–5 • Beginner Tier TSI scores between 1 and 17	→ Go to Chapters 5 and 6 for instructional activities for beginning readers
• Beginner Tier TSI scores 18–20 • Transitional Tier TSI scores above 0	→ Go to Chapters 7 and 8 for instructional activities for transitional readers

FIGURE 2.14. Correct scores to stage chapters.

with as much letter–sound information as possible. In Form 1 of online Appendix A, we probe 10 different consonant sounds and scan across all five short vowel sounds. The feature scores will allow you to know if any letter–sound connections were established, and a closer look will provide information about specific letter–sound connections that need instruction.

Grouping is a critical first step for your word knowledge instruction. Targeted small-group instruction allows you to provide timely, appropriate instruction. The following guidelines may be helpful when considering group formation.

- Three to four groups are manageable. More groups are often difficult to manage, resulting in less instructional time.
- Consider the number of children in each group. If you have a group of students working below your district's grade-level expectations, then you may want to have a smaller group size. A group comprising fewer students allows you to provide more intensive instruction.
- You will find that rank ordering your students (by correct scores) on the class record will reveal clusters of similar scores that can be used to determine your groups.

While the TSI is a tool designed to help you make grouping decisions and guide you to the stage chapters in this book, it can also assist you in monitoring student progress across the year. The correct score is an appropriate score to use for the purpose of monitoring your students' movement across stages; however, feature scores are also helpful as they help you obtain evidence of movement within a stage. The next section discusses progress monitoring in more detail.

Ways to Monitor Your Students' Progress

Progress monitoring is an important part of your classroom procedures and records. Monitoring provides you with a record of student performance to determine the effectiveness of your classroom instruction. Armed with this information, you can determine whether (1) you need to explore instructional modifications, (2) a student needs supplemental instruction, or (3) you should move forward in your instruction. For example, a student may move from the emergent stage to the beginner stage of development, signaling you to move to the activities outlined in Chapters 5 and 6 on the beginning reader. You must have multiple pieces of evidence of your students' basic understanding of the features, as well as evidence of application. Progress monitoring should allow your students multiple opportunities to *demonstrate* their understanding, as well as show *maintenance* and *transfer* of these understandings. Your weekly assessments demonstrate your students' knowledge, cumulative assessments allow you to check for maintenance over time, and observations of your students' reading and writing give you a glimpse into their transfer of knowledge. Taken together, these three types of monitoring progress help you look for evidence of your students' word knowledge in a more purposeful, targeted way. We have identified ways to assess all three of these types of monitoring (see Figure 2.15).

Demonstrate Knowledge

You should assess your students every week or so on how they initially *demonstrate* their understanding of recent word knowledge instruction. You can easily use the "back end of the zone" word lists in online Appendix B: Toolkit Activities to make lists of 10 or more words to call out for your students to spell. Like the TSI, these quick weekly or biweekly checks provide you with information about your students' understanding of words and how they work. If you have been studying the blend features in Chapters 5 and 6 on the beginning reader, then you would have your students spell this set of 10 words that were all compiled from these "back-end-focused" word lists for blends in online Appendix B: Toolkit Activities. We suggest an 80 to 20% ratio of words studied during your instruction/practice versus "transfer" words. Transfer words are words that have not been included in your sorts but have the target feature. For example, the words below include 8

Demonstrate Knowledge (*initial demonstration of understandings*)	Maintain Knowledge (*maintenance of understandings over time*)	Transfer Knowledge (*transfer understandings to reading and writing*)
• Weekly or biweekly spell checks	• Cumulative spell checks • TSI beginning, middle, and end of year	• Writing samples • IDI

FIGURE 2.15. Ways to assess: Demonstrate, maintain, and transfer of word knowledge.

words from the instructional sort (*slip, crab, snack, grab, smug, flag, clap, brick*) and two transfer words (*grit, fled*).

slip	*flag*
crab	*clap*
snack	*brick*
grab	*grit*
smug	*fled*

As you can see, the list looks across *s*-blends, *l*-blends, and *r*-blends. It will be critical for you to note whether your students are representing both consonants in these blends, spelling *grab* with GR rather than GAB. Notice also that this list includes only short vowel words; therefore, this selection allows you to also check their short vowel knowledge as well.

Emergent readers will not have spell checks but can easily demonstrate their growing letter–sound knowledge through letter–sound assessments. You can also ask them to write letters for target sounds: (1) you can simply produce the target sounds such as /m/ or /ă/ or (2) you can ask them to write the initial sound of a target word such as *mop* or *add*. In either option, the students would only be required to write one letter for the target sound.

Maintain Knowledge

You may have noticed that your students often know words on a weekly spelling test but do not consistently retain that knowledge. We suggest that you continue to include weekly spelling tests that focus on your current word knowledge features of study as well as cumulative spell checks. These cumulative checks include words that exemplify features you have been working on and provide you with a record of the maintenance of the word knowledge features studied. You can easily create targeted, cumulative spell checks with the word lists from online Appendix B: Toolkit Activities. These checks are 10 or more words that show multiple word knowledge features from previous study. For example, the group that completed the weekly blend assessment just discussed would also be good candidates for a cumulative spell check surveying blends, as well as digraphs. We suggest incorporating a cumulative check approximately every 6 weeks. Their cumulative check might look like this:

slug	*smug*
chat	*this*
snag	*shut*
flag	*clip*
shop	*chum*

The TSI can be used several times during the year to assess your students' progress and check for maintenance of their understandings over time. We have provided three forms that could be used in the fall, winter, and spring. The words chosen exemplify target word knowledge features so that you can compare "apples to apples" and feel confident about your students' records of progress. These words will show up in your word knowledge instruction; however, students will not specifically study the words probed on the TSI to avoid inflating their scores. See Figure 2.16 for a first grader's progress across the course of a year. This student's correct scores increased over the year, as do her feature scores. Her fall scores indicate that she should work within Chapters 5 and 6 for beginning readers, and her spring scores point her teacher to move to Chapters 7 and 8 for transitional readers.

Your emergent students can also demonstrate their maintenance of letter–sound knowledge. They can do so by following the same cumulative task described above in which you have them write the letter for an orally presented target sound or the initial sound of the target word. You would use words targeting those sounds that have been taught, such as *map* after learning /m/, /ă/, and /p/. You can also consider your students' performance on the activities in Chapter 4. For example, the sound card activity provides you with evidence of their letter–sound recognition with attention to both their accuracy *and* their automaticity.

Transfer Knowledge

To confirm your students' understanding of word knowledge instruction, you will need more evidence. You should not only keep records of your students' performance on spell checks but should also look for evidence of transfer to reading and writing. The ultimate goal of your instruction is the transfer of this knowledge to their reading and writing; specifically, your students use this knowledge when decoding and encoding.

Evidence of Transferring Word Knowledge to Writing

Your daily observations can be helpful, and we have created activities that allow you to more systematically observe and note evidence from your students' writing

	Consonant	Short Vowel	Digraph and Blend	Correct
Fall	20	10	3	5
Spring	25	20	14	19

FIGURE 2.16. First-grade TSI across the year.

samples. Within the course of a grading period, you should plan to utilize multiple writing samples in observing their transfer. We suggest collecting four to six writing samples in order to have enough information about their consistent transfer of the word knowledge you have been targeting during instruction. To help in keeping records of students' word knowledge application, we suggest using the observation guides offered in online Appendix A: Assessments. These observation guides are designed to reflect the target features of each stage. For example, the Writing Observation Guide: Beginning Reader prompts you to look for evidence of short vowels, consonant blends, and consonant digraphs. Refer to Chapters 4, 6, or 8 for details on how to use the guides as you reflect on writing samples at the three different stages.

As you work through the Word Knowledge Toolkit chapters (Chapter 4 for emergent readers, Chapter 6 for beginning readers, and Chapter 8 for transitional readers), you can use the activities in the Transferring Words section of the toolkit for evidence of their word knowledge during reading and writing tasks, such as the word hunt in writing in Chapter 8 and the dictated sentences in Chapter 6. Dictated sentences require students to write sentences dictated by the teacher. These sentences are constructed to include many exemplars of the word knowledge features being studied. Our first grader from Figure 2.16 wrtoe the following dictated sentences during her consonant blend study (e.g., *sl* in *slip, sm* in *smock, cr* in *crab*):

Slip the block in the smock.
Will the crab snip the flag?

This student also wrote dictated sentences meant to seek evidence of her maintenance of her digraph knowledge (e.g., *th* in *that, sh* in *shop, ch* in *chip*):

That clock is in the shop.
Did you chip the clock?

Evidence of Transferring Word Knowledge to Reading

To ensure a full picture of your students' understanding of the features, you need to see how they use their word knowledge when decoding unknown words. We have chosen the Informal Decoding Inventory (IDI) created by Walpole, McKenna, and Philippakos (2011) as a tool for this purpose. The IDI in its entirety (both Forms 1 and 2) is provided in online Appendix A: Assessments. The inventory is an individually administered assessment divided into two parts. Part I assesses features used to decode single-syllable words. These features are often seen in the texts read by beginning readers; therefore, we will use Part I to assess transfer of features in reading for beginning readers. Part II assesses skills used by transitional readers—multisyllabic word reading. Figure 2.17 details the features found within Parts I and II.

Each assessed set includes 10 words exemplifying the feature along with 10 nonwords to ensure your student is transferring knowledge to unknown words. Begin each feature set by asking what the word is and move left to right on your scoring sheet while the student moves top to bottom on the student sheet. Ask "What is this word?" with each word if necessary. Follow this same procedure as you move to the nonword reading. For your initial administration, give all sets in either Part I or Part II, depending on your reader's stage. As you move through the year, you should give the IDI multiple times. However, with subsequent administrations, you should only administer the set that has been targeted in your instruction.

Use the benchmarks provided by Walpole et al. (2011) to assess your students' performance and transfer. See Figure 2.18 for scoring benchmarks. Notice the real-word criteria is higher than the criteria used for nonwords, because real words should be more familiar and, therefore, more easily identified by sight.

Let's consider our first grader from Figure 2.16. Her teacher had her read each set in Part I twice in the year, starting in January and again in March (see Figure 2.19). Notice her consonant blend and digraph score of 7 out of 10 reading real words and 2 out of 10 reading nonwords in January. Here we can see her ability to read real words with much more success compared with her relative weakness transferring this knowledge to nonwords. In March, after targeted instruction, her growth is significant. She moves to 10 out of 10 reading real words and 8 out of 10 reading nonwords. This performance demonstrates, and provides further evidence of, the transfer of her consonant blend and digraph knowledge. Taken together with the observations of her dictated sentence writing and cumulative spell checks, we can feel assured of her strong understanding of the feature and, therefore, the decision to move forward in our instruction. Moreover, we can also see the student beginning to use long and abstract vowel patterns while decoding in the March results.

Part I *Assessing Beginning Readers*	Part II *Assessing Transitional Readers*
• Short Vowels • Consonant Blends and Digraphs • *R*-Controlled Vowel Patterns • *V*–Consonant–*e* • Vowel Teams	• Compound Words • Closed Syllables • Open Syllables • Vowel–Consonant–*e* Syllables • *R*-Controlled Syllables • Vowel Team Syllables • Consonant-*le* Syllables

FIGURE 2.17. Parts I and II of the Informal Decoding Inventory.

Part I: Decoding for Beginning Readers

	Real Words		Nonwords	
	Mastery	Instruct Here	Mastery	Instruct Here
Short Vowels	8–10	7–0	6–10	5–0
Consonant Blends and Digraphs	8–10	7–0	6–10	5–0
R-Controlled Vowel Patterns	8–10	7–0	6–10	5–0
Vowel–Consonant–e	8–10	7–0	6–10	5–0
Vowel Teams	8–10	7–0	6–10	5–0

Part II: Decoding for Transitional Readers

	Real Words		Nonwords	
	Mastery	Instruct Here	Mastery	Instruct Here
Compound Words	8–10	7–0	6–10	5–0
Closed Syllables	8–10	7–0	6–10	5–0
Open Syllables	8–10	7–0	6–10	5–0
Vowel–Consonant–e Syllables	8–10	7–0	6–10	5–0
R-Controlled Syllables	8–10	7–0	6–10	5–0
Vowel Team Syllables	8–10	7–0	6–10	5–0
Consonant-le Syllables	8–10	7–0	6–10	5–0

FIGURE 2.18. IDI scoring benchmarks.

	Short Vowel	Blend and Digraph	R-Controlled Vowel	Vowel–Consonant–e	Vowel Teams
January Real Nonword	6 4	7 2	0 0	1 0	0 0
March Real Nonword	10 10	10 8	6 5	4 4	5 3

FIGURE 2.19. First-grade IDI.

	Demonstrate	Maintain	Transfer
Emergent	• Weekly or biweekly checks	• Emergent TSI (Appendix A) • Letter–sound check	• Concept of word performance (Chapter 4) • Emergent Writer Observation Guide (Chapter 4) • Transferring words activities from Emergent Toolkit (Chapter 4)
Beginner	• Weekly or biweekly checks	• Beginner TSI (Appendix A) • Cumulative spell checks	• Informal Decoding Inventory Part I (online Appendix A) • Beginning Writer Observation Guide (Chapter 6) • Transferring words activities from Beginner Toolkit (Chapter 6)
Transitional	• Weekly or biweekly checks	• Transitional TSI (Appendix A) • Cumulative spell checks	• Informal Decoding Inventory Part II (online Appendix A) • Transitional Writer Observation Guide (Chapter 8) • Transferring words activities from Transitional Toolkit (Chapter 8)

FIGURE 2.20. Progress monitoring options.

Tools to monitor progress over time are discussed in more detail in Chapters 4, 6, and 8. Each reader stage includes options to monitor demonstration of understanding, maintenance of use, and transfer of knowledge. Figure 2.20 outlines assessment options throughout this book.

You will use assessments, particularly the TSI, to help guide your instruction and monitor your students' progress. Your initial testing with the TSI will help move you to the appropriate instructional chapter in this book. In addition, your continued testing with the TSI will help you monitor student progress over time. More frequent spelling tests and cumulative spell checks are equally important as you build evidence of student growth. As you gather more data on your students, you will need to adjust your groups accordingly. Student use of word knowledge features studied in their reading and writing highlights student proficiency with the features.

Conclusion

This chapter has presented you with assessments that will help you systematically assess both ends of the word knowledge zone. First, the TSI provides you with information about your students' word knowledge they can use while spelling, the back end of the word knowledge zone. Second, the IDI allows you to assess your students' knowledge of how words work when decoding, the front end of the zone.

You can use the TSI results to guide you to the stage chapter in this book that will inform your instructional decisions. The IDI will help you consider features of study for decoding practice. Both assessments will also factor into your progress monitoring. In addition, the word knowledge toolkit chapters for each stage will provide you with activities to observe the transfer of your instructional word knowledge practice. Armed with multiple pieces of evidence, you can gauge your students' mastery of word knowledge features.

CHAPTER 3

· · · · · · · · · · ·

The Emergent Reader and Writer

BUILDING FOUNDATIONAL SKILLS
THAT FACILITATE WORD LEARNING

GUIDING QUESTIONS

· ·

- What are the reading characteristics of the emergent reader?
- What are the writing/spelling characteristics of the emergent writer?
- How do the feature scores in the Tiered Spelling Inventory (TSI) guide your word knowledge instruction at this stage?
- What are the instructional milestones of this stage?
- How might you organize your literacy block for word knowledge instruction at this stage?

Janya is a kindergartner whose parents immigrated from India when Janya was 1. Her parents speak Hindi at home but are both fluent English speakers and have provided Janya with a literacy-rich home. Janya, also fluent in English, has entered kindergarten like many of her classmates—an emergent reader. Mr. Moore, her teacher, has been taking observational notes about his students' concepts of print. Janya knows quite a bit about texts and how they work. Mr. Moore has noted that she knows the difference between print and pictures, where text starts on the page, and that print moves from left to right. However, she does not know the return sweep of lines in text and does not understand that text consists of letters that make up words. It is clear that Janya has had some experience with books prior to coming to school. She frequently picks up books to pretend read; Janya retells stories or uses the illustrations to help her build a story.

Janya loves journal time. She enjoys drawing pictures and then writing about them. Janya does not yet understand the connection between letters and sounds, so her writing is pretend. It is composed of the handful of letters and numbers she already knows how to write, presented randomly. Her alphabet knowledge is building; she can identify many uppercase letters and some lowercase letters and knows the sound /j/. She wrote about recess on the playground the other day (see Figure 3.1). Notice that Janya uses a combination of letters and numbers, and the letters she has chosen are found in her name.

Every day after lunch, Mr. Moore reads aloud to his students. One book his class enjoys is *I Was Walking Down the Road* by Sarah Barchas (1987). With this book, Mr. Moore invites the students to participate in the refrain with hand motions. Janya loves chorally reciting, "I caught it. I picked it up. I put it in a cage." From time to time, Mr. Moore demonstrates pointing to each word in the refrain as the students recite and will invite the students to help point. This practice helps Janya and her classmates begin to develop an understanding of how words work in print. When Janya attempts to point to the words as she recites the refrain, she sweeps across the line with her finger.

Mr. Moore also takes advantage of the rhyming couplets in the story, such as "I was looking at the sky. Then I saw a butterfly." The class enjoys whispering the rhyming words, supplying the rhyming words when Mr. Moore pauses, and playing games with the rhyming pairs: *sky/butterfly, road/toad, rake/snake, log/frog, mail/snail, house/mouse, mitten/kitten,* and so on. Through these language play activities, Janya has developed her sense of rhyme. Mr. Moore has noticed Janya is beginning to grapple with syllables in words. After having the class play Concentration with the rhyming pairs from the book, Mr. Moore invites Janya and her classmates to take the animals from the story and sort them by the number of syllables: one syllable— *toad, snake, frog, snail, mouse*; two syllables—*kitten*; three syllables—*butterfly*. He observes Janya making many syllable connections and even extending by putting her name in the two-syllable category.

Janya and her friends enjoy the centers' rotation, particularly the writing center, when not with Mr. Moore during the small-group rotations of the language block. Janya creates menus while playing restaurant, makes lists for the grocery store, and

FIGURE 3.1. Janya's writing sample.

leaves notes to friends in the post office. Each of these activities give Janya and her classmates opportunities to navigate the waters of written language and experiment with their building knowledge of letter sounds. Another aspect of centers Mr. Moore strives to reinforce is oral language. He knows this is an opportunity for Janya to learn new vocabulary and practice in an authentic setting. This month in the library center, he has included objects from another favorite read-aloud, *The True Story of the Three Little Pigs* by Jon Scieszka (1996), for children to engage in dramatic play.

Janya is beginning the year with many skills that will help her move into the beginner stage of reading. She knows some letter names and can form some letters to engage in pretend writing. Although she does not have an awareness of phonemes, she has a solid understanding of rhyme and is building her syllable awareness. Janya is an emergent reader and is starting to practice tracking words in print with Mr. Moore's help. Let's read more about students like Janya.

In this chapter, we describe the emergent reader and writer. We will first acquaint you with the defining characteristics of the emergent reader, as well as the emergent writer and speller. Then we outline two foundational concepts your emergent students must gain: phonological awareness and the alphabetic principle. Next, we provide guidance on how word knowledge instruction fits within the language arts block for the emergent reader. The chapter concludes with scheduling ideas and ways to monitor your students' word knowledge progress.

Characteristics of Emergent Readers and Writers

The emergent stage of literacy development encapsulates the period when children imitate and experiment with print. Students at this stage are typically found in kindergarten classrooms but can be found throughout the primary grades. Emergent readers do not spell or read in the conventional sense. Like Janya, emergent students pretend read and write, because they have a limited understanding about how oral language and print are related. Many of the literacy characteristics of the emergent student are foundational to reading and writing; they are core skills necessary to take part in conventional reading and writing.

Reading Characteristics: The Foundational Work of the Emergent Reader

The emergent reader is building the awareness that letters are put together in various ways to build words and words are put together in texts to tell a story or give information (see Figure 3.2). Emergent students do *read*, but the reading they engage in is mostly pretend. During pretend reading, we can observe a child's understanding of story language. Students move through stages of storybook

Emergent Reading Characteristics

- Reads texts at a kindergarten level (e.g., simple, predictable, repetitive texts).
- Pretends to read by retelling familiar books.
- Does not have a concept of word—unable to match speech to print.
- Explores elements of story structure and language.
- Rehearses concepts of print while interacting with books.

FIGURE 3.2. Reading characteristics of the emergent reader.

structure and language as they retell stories (Sulzby, 1986). Children first begin to label pictures in books without attention to the story. Justice, Skibbe, Canning, and Lankford (2005) found preschoolers did not often attend to print in picture books. Rather, their focus remained on the illustrations. As children become more experienced with books, their retellings revolve around the plot of the story with attention to storybook language, using phrases such as "Once upon a time" or words like *meanwhile*.

Pretend reading is a critical event. Students need opportunities to practice the conventions of print (see e.g., Clay, 2006), holding books right-side up, turning pages from front to back, gazing from left pages to right pages. As children start to pay attention to the print, realizing words carry a great deal of the meaning in picture books, they begin to understand that you start reading at the top of the page. They will also begin to notice reading characteristics, such as moving from left to right in a line of print and the return sweep moving from one line to the next. You may even see children pretend reading with their own very engaging versions of stories while sweeping their fingers across the page to mimic the adult readers in their lives. Much of this develops through experiences with literature and, with some children, prior to coming to school. However, many children develop their concepts of print as a result of teacher-led instruction.

Another type of reading an emergent child will use is memory reading. Emergent-level books are designed for memory reading. These texts include limited word choice, using repetitive phrases or sentences with predictable language. Each page brings a one-word change in the phrase or sentence with heavy illustration support to cue the child to the one-word change. Consider the two-page spread from an emergent-level text that we wrote (see Figure 3.3). Notice the repetitive sentence frame ("I have my ____________.") as well as the picture support for the word change. Students are able to easily memorize these texts and then practice

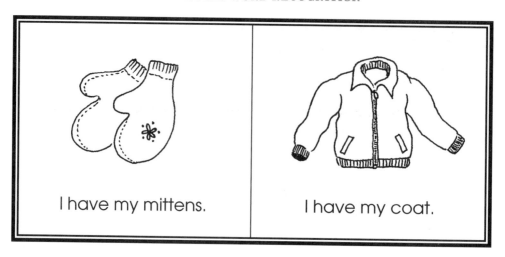

I have my mittens.   I have my coat.

FIGURE 3.3. Emergent-level text.

coordinating the spoken word to the printed word. The ability to track print to match speech is called concept of word. Students memorize little books, jingles, and rhymes to fingerpoint while taking part in this memory reading. Refer to guidelines for concept of word assessment in Chapter 4. During a concept of word assessment, we can find out whether a student can accurately track print while memory reading and identify words. An emergent reader will *not* be able to demonstrate a concept of word.

Emergent readers will follow a continuum of skill in tracking memorized print (Gill, 1992). Novices may simply sweep a line with their fingers while reciting. They may or may not demonstrate a return sweep moving from one line to the next. Students will then become aware of some sort of discernible unit; however, that unit will not be a word. Often at this point, you will see students "bouncing" their fingers across the line to the beat of the rhyme. Students may be saying words with their fingers in the air; the bounce, in other words, is not coordinated with words. Sometimes you may even see a student bounce while pointing to individual letters. This student knows about the unit in a global sense but does not understand differences between letters and words. Students will then begin to coordinate pointing with the written words, but this coordination will still not be an absolute match. They will have difficulty negotiating the two-syllable words. These students will get to the end of the line and run out of words. See Figure 3.4, which illustrates student movement through this continuum. The figure has what the child says in quotes, the text as it matches to his speech, and how he is tracking. As you move down the figure, the child's concept of word further develops. Through ample opportunities of teacher-led concept of word activities, children will move along this continuum and develop a firm concept of word in print.

Building the foundation: *Sweeps across the page with or without directionality.*

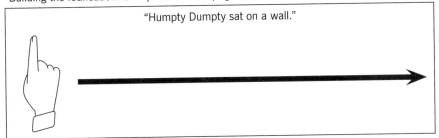

"Humpty Dumpty sat on a wall."

Emerging: *Points to letters while verbalizing words.*

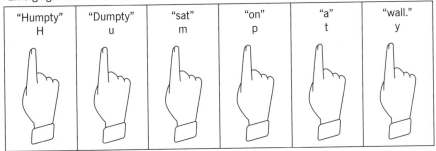

| "Humpty" H | "Dumpty" u | "sat" m | "on" p | "a" t | "wall." y |

Developing: *Bounces finger across the page while verbalizing the words.*

| "Humpty Dumpty" Hump | "sat" ty | "on" Dump | "a wall." ty |

Nearing proficiency: *Gets off track because of two-syllable words.*

| "Humpty" Hump | "Dumpty" ty | "sat" Dump | "on" ty | "a" sat | "wall." on |

FIGURE 3.4. Concept of word development: Matching speech to print.

Writing and Spelling Characteristics: The Orchestration of Connecting Letters to Sounds

Students in the emergent reading stage are most often simultaneously in the emergent stage of writing and spelling (see Figure 3.5). Emergent students do not understand the connection between letters and sounds. At first, children will scribble when writing. Children at this level of development often refer to writing as drawing, saying they are *drawing* their name. In fact, they think of their names as a series of shapes rather than a series of letters put together to spell their name. As children have more experience with print and start becoming more observant, they begin mimicking the global contours of written language. You may see your students use mock-linear writing or letter-like forms. Figure 3.6 shows emergent spellings of *lip* from the Tiered Spelling Inventory in Chapter 2 (Figure 2.1). Notice the first three spellings, moving from scribbles to mock-linear to letter-like forms.

Later in the stage, students will learn about letters and numbers and their forms through targeted instruction. At this point, they begin to develop the understanding that writing involves some sort of symbol, so they begin to try it out for themselves. Look at Figure 3.6 where we next see a child using "symbol salad" (Bear et al., 2012). Late in the stage, students have learned even more about written language; they have learned some letter sounds and have started to think more about the sounds they hear in words. This attention to salient sounds is often found when there is a tangible event, such as your lips popping for the /b/ in *baby* or friction in the mouth with the /f/ in *fish* or the continuant sound /m/ in *mom*.

Critical to writing and spelling is alphabet knowledge, including letter naming, letter sounds, and letter formation. Emergent writers and spellers may or may not have a developing knowledge of letter names. Students enter kindergarten with a variety of experiences and knowledge, knowing some uppercase letters and few, if any, lowercase letters. Others will enter kindergarten knowing no letter names,

Emergent Writing and Spelling Characteristics

- Writes with scribbles, letter-like forms, or symbol salad.
- Has no connection between letters and sounds.
- Begins to include salient sounds at the end of the stage.
- Depends on letter knowledge and letter formation.

FIGURE 3.5. Writing and spelling characteristics of the emergent reader.

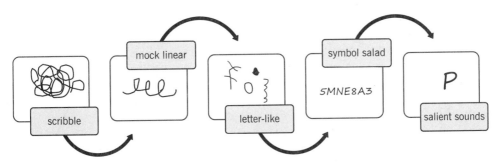

FIGURE 3.6. Emergent spellings of *lip*.

not even knowing the ABC song, while others will come to kindergarten knowing almost all upper- and lowercase letter names. All of these students can still be emergent. The deciding factor is whether they have an awareness that letters can represent sounds—the alphabetic principle. As just discussed, emergent students do not have an understanding of the alphabetic principle; they have yet to make that connection between letters and sounds. Emergent students are learning about the formation of letters. The letters in their names are often the first ones learned. Uppercase letters are considered more distinct, so children often learn them before their lowercase counterparts. Students have difficulty with reversals, such as static reversals (e.g., 2 for S). They may confuse letters and numbers.

Their writing samples will reflect their knowledge of letter sounds and letter formation. If they are scribbling in their spelling samples and consider their written name a drawing, their other writing attempts will follow suit. Students who have begun to understand written language as a series of symbols and have learned how to form some letters will start to explore their use in their writing. As they begin to learn some letter names, you will notice the occasional letter–sound connection in their writing. As students move through the stage and become more aware of the alphabet, their writing samples become shorter. As they learn more about letters and sounds through targeted instruction, they become much more selective, only committing to paper the sounds they know. Figure 3.7 shows two emergent writing samples: (1) a kindergartner writing a long story about the winter holiday with her cousins and (2) a first grader with the sentence "My mom wakes me up in the morning." Regardless of their level of letter–sound knowledge, emergent writers do not attend to the letters and sounds that make up words, much less spaces between words.

The Development of Phonological Awareness

How do children move from this wonderful pretend stage into conventional literacy behaviors? First, with targeted instruction, they learn to process oral language as

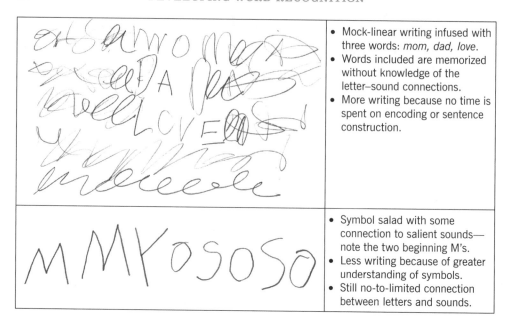

| | • Mock-linear writing infused with three words: *mom, dad, love*.
• Words included are memorized without knowledge of the letter–sound connections.
• More writing because no time is spent on encoding or sentence construction. |
| | • Symbol salad with some connection to salient sounds—note the two beginning M's.
• Less writing because of greater understanding of symbols.
• Still no-to-limited connection between letters and sounds. |

FIGURE 3.7. Emergent writing samples.

a sequence of sounds—they develop phonological awareness. Phonological awareness is at the core of learning to read and write in an alphabetic written language. This awareness of phonology reflects one's ability to detect and manipulate the sound structure of words. As children begin to become phonologically aware, they leave their meaning-based processing of language and realize that *mouse* rhymes with *house* in addition to the fact that a *mouse* might be in your *house*. A student's phonological awareness entering school is highly predictive of later reading success (Badian, 1994; Bryant & Bradley, 1985; Lonigan, Burgess, & Anthony, 2000; Torgesen, Wagner, & Rashotte, 1994), and a student's participation in teacher-directed phonological activities in school directly impacts the ease and pace of learning to read and write (Byrne & Fielding-Barnsley, 1991; Goswami & Bryant, 1990; Walton, 1995).

It is important to make a distinction between phonological awareness and phonemic awareness. Phonological awareness is an umbrella term, and phonemic awareness is a subtype. The phonology umbrella covers all levels of awareness with phonemic awareness being the most sophisticated. Students typically move through a progression of increasingly more sophisticated phonological skills. See Figure 3.8.

Many children enter the phonological system by first considering rhyme. Children begin to notice how words sound the same, such as *cat, hat,* and *bat*. Typically, rhyme awareness starts to develop in the preschool years. Children who have not developed rhyme awareness will depend on making meaning of language when

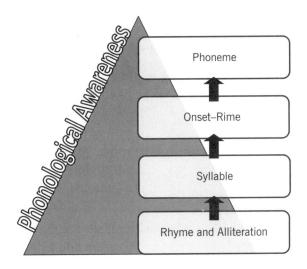

FIGURE 3.8. Phonological awareness progression of development.

faced with a rhyming task. For example, when shown the pictures of a wall, a cat, and a hat, the child might say, "Cat and wall . . . the cat sits on the wall" when asked for the rhyming pair.

As children start to develop an awareness of rhyme, they also begin to notice how words sound at the beginning as a result of teacher-led instruction—they develop an awareness of alliteration. Children will begin to notice that their name begins like a friend's name, such as Bella and Benita. They will enjoy books like *Four Famished Foxes and Fosdyke* (1995) and *Some Smug Slug* (1996), both by Pamela Duncan Edwards. These students are able to sort objects or pictures by like beginning sounds.

Refining their phonological understanding more, children will then begin to develop the syllable awareness that Janya had at the beginning of the chapter. A syllable is a unit of sound anchored on a vowel. Children will clap syllables in words, clapping twice for *ti-ger*, three times for *kan-ga-roo*, and four times for *rhi-no-cer-os*. Throughout this stage, emergent children are continually developing a more sophisticated awareness as they interact more with spoken language. This syllable awareness propels students toward the understanding that spoken language is made up of words.

As they work through syllables during targeted instruction, they begin to move inside the syllable and work on initial sounds in syllables. Children at the end of the emergent stage, entering the beginner stage, will begin to process sounds within the syllable. They can segment the initial sound in words, solidifying their awareness of onset and rime. An onset is the initial sound of a syllable, including single consonants, digraphs, and blends (e.g., the *c* in *cat*, *sh* in *ship*, *bl* in *blade*). The rime is the vowel and everything that follows (e.g., the *at* in *cat*, *ip* in *ship*, *ade* in *blade*). This ability to process the onsets of words will equip emergent readers with the foundational skills necessary to begin developing a full concept of a word in text. They can now identify the beginnings and endings of words, enabling them to track accurately.

As they are developing their concept of word in text, they are also negotiating words in spoken sentences. These phonological skills will help them develop a full concept of word in text (Flanigan, 2007; Morris, Bloodgood, Lomax, & Perney, 2003). They will also begin to distinguish among words in a spoken sentence. When asked to push a marker for each of the spoken words in "I like school," an emergent reader might be able to push one marker for each of the three words. Emergent children often attach articles to nouns or keep participle phrases intact while pushing for words in a sentence, pushing three markers for "I ride"—"the bus"—"to school." They will also push multiple markers for multisyllabic words, pushing six markers for "I like to eat piz-za."

Last, children will be aware of all sounds in a word, otherwise known as phonemes. Once children are aware of phonemes, they have entered the beginner stage. Therefore, our children in the emergent stage will focus on rhyme–alliteration, word–syllable, and onset–rime, depending on their assessed needs.

Developing a Comprehensive Understanding of the Alphabet

Another critical awareness emergent readers must gain is the alphabetic principle. This is the awareness of understanding letters are connected to sounds. In fact, preschool and first-grade children's knowledge of alphabetic print predicts later reading development (Lonigan et al., 2000; Storch & Whitehurst, 2002). Students must learn letter names and their corresponding letter sounds. The feature scores from the TSI can give you information about your students' knowledge of letter sounds. To gain a more comprehensive picture, you should also use an informal assessment of their letter–sound knowledge as well as their ability to name letters. Armed with this data, you can strategically choose letters for alphabet instruction.

Students must also learn how to form letters. The act of forming letters, much less spelling words, is very laborious for emergent writers (Berninger, 1999; Graham & Harris, 2000). While many recognize the support of letter names in learning letter sounds (e.g., Scanlon, Anderson, & Sweeney, 2010), Graham (2009–2010) contends that learning letter names is equally important for writing because the name can "serve as a cue for retrieving from memory the motor program for writing it" (p. 23). Students must practice letter formation to reach automaticity so that they can extend the majority of their cognitive energy on letter–sound connections. Handwriting instruction can positively impact writing fluency, length, *and* quality (Graham, 2009–2010) and is, therefore, warranted in a comprehensive primary literacy diet. Explicit handwriting instruction is more beneficial than incidental instruction (Graham, Harris, & Fink, 2000) and should, therefore, be the mode of instructional practice.

Your explicit instruction and practice can include verbal rehearsals of formation, such as "up, around, down, and across" for lowercase *f*. However, Graham cautions teachers not to have students use this language while practicing letter formation (2009–2010) because this may possibly tax memory during the task. Letter-formation guides that include numbered formation cues are particularly helpful (Berninger et al., 1997). Additionally, learning letter names is important since the names can work as a cue for formation as well (Berninger & Graham, 1998). Taking all of these handwriting points together, we suggest that in addition to teaching letter sounds you focus on the formation of the letters, providing (1) explicit instruction of the formation, (2) letter-name instruction, and (3) many opportunities for your students to practice using numbered models.

Common Core Alignment

The previous section describes what children at the emergent stage should *know* about phonology, letter–sound correspondence, and concepts of print (e.g., beginning sound awareness). The Emergent Word Knowledge Toolkit in Chapter 4 describes activities that promote what children should *be able to do* with this emergent reader knowledge (e.g., sound sorting promotes children's ability to write a letter for consonant sounds). Figure 3.9 identifies the Common Core State Standards (CCSS) foundational skills that children *should know and be able to use*, which are targeted in this chapter.

Emergent Readers and Writers: A Balanced Literacy Diet

Reading instruction for emergent readers, writers, and spellers should follow what we will call a literacy *diet*. As with the nutritional diets we follow, a literacy diet should be balanced and comprehensive, comprising all necessary components. To build upon this analogy, each component can be further refined by *portion size*. In the literacy diet, the portion size relates to the allotted instructional time in the classroom. Teachers who employ a well-balanced and appropriately proportioned literacy diet will help their emergent students develop into healthy, achieving readers.

The literacy diet for emergent readers consists of targeted, assessment-based instruction to develop foundational skill in reading skills, word knowledge, writing, and oral language. While addressing these components, we build upon the defining characteristics of the emergent stage as we work to increase our students'

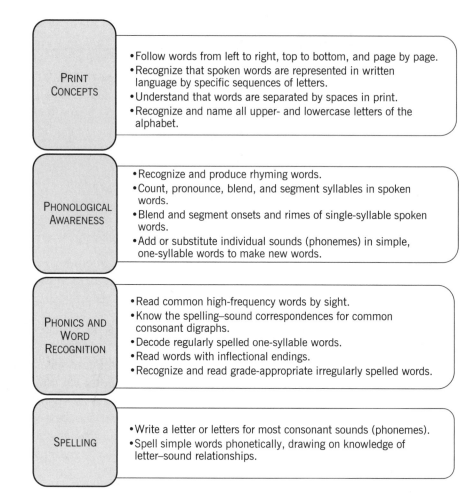

FIGURE 3.9. Common Core alignment.

strengths and match our instruction to their developmental needs. See Figure 3.10 for more detail about the components and their corresponding time allotments.

Although all components of the literacy diet factor into successful word knowledge development, the rest of this chapter is devoted to the components most directly related to word knowledge in emergent instruction: (1) small reading groups and (2) instruction in word knowledge. However, some of the suggested activities will fall within writing instruction and practice, as well as read-aloud components. Literacy instruction in the emergent classroom is incorporated throughout the day, and many activities are built to encourage foundational literacy skills. Chapter 4 presents instructional strategies to use during the word knowledge portion of the literacy diet.

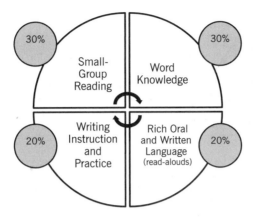

FIGURE 3.10. A balanced literacy diet for emergent readers.

Emergent Milestones

As you plan a balance across the components of the toolkit, you should also keep the milestones of this stage in mind. Ensuring student growth, and success, will rest both on the ways you balance activities and on your attention to milestones. The first step is using assessment to determine what your students already know and where you should target your instruction. This assessment data should help you measure progress toward the milestones. Throughout the stage, an emergent reader/writer must:

- Spell with initial and final sounds.
- Begin to use letter–sound correspondences when writing.
- Use initial sounds to help them track memorized text more accurately.
- Track accurately during memorized reading with self-corrections.

You must guard against instruction that is just a bank of activities. Rather, you will strategically plan your instruction with student assessment information and these milestones in mind.

Daily and Weekly Schedules

The activities detailed in Chapter 4, The Emergent Reader's Toolkit, can easily be incorporated into your language arts block. Let's return to Janya and Mr. Moore's kindergarten classroom to see how he incorporates word knowledge instruction into his 120-minute literacy block. Mr. Moore organizes his literacy instruction around the four components of the literacy diet with close attention to the portion sizes outlined in Figure 3.10.

1. *Small-group reading instruction* (60 minutes). Mr. Moore has three groups established in his classroom and meets with each group daily for approximately 15–20 minutes each. He organizes these flexible groups according to student literacy strengths and needs; the groups change as needed. Students not meeting with Mr. Moore rotate through two other stations: (a) small group with teacher-directed extension work with the push-in reading specialist, Ms. Greer, and (b) academic centers that focus on literacy, math, and thematic units. (*Note*: Janya's school has scheduled two reading support teachers to "push" into the kindergarten and first-grade classrooms during small-group rotations of language arts.)

2. *Word knowledge* (15 minutes). This work is incorporated into the small-group reading instruction. See below for a description.

3. *Writing workshop* (15 minutes). Mr. Moore usually organizes his writing workshop in the following two parts: (a) whole-class shared writing and (b) individual writing time while Mr. Moore and Ms. Greer conference with students.

4. *Read-aloud* (30 minutes). Mr. Moore uses this time to read aloud rich language texts, using both narrative and informational texts. He focuses his read-alouds on a variety of purposes and frequently rereads books for different purposes. For example, he will read from the *Let's Read and Find Out Science* series *Animals in Winter* (Bancroft, 1997) to focus on science concepts about adaptation as seasons change. During this initial reading, he will attend to vocabulary/concept development as well as early comprehension strategies for informational texts. Subsequent readings will focus on other aspects, such as print referencing or extending to phonological skills. With this book, he extends to syllable awareness with a syllable sort of various animals: fox, squirrel, and porcupine.

How do the students in Mr. Moore's class spend their daily small-group instruction across a week? Figure 3.11 illustrates a typical week. Since Mr. Moore includes word knowledge instruction in his small group and extends to Ms. Greer's group, the following details both Mr. Moore's and Ms. Greer's work. The activities in his schedule are detailed in Chapter 4.

Notice how Mr. Moore has chosen word knowledge activities from each of the parts of the instructional Word Study Toolkit: reading words, writing words, manipulating words, and transferring words. Attending to each part ensures his students are building a strong foundation of word knowledge:

- *Reading words*—Tracking Text; Get to the Word
- *Writing words*—Initial Sound Sort; Quick Write

	Monday	Tuesday	Wednesday	Thursday	Friday
Mr. Moore	Initial Sound Sort	Sound Hunt; Tracking Text	Initial Sound Sort; Tracking Text	Tracking Text; How Many Words?	Head, Shoulders, Knees, and Toes; Quick Write
Ms. Greer	Lowercase Formation; Syllable Sort	Get to the Word	Syllable Concentration	Targeted Word Hunt	Syllable Racetrack Game; Sentence Frames

FIGURE 3.11. Weekly word knowledge schedule in Mr. Moore's class for Janya's group.

- *Manipulating words*—Syllable Sort; Syllable Concentration; Syllable Racetrack Game; Head, Shoulders, Knees, and Toes; How Many Words?
- *Transferring words*—Sound Hunt; Sentence Frames; Targeted Word Hunt

However, Mr. Moore knows literacy instruction permeates the entire school day, especially in a kindergarten classroom.

- During morning message, he starts the day with jointly constructed message. Students assist by helping identify letters for sounds as they stretch out words. He invites students to "share his marker" to help form target letters. Students discuss where he starts writing on the page and where he goes once he has gotten to the end of a line.
- During writing workshop, he and Ms. Greer move around the room and support students as they explore written language. They assist with letter formation, letter–sound connections, directionality, and sound segmentation.
- While reading aloud, he frequently invites students to assist with reading by asking questions about print concepts. He also will pull out key sentences to highlight tracking text, matching his speech to print. Many read-alouds are followed by a modeled writing experience where Mr. Moore thinks aloud while writing a sentence about the read-aloud.

This kindergarten sample incorporates a teacher-created curriculum as the core reading program. You may be in a district or school using a basal reading program. To see an example of how the Word Knowledge Toolkit can be incorporated within a basal reading program, refer to Chapter 5 (pp. 125–126). In this example, Mr. Ramos, a first-grade teacher, uses the toolkit within his basal reading program.

When Will Your Students Be Ready to Move to the Next Stage?

As you move through the activities detailed in Chapter 4, you will begin to see your students applying the targeted skills. You will observe your students demonstrating the milestones of the emergent stage:

- Demonstrating accurate letter–sound knowledge.
- Spelling with initial sounds.
- Beginning to use letter–sound correspondences when writing.
- Using initial sounds to help them track memorized text more accurately.
- Tracking accurately during memorized reading with self-corrections.

These milestones should be met in the spring semester of the kindergarten year. Students should end kindergarten as beginning readers, the next stage of reading.

We suggest administering the TSI from Chapter 2 at least three times in a year in order to monitor your students' progress. The TSI provides you with specific information about letter–sound correspondence as well as phoneme segmentation skill. When you see students representing initial sounds or initial and final sounds, you know your students are segmenting sounds, or phonemes, in words. You may also have additional data from your students, such as letter–name and letter–sound knowledge (see Chapter 2) as well as concept of word development (see Chapter 4). Taken together, these assessments provide you with multiple pieces of evidence about your students' ability to:

- *Demonstrate* their understanding.
- Show *maintenance* and *transfer* of these understandings.

Our ultimate goal is for students to *apply* the phonics and spelling skills while reading and writing, demonstrating their growth in word recognition. Figure 3.12 provides guidelines for using assessment data to gauge these milestones.

The ultimate goal of instruction is to transfer word knowledge into contextual reading and writing. Observations of your students developing concept of word as outlined in Chapter 4 will help you look for reading transfer. You can observe your students' performance on the activities from the Word Knowledge Toolkit for writing transfer in Chapter 4. You can also take note of their writing samples. We have created the Writing Observation Guide: Emergent Reader to help you observe your students' writing on both toolkit activities and writing samples. A printable form is found in online Appendix A: Assessments (*www.guilford.com/hayes4-forms*). (*Note*: You will not use the guide until your students have demonstrated they are later in the stage.) You will need to observe the quality of their writing. If your students' writing is scribbles or mock linear, you will not use the guide. Likewise,

Milestone	Assessment Evidence
• Spelling with initial and final sounds • Beginning to use letter–sound correspondences when writing	• TSI: Score of 1 or higher • Letter–sound assessment • Emergent writing observation • Activities from the Emergent Reader's Toolkit
• Using initial sounds to help them track memorized text more accurately • Tracking accurately during memorized reading with self-corrections	• Concept of Word assessment

FIGURE 3.12. Emergent stage milestones and assessment evidence.

if your students' writing is letter-like or symbol salad, you will not use the guide. Once your students are using salient sounds or representing initial sounds, the guide will be useful.

The guide is designed to help you look for evidence of their application of letter–sound knowledge. Notice in the student example in Figure 3.13 that the observation guide is designed for individual student performance and provides you with six opportunities to note your students' transfer of their burgeoning letter–sound knowledge. We suggest you look for multiple points of evidence of transfer—4–6 points of evidence. Also notice the student in the sample has 4 points noted thus far with the teacher checking off evidence of letter–sound use and quality of writing. In preparation for parent–teacher conferences, the teacher noted evidence across multiple writing activities and samples, marked the dates of the work, and checked all letter sounds that were used accurately.

The teacher has completed instruction on four initial sounds: *B*, *M*, *S*, and *A*. After a review of the writing samples and activities, the teacher was able to systematically observe the student's letter–sound use. As you can see, this student is demonstrating good use of *B* and *M*. In contrast, the child is still not consistently using *S* and *A* accurately because at least four cells were not checked. The teacher made note of this and has made instructional decisions for the coming week to reflect this need. Moreover, the teacher was able to clearly communicate with the parents (using child samples) that the child is beginning to make letter–sound connections.

The assessments are presented in this book to provide you with the necessary information to build evidence of your students' growth. Armed with multiple pieces of evidence, you can confidently make decisions about the needs of your students that will ultimately guide your instruction. You will also have information about students who need more instruction and those who are ready to move forward. The milestones for the emergent stage help you make decisions about moving students to the next stage of word knowledge development—the beginner stage.

Writing Observation Guide: Emergent Reader

Dates	10/15	10/21	10/29	11/1	11/5	11/12
Consonants						
B	✓	✓		✓	✓	
M	✓	✓	✓	✓		✓
S		✓	✓	✓	✓	
T						
N						
R						
P						
C						
F						
D						
G						
H						
L						
K						
J						
W						
V						
Y						
X						
Q						
Z						
Vowels						
A	✓		✓		✓	✓
E						
I						
O						
U						

FIGURE 3.13. Emergent Writer Observation Guide.

Conclusion

Emergent readers are just setting out on their literacy journeys. They are increasing their understanding of how texts work and that the text carries the message separate from illustrations. Emergent writers and spellers are not making connections between letters and sounds. They are hampered by their limited letter–sound knowledge combined with their limited phonological awareness. The labor of their writing is exacerbated by a lack of letter formation knowledge. The Emergent Tier of the TSI provides you with information about their emerging letter–sound knowledge, as well as their awareness of the phonemes that make up words. By using the activities in Chapter 4 within a comprehensive literacy diet, you will be able to strategically plan instruction to help your students meet the milestones of the stage and move to the beginner stage.

The Emergent Reader's Toolkit

ACTIVITIES AND STUDENT STRATEGIES

GUIDING QUESTIONS

- What are the four categories of the Word Knowledge Toolkit for Emergent Readers that promote deep word learning?
- What activities promote emergent reader and writer transfer of word knowledge to contextual reading and writing?
- What activities in the Word Knowledge Toolkit help emergent readers develop a concept of word?
- What activities in the Word Knowledge Toolkit help emergent readers build their letter–sound knowledge?
- What activities in the Word Knowledge Toolkit promote letter–sound connections while writing and spelling?
- How do you know when your emergent readers have moved beyond the emergent reader stage to the beginner stage?

You will see that our description of the emergent stage has clear instructional implications. The activities presented in this chapter are organized into a Word Knowledge Toolkit for Emergent Readers. Our toolkit of instructional strategies for the emergent stage includes targeted strategies that allow you to focus on your students and the strategies that best meet their developmental needs. Our tools, or strategies, are chosen to get the job done—to increase student learning. Each instructional strategy introduced in this chapter will include its purpose so you can make good choices. Your students need to explore words in great depth; therefore, the toolkit will direct you to have your students:

- *Reading words*: Build alphabetic principle.
- *Writing words*: Letter–sound application.
- *Manipulating words*: Letter–sound analysis.
- *Transferring words*: Connect to context.

As you move through the week, you will work to ensure instruction across these four categories (see Figure 4.1), providing students many opportunities to read and write words while deeply exploring how words work.

Word Knowledge Toolkit Part I: Reading Words

Instructional Strategy: Concept of Print

- Purpose: to orient students to the macro- and micro-elements of books.

Children born into a literate society enter into a world of print. As children develop these print concepts, they begin to recognize the difference between print and pictures, they know the orientation of a book and can hold it right-side up, where text begins on a page, and how to transition from one line to the next. While they learn these more global aspects of print, they are also learning more about the micro level of print—letters and words. Justice and Sofka (2010) have taken the concept of print described by Clay (2006) and extended it to include a variety of print-referencing activities.

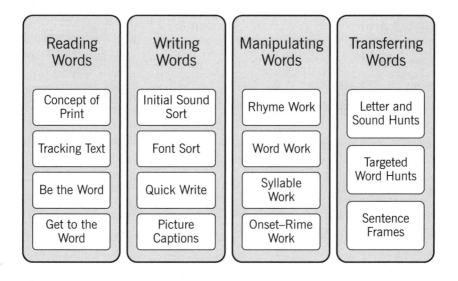

FIGURE 4.1. Emergent Word Knowledge Toolkit.

1. Use informal surveys like Clay's Observational Survey (2006) or simply observe children's interactions with text to see the print concepts your students need to develop. As you read aloud, invite your students to interact with the text making sure to include questions within the print-referencing categories in Figure 4.2 (adapted from Justice & Sofka, 2010).

2. Once you have information about their concept of print, you can start to organize your read-alouds to incorporate questions to encourage students to interact with print, using the print-referencing categories.

3. Invite your students to interact with the text during read-alouds with targeted questions revolving around their observed print concept needs. You can also encourage these types of interactions while your students engage in pretend and memory reading. Here is an example of what this approach might look like in a classroom. Begin a read-aloud of *Chrysanthemum* by Kevin Henkes (1991) with:

"Today we are reading this book. It's title is *Chrysanthemum*. [Point to the title.] The author is Kevin Henkes. What does the author do? That's right. The author writes the words, so Kevin Henkes wrote the words we will read. He also illustrated the book. What does the illustrator do? You got it. He also drew the pictures we get to look at. How do I get to my first page? Thanks. You are right. Now that we are on the first page, show me the first word on the page. That's right. Now which way do I read?"

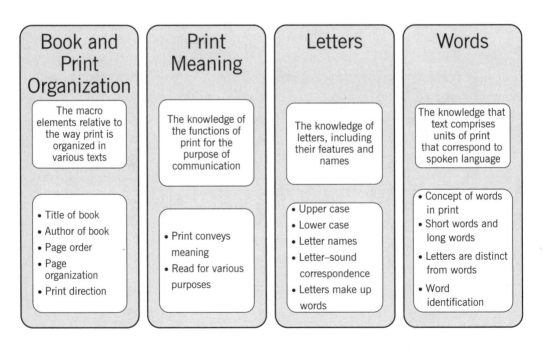

FIGURE 4.2. Print-referencing categories for emergent readers.

Notice that in this brief introduction before reading the book, the teacher has quickly included many aspects of book and print organization. See online Appendix B: Toolkit Activities (*www.guilford.com/hayes4-forms*) for an extensive list of questions you would ask your students organized around these print-referencing categories, as well as a checklist to gauge your students' progress in concepts of print.

Instructional Strategy: Tracking Text

- Purpose: to focus student attention to individual words in written texts.

Before you can begin this activity, you must assess your students' concept of word. You can use this informal assessment for your initial decisions about instruction as well as monitor progress over time. We provide the following guidelines for concept of word assessment:

- *Choose the text*. Choose a rhyme or predictable book that will be easy to memorize and has some instances of two-syllable words. For example, many nursery rhymes lend themselves to this: *Humpty Dumpty, Little Bo Peep*, and *Five Little Ducks*. If you choose a rhyme, we suggest converting the rhyme into a booklet, putting each line on a different page with a picture. You can easily find pictures for this purpose online.

- *Memorize the text*. Help your students memorize the rhyme or book you have chosen. We suggest using the pictures from your book to help. Using the picture assists the memorization process but it also helps cue your students to the line when they are doing the concept of word task. The most important consideration here is that you have ensured that your students have memorized the rhyme or book.

- *Read the text*. After memorization, you will model fingerpoint reading the rhyme or book for students. Tell them you are going to read the book and point to each word as you say them. Next have students fingerpoint read the memorized text. You will observe the tracking to note whether or not students can orchestrate speech to print, demonstrating a concept of word. Refer to Chapter 3 for a discussion about the continuum of concept of word development. Emergent readers will not be able to accurately track text.

- *Identify words in the text*. It is not enough to measure students' skill at tracking. You must confirm their concept of word by asking them to identify individual words within a line of text. To do this, you will choose one word per page. Point to the word and ask, "What word is this?" Students will provide a variety of answers based on their level of development. Some students may simply recite the line on that page or a phrase from the page, such as "sat on a wall." Other students will guess any word from the line without regard to letter–sound matches.

Still other students will try to use initial sounds as clues or reread the line to "get to the word." Whichever way, you will be noting whether they can identify words.

• *Interpret the text reading.* Take the tracking information combined with the word identification in text to make a determination about your students' concept of word. If your students are able to demonstrate a concept of word in text, then you will need to reconsider their Tiered Spelling Inventory (TSI) performance. A concept of word is characteristic of a beginning reader; emergent readers do *not* have a concept of word.

As your students read memorized texts for reading practice, have them track the print. This activity will help develop their concept of a written word as they orchestrate their speech with the print on the page. Fingerpoint reading, or tracking text, is a critical *first* step in helping your students become aware of words in print.

1. The first step is the choice of text. You can choose nursery rhymes, poems, jingles, emergent-level predictable texts, songs, or child-dictated texts. These texts must be easily memorized (remember, this is memory reading). Be careful of your choices. It is tempting to use seasonal songs or poems; however, these choices are not always ideal. For example, we often put movements to songs. It is difficult for children to move from singing with movements to reciting while pointing to words without movements. When choosing texts, you should consider the following:

- *Length of overall text*
  - Should be short with few lines per page.
- *Length of lines in text*
  - Should not have too many words in a sentence.
- *Ease of memorization*
  - Should be quick and easy to memorize; familiar rhymes, etc., are good options.
- *Number of single-syllable words*
  - Students just beginning benefit most from texts with only single-syllable words.
- *Number of multisyllabic words*
  - As students develop their awareness, bring in multisyllabic words.
- *Position of multisyllabic words*
  - At first, having multisyllabic words at the end of the line is more supportive.

2. Once you've chosen an appropriate text, make sure your students have it memorized. If using a poem or a jingle, orally memorize it prior to the tracking activity. If using an emergent-level, predictable book, use the book to help your students memorize. This memorization is often easy, because the students must only memorize the repetitive sentence frame as you point out the one-word change cued by the picture (see discussion in Chapter 3).

3. Now that the text is memorized, you should model tracking while you read aloud with very deliberate, clear pointing. Keep this slow and make sure to orient your text so that it is right-side up for your students.

4. Have children point as they read/recite the text page by page. You will model reading tracking the words on the page and then have the students point and chorally read the same page. Now move to the next page, with you modeling before they chorally point and read. Proceed through the book in this manner.

5. After your students have gone through each page, have them chorally read/recite the entire text as they point to each word. Monitor their speech-to-print match. To help monitor after they have pointed and read the entire book in unison, invite students, one at a time, to point and read a single page.

Modifications

- If students have difficulty, let them "piggyback" your finger. To do this, a student will put his or her finger on top of yours as you take the lead pointing while you both read aloud.

- For novelty, you can have a variety of pointers on hand. These pointers not only provide motivation but they also help exaggerate the act of pointing.

- If your children have difficulty tracking, consider your text choice. You may possibly need a shorter text with only single-syllable words in short, simple sentences.

- You should begin your early decoding strategy instruction even with emergent students building a concept of word. The main decoding focus for your emergent students is using the beginning sound. After your students track text, you will have them identify words within a line of text. During this activity, you will model, provide guided practice, and reinforce using the initial sound to identify words. We offer the following guidelines to help you respond to your students as they work to identify your target words. These guidelines are based on the work of Johnston et al. (2009), Morris (2005), and Clark (2004). A quick reference for responding to emergent students during reading is in online Appendix B: Toolkit Activities.

  o First, do nothing. Allow the child to try to identify the word.
  o If the child is not successful, ask what sound the target word begins with and what letter represents that sound. For example, you would ask a student trying to identify the word *sat* in *Humpty, Dumpty Sat on a Wall*, "What sound do you hear at the beginning of *sat*? Yes, /s/. What letter makes that sound?"
  o If the child correctly identifies the word, reinforce using the initial sound to identify the word. For example, you might say, "You used the first sound you hear in *sat*, /s/, to help you look for the word beginning with an *S*. There it is: *sat*."

o If the child incorrectly identifies the word, ask: Could that be _____?
Why not? These two questions allow you to discuss initial sounds of
words and matching the sounds with their corresponding letter.

o If the child remains stuck on a word, you can prompt with some general
questions:

"What is the first sound you hear?"
"What letter makes that sound?"
"Reread the sentence to find the word."

Instructional Strategy: Be the Word

- Purpose: to focus student attention to individual words
  in written texts.

As your students read memorized texts, have them track the print. This activity
will help develop their concept of a written word as they orchestrate their speech
with the print on the page.

1. Again, have students memorize the text to be used.
2. Make a card for each word in the memorized text, printing each word on
   an individual card.
3. Allow students to match their word cards to the printed text.
4. Students *read* the text in unison. Each student stands or holds his or her
   card up when his or her word is said.
5. Do this multiple times with students keeping their same cards. Then you
   can switch cards and do it again.

Modifications

- If working with a small group, you can use only one line from a text or
jingle to have children "be the word."

- Pair students to "be the word" when a student is struggling. Being the word
with a stronger buddy can help them participate.

Instructional Strategy: Get to the Word

- Purpose: to focus student attention to individual words
  in written texts.

You are accentuating words as you provide multiple opportunities for your students
to track print. However, children need many opportunities to identify individual
words. We have seen many children track print accurately, but then they cannot
identify an individual word in text. For example, one student successfully tracked

the line "Hands can tie." Her teacher then pointed to *tie* and asked the student, "What word is this?" The student replied, "Hands can tie." Not only could she not identify the word, she could not demonstrate that she had a concept of what a word really is. By engaging your students in activities that "get to the word," you are helping them build a well-developed concept of a word.

1. Give your students multiple opportunities to track the text you are working on in your small group.
2. Put individual lines from the text on a sentence strip. Make sure to put large spaces between the words.
3. Give one sentence strip to each child and have the children match their sentences to the text. Invite each child to point and read each of the sentence strips.
4. Give a pair of scissors to each child, having the children cut the line of text into individual words.
5. Have children count their words and compare sentences, deciding which sentences are longer or shorter. As students compare, have them "push" each word forward on the table as they say them.
6. Have students mix up their words and then rebuild the sentences. Students can refer to the original text if they need help.

Modifications

• If students have difficulty recognizing where to cut, you can support them in a variety of ways. Have students put a marker or sticker under each word before cutting the sentence strip into individual words. Or you can have students use a pencil or highlighter to make a line in between each word and have them cut on the line.

• To further emphasize the words, have students place the cut-up words on top of sentence strips with the text placed in a pocket chart. Matching the words as they say them will help them make the connection between speech and print.

Word Knowledge Toolkit Part II: Writing Words

Instructional Strategy: Initial Sound Sort

• Purpose: to focus attention to initial sounds as a way to develop letter–sound connections.

To develop letter–sound knowledge, you should focus first on beginning sounds of words. We suggest that you also call attention to the letter names. Many letter names provide information about the letter sound. For example, you hear the sound /b/ at the beginning of the name, *B*. The letter *M* has the target sound, /m/, at the end of its name. Children tend to learn the letters with the target sound at the beginning more readily (Treiman, Pennington, Shriberg, & Boada, 2008); however, these connections are generally helpful, whether at the beginning or end of the letter name (Bear et al., 2012). Once your students have some letter–name knowledge (they know at least 12 letter names), begin your initial sound instruction. Armed with some letter–sound knowledge, your students will be able to begin to participate in writing activities.

The sorting activity provides a critical backdrop to your letter–sound instruction. Sorting pictures or objects into categories provides your students with an engaging, hands-on activity. You will compare and contrast by initial sounds based on similarities (e.g., *mat, man,* and *moon* all begin with /m/ like *mouse*) and differences (e.g., *mat–mouse* or *mat–ball*; *mat* begins with /m/ like *mouse* and not /b/ like *ball*). In this way, learning letter sounds is a conceptual process requiring your students to recognize and use the similarities and differences among the pictures/objects through comparisons. This type of activity allows students to organize newly learned concepts and make generalizations about all members of the category. In other words, your students are thinking about how *mat* and *man* begin, as well as why they belong with *mouse* and the initial sound /m/. Notice how the steps in this activity revolve around helping your students make these generalizations. Your sorts should always be constructed to review previously taught sounds as you bring in new sounds. This way, students are always reviewing and solidifying as they learn new sounds. This recursive type of teaching helps students build accuracy and automaticity.

Online Appendix B: Emergent Toolkit Activities (Initial Sound Sorting) provides a suggested sequence: *B, M, S, A, T, N, R, O, P, C, F, I, D, G, H, E, L, K, J, U, W, V, Y, Z, Q, Z*. We offer this sequence based on: (1) the letters that occur more frequently in simple words are taught first, (2) letters that have similar sounds and are easily confused are separated, (3) vowels are incorporated early, and (4) the first letters taught will allow you to make simple consonant–vowel–consonant words through oral blending (e.g., *mat, sat, bat*). You will modify the sequence based on student performance on the Emergent Tier of the TSI and your letter–sound assessment. The sequence is not meant to be used in a "letter-a-week" approach. Rather, we present the sounds in sorting contrasts so you will teach multiple sounds during any given week. Notice how we begin the contrasts. We start with two and then add another before moving to the third sorting contrast as a review plus a new vowel sound. This allows you to teach and provide recursive practice in a fraction of the time relative to a letter-a-week approach.

1. You will need to assess your students' letter–sound knowledge to identify sounds they know and those they have yet to learn. For letters with more than one sound (e.g., *g* in *girl* vs. *g* in *gentle*), our targets are:

- Short *a* as in *apple*
- Short *e* as in *Ed*
- Short *i* as in *igloo*
- Short *o* as in *octopus*
- Short *u* as in *up*
- Hard *g* as in *girl*
- Hard *c* as in *cat*

2. Consider your sequence of study. We will first target more frequent letter sounds (e.g., /m/ is more frequent than /y/), and at first, we will separate those that are visually and/or phonetically too similar (e.g., M and N). Last, you should compare and contrast two to four sounds during sorting. Although it may seem counterintuitive, teaching the letters in sets is more effective than teaching them one at a time. You should also bring previously taught sounds back into the sorting contrasts to ensure maintenance. Again, refer to online Appendix B: Emergent Toolkit Activities for an extensive set of possible sorts presented in a suggested sequence.

3. Now that you have your target letter sounds and a sequence of study, create your initial sound sort. These sorts are done with pictures, emphasizing the initial sounds. Be careful not to use pictures with initial blends or sounds outside our target. For example, do not use a picture of *clock* for C. Emergent children need to hear the sound without the complication of the blend. You would also not use a picture of a *giraffe* for G because our target sound will be hard *g* as in *girl*.

4. Choose a key word/picture to use as a *consistent* reference for each letter sound. See online Appendix B: Emergent Toolkit Activities, where a keyword is suggested for each sorting contrast (e.g., *mouse* for /m/). We have offered a set of keywords for each initial sound you will teach. These can be enlarged and posted in your classroom for easy reference. These keywords/pictures will be used with each sorting contrast you use.

5. Introduce the key word/picture to your students by emphasizing the letter name as well as the letter sound and the initial sound keyword. For example, see Figure 4.3 with the sort contrasting /b/ and /m/. You would introduce /b/ by saying:

> "Here is a picture of a ball. *Ball* starts with the /b/ sound. /b-b-b-awl/. You say it: /b/. *Ball* starts with the sound /b/. The letter B makes the /b/ sound we hear at the beginning of *ball*. What sound do you hear at the beginning of *ball*? Yes, that's right, /b/."

6. Model sorting at least one picture while thinking aloud.

> "Here's a picture of a bird. /b-b-b-ərd/. I hear a /b/ at the beginning of *bird*. *Bird–ball. Bird–mouse. Bird* and *ball* both begin with the same sound, /b/. I hear /b/ at the beginning of *bbb-bird* and *bbb-ball*."

7. Invite your students to continue with the sort. Identify any pictures they are unsure of right away to keep the focus on the target initial sounds. Have your students name each picture as they sort.

8. If students have any confusion, refer them back to the key word. You can also refer them back to an entire category. For example:

> "So, we have a picture of the moon. *Mmmmmmoon*. Does *moon* start like *bird* or *mouse*? *Mmmmmoon–bbbbird*. *Mmmmoon–mmmmouse*. I'm thinking *moon* begins with /m/ like *mouse*. Let me check with the other pictures. *Mouse, mop, man, moon*. Yes, they all begin with /m/."

9. After all picture cards are placed, you should review each category. Make sure to have your students think about one key question: Do the categories "sound right"? Does the /m/ group with *mouse* have only pictures of words beginning with /m/? Does the /b/ group with *ball* have only pictures beginning with /b/? Also, make sure to bring your students back to the letter name of the target sound: *mouse* begins with /m/ and the letter that makes that sound is *M*.

Modifications

• Sometimes you may want to have your students explore the initial sounds of pictures themselves, deciding on the categories and identifying the initial sounds. For example, you could have provided your students with all of the pictures for the /b/ versus /m/ sort in Figure 4.3. Invite the children to sort the pictures by their beginning sound. If they have any difficulty at first, you can start the sort and invite them to finish. After they have placed all pictures into their categories, talk about the initial sound of each category and then bring in your key word/picture card to talk about the letter that maps onto the initial sound.

• Play initial sound games. You can take just about any well-known game, such as Concentration or Bingo, and turn it into an initial sound game. For Concentration, you would match pictures by their initial sound. For Bingo, you would choose a picture card and then put a marker on your Bingo board if you have an initial sound match. You can also play a racetrack game in which your students pick a picture card and move spaces to get to a picture beginning with the same sound. See online Appendix B: Emergent Toolkit Activities for printable forms and example games.

• Sound cards are also a fun extension. These are used to help develop automaticity with letter sounds. See Figure 4.4. At the top is a quick-practice box. You can use this to demonstrate and/or have your students practice providing the letter sounds before getting started. Then they simply read across each line, saying each letter sound.

FIGURE 4.3. /b/ versus /m/ sort.

Instructional Strategy: Font Sort

- Purpose: to call attention to the visual aspects of letters to assist in letter recognition, and ultimately, letter formation.

Knowing the ABC song is a first step to learning the alphabet. However, children must go beyond the song and develop a deep knowledge of the alphabet. They must know the names and shapes of each letter. To do this, they must recognize the visual aspects of letters and learn how to form them. Not only do they need to learn the 26 letters, they must know the upper- and lowercase versions of each. Having your students track an alphabet strip while singing the "Alphabet Song" is a mainstay kindergarten activity. Inviting children to find target letters after tracking/singing the ABC's is another common kindergarten activity. Font sorts take this work a step further. A font sort allows your students to further explore the visual aspects of letters. Moreover, font sorts are an effective extension of

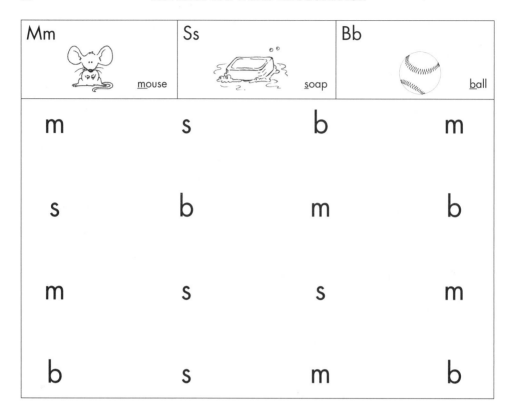

FIGURE 4.4. Sound card for /m/, /s/, /b/.

explicit formation/handwriting instruction, while at the same time reinforcing letter names.

1. Using your word processing program, select a variety of fonts for your target letters. Make sure the fonts chosen remain true to the characteristics of each letter you must emphasize for your students. Do not choose fonts with too much embellishment. Usually, six or eight fonts provide enough examples. See Figure 4.5 for an example font sort. As you begin, use a basic, primary font for your header card. Talk about the visual aspects of the letters. You probably already have language you use to describe these aspects of letters. For example, the Handwriting Without Tears curriculum uses the following language for lowercase *b*: "dive down, swim up and over, then around and bump" (Olsen, 2013). With each of your font samples, you will use this same language to emphasize the main visual characteristics of the letter despite the font.

2. After the font sort is completed, invite your students to review each letter and its formation. Last, they should have practice forming the letters themselves. As students write letters, use the formation language to guide them.

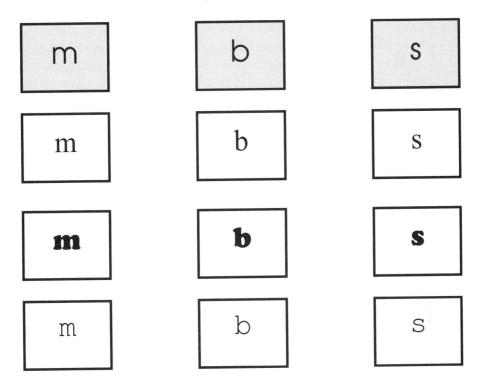

FIGURE 4.5. Font sort for *m, b, s.*

Modifications

• To further emphasize letters, you can engage your students in letter hunts. Students can hunt for letters in the ABC charts you use for tracking while singing the ABC song. They can hunt in the texts you use to practice tracking print to develop a concept of written word. You can invite students to hunt for target letters during read-alouds or during shared writing activities.

• For additional practice recognizing letters, invite your students to play games such as Concentration and Bingo where they match upper- to lowercase letters. See Figure 4.6. Notice this Bingo board has only eight cells. Students play quick games to match upper- and lowercase as they work to get four in a row.

• Students can also get extra practice recognizing letters by tracking the alphabet while singing the "Alphabet Song." For engagement, you can sing the alphabet to various tunes. Use different fonts to build identification skills. We suggest setting up your ABC chart to match the tune. Figure 4.7 illustrates this point with a few common children's songs. This modification will allow for easier follow-up. After singing and tracking, play a quick game of I Spy. Having students identify letters is critical for learning. If students have difficulty, they can "sing

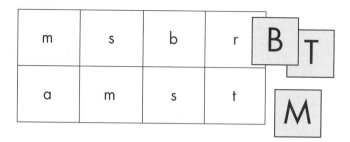

FIGURE 4.6. ABC Bingo.

back" for the letter. Setting your ABC chart to match the tune allows you to more easily start within the song for students to sing back.

Instructional Strategy: Quick Write

● Purpose: to provide repeated practice with letter formation, working toward automaticity.

In order for children to write words, they must orchestrate a variety of skills. They need to segment sounds, make matches between letters and sounds, and form the appropriate letters. Your work across all categories of the Word Knowledge Toolkit will provide practice with each of these skills. The Quick Write activity will provide your students with fun, repetitive practice of letter formation. As your students practice, they will become more automatic and confident when forming letters.

"Alphabet Song"					"Mary Had a Little Lamb"				"Are You Sleeping"					
a	b	c	d	e	**a**	**b**	**c**	**d**	a	b	c	d		
f	g				**e**	**f**	**g**		e	f	g	h		
h	i	j	k		**h**	**i**	**j**		i	j	k			
l	m	n	o	p	**k**	**l**	**m**		l	m	n			
q	r	s			**n**	**o**	**p**	**q**	o	p	q	r	s	t
t	u	v			**r**	**s**	**t**		u	v	w	x	y	z
w	x	y	z		**u**	**v**	**w**	**x** **y** **z**						

FIGURE 4.7. Singing the alphabet.

1. For a Quick Write all you need is a personal dry-erase board or chalkboard for your students. Your Quick Writes can focus on letter names or letter sounds. Pass out enough dry-erase boards for each child with markers and erasers.

2. Tell students to write your target letter name or letter sound. You would say, "Quick write the letter for /m/."

3. Students will write their responses and then flip their boards to show their Quick Write. Once all are monitored, have them erase and move to your next target.

Modifications

• Some students may require additional assistance as they are learning letter names and sounds. You can provide additional support, for example, by adding your key word for the target sound. "Quick write the letter for /m/ as in *mmmmmouse*." Or "Let's quick write a lowercase *m*."

• Students may also struggle with learning letter formations. You can use the talking prompts to verbalize the steps in forming a letter, such as "Start with *n* and swim up and over. Remember *m* has two humps" for *M* (Olsen, 2013). In fact, these types of prompts are commonly used in preschool and kindergarten classrooms. These prompts may be helpful in *teaching* formation with your model; however, they have not been proven to be helpful for students to rehearse while *practicing* (Graham, 1983). Emergent readers have many balls to juggle while writing/spelling, and the rehearsal/verbalization may just be an overload. Therefore, if you have students who are struggling with formation, you may choose to forgo the verbal rehearsing/prompts and stick with a numbered model for practice where the letter has numbers to represent a sequence of strokes and lines a student makes to form a letter.

Instructional Strategy: Picture Captions

• Purpose: to build letter–sound connections through writing for sounds.

Writing helps your emergent students work within a written language in meaningful ways. Beyond exercises emphasizing letter formation, your students need opportunities to explore written language in meaningful ways. You may encourage pretend writing to facilitate a flow of writing. However, emergent writers need to engage in purposeful activities where they write for sounds. The Picture Captions activity is a way to engage your students in writing for sounds during an authentic writing event.

1. Provide your students with engaging pictures. Students enjoy writing about pictures of animals, for example, or events where a problem has arisen. They also enjoy writing about their personal artwork or the artwork of their classmates.

2. Have plenty of supports on hand. Make sure that the supports are regularly used throughout the school day so your students are familiar with them. For example, each student should have an ABC chart readily available at his or her seat. Your students should also have easy access to the class word wall, as well as supported practice using it.

3. Discuss what students will write about. Encourage them to concentrate on one simple sentence. This way they can concentrate on writing for sounds as you help them stretch out words and apply their burgeoning letter–sound knowledge.

4. After they have decided on a sentence, verbally count the number of words in the sentence. Then write a line per word on the student's paper. This step will further help them develop their awareness of a word.

5. Assist your students while writing, helping them stretch out words and apply letter sounds.

6. Follow up by having your students point and read their sentences when done.

Modifications

• If working with a group, you can jointly create a sentence and follow the steps above as a group.

• Writing a sentence may be too overwhelming. Rather than creating a sentence, you could have your students write a single word related to the pictures. You would help them stretch out the word and apply letter sounds. Or you can supply a sentence frame, having the students write only one or two words to complete the sentence. For example, if the students created the sentence "The panda eats bamboo," you would write: The _____ eats _____.

• Students who are just learning about letter sounds can write initial sounds only.

Word Knowledge Toolkit Part III: Manipulating Words

Instructional Strategy: Rhyme Work

• Purpose: to encourage awareness of rhyme in spoken words.

The entry level for phonological awareness is rhyme awareness. Kindergarten classrooms are filled with read-alouds of fun, engaging rhyming books. These read-alouds introduce rhyme to your students, but we need to follow up with activities to emphasize rhyme. To facilitate their skill at rhyming, we have offered a variety of activities to give your students plenty of fun, repetitive practice. These activities revolve mostly around identifying rhyme, because it is easier for children to identify rhymes in a text than to generate rhyming words. We will note whether the activity is identification or generation. Just remember to begin with those activities that identify rhyme, moving to generate activities when your students are accurate at identifying rhyming words. All of the following activities are provided to help build the rhyme awareness of your students.

All games presented in this section and the next are ubiquitous activities we have all seen in classrooms and used ourselves; we do not know their archival sources. We have selected them because we have seen them work in classrooms to provide targeted practice while engaging students. Our directions for each game come from our own observations about how to make them work best in a classroom environment.

Rhyming Picture Sorts: Rhyme Identity

1. Select pictures of rhyming words that will provide your students with at least two rhyming contrasts; do not use more than four contrasts. For example, you may choose to focus on words that rhyme with *mop* and words that rhyme with *cat*. You could choose the following pictures: *hop, stop, top* and *hat, rat, bat*.

2. Model placing one or two rhyming pictures. Emphasize the rhyming chunk. For example, you would say:

> "I'm going to look for pictures that rhyme with *cat* or *dog*. Here's my first one. *Hat. Hat–cat. Hat–dog. Hat* and *cat* rhyme or sound the same at the end. They both end with /ăt/. *Hat–cat*."

3. Have students say each picture as they place them into their rhyming categories.

4. Once they are finished sorting their pictures, have students "read" their pictures and discuss their categories.

See You Later, Alligator!: Rhyme Identity

1. Collect three pictures, two rhyming pictures and one that does not rhyme with the other two. This is an oddity task, where students choose the odd man out.

2. Show the pictures to your students, naming each one. Challenge them to find the one that does not rhyme. When they have their answer, have them push the picture that does not rhyme while saying, "See you later, alligator!"

3. Reinforce their answer by emphasizing the rhyming chunk. For example, if shown pictures of *hat, cat, mop*, your students would say, "See you later,

alligator!" to *mop*. You would reinforce their answer by saying, "Yes. *Hat* and *cat* both end with /ăt/."

Make a Match: Rhyme Identity

1. Collect four pictures. One picture will be your target picture and the other three will contain one that rhymes with your target and two that do not. The goal with this activity is not to find the odd one out like in See You Later, Alligator! Instead, you are finding the one to keep in—to make a match.

2. Show the pictures to your students, naming each one. Tell them which picture is your target and challenge them to find the one picture that rhymes with the target.

3. Reinforce their answer by emphasizing the rhyming chunk. For example, if your students are shown the target picture *frog* along with *bat, gum,* and *log,* they would "make their match" between *frog* and *log*. You would respond by saying, "Yes. *Frog* and *log* both end with /ŏg/. They rhyme."

Rhyming Go Fish: Rhyme Identity

1. Collect a bank of picture cards. Thirty or so pictures of rhyming pairs will be plenty for a group of four children with each child getting four cards. Make sure to have enough variety in the rhyming pairs for an enjoyable game.

2. Shuffle and deal the picture cards. Continue play using the same general rules of traditional Go Fish.

3. Encourage students to lie down any rhyming pairs they have in their hands. Before play begins, the rhyming pairs must be verbally presented to the group and agreed upon.

4. The first player asks another player if he or she has a rhyming picture. For example, if the player has a picture of a *pig*, then that player would ask, "Do you have a picture that rhymes with *pig*?"

5. If the child does not have a rhyming match, then the child says, "Go fish!" Then a card must be drawn. If the child does have a rhyming match, the child hands it over, and the rhyming match is laid down.

6. Play continues until a player runs out of picture cards. Then the group reviews the rhyming matches to see which player has the most rhyming matches.

Hot Potato: Rhyme Generation

1. Have a "hot potato" of sorts. This can be a beanbag, a stuffed animal, and so on. The students form a circle to get started.

2. Start playing by holding the hot potato and saying a word. Then pass the potato. The child getting the potato must then supply a rhyming word. For example, if you begin play saying "mat," then the next player must say a word rhyming with *mat*. To encourage a class collaboration rather than competition, players can always get help from classmates.

3. Play continues until the class cannot think of another rhyming word.

Rhyming Head, Shoulders, Knees, and Toes: Rhyme Generation

1. Have students stand in a circle. You begin by modeling. While touching your head, say your target word. As you touch your shoulders, knees, and toes, say another rhyming word as in Figure 4.8.

2. Play moves to the next child. Provide the rhyming target. Then the child must say the target while touching his/her head. Then the child touches his/her shoulders, knees, and toes while generating words that rhyme with the target.

Instructional Strategy: Syllable Work

- Purpose: to build an awareness of syllables in spoken words.

Children will work on their syllable awareness as they refine their understanding of a spoken word. Their awareness of syllables can be facilitated by the activities in this section. Some of these activities encourage them to segment syllables while others direct them to blend syllables. Regardless of segmenting or blending, the activities emphasize syllables and help students extend their understanding. The activities in this section will help you build children's awareness of syllables in spoken words.

FIGURE 4.8. Rhyming Heads, Shoulders, Knees, and Toes.

Guess My Word

1. You can choose to use a puppet for this activity if you like. There is no need to buy one; you can use an old sock with eyes and a mouth. Explain to your students that the object of the game is to figure out what word you (or the puppet) are trying to say. Explain that the word will be spoken one part at a time. The students will need to put the parts together to make the word.

2. Begin with two-syllable words and orally present the word one syllable at a time. For example, say "ta-ble." A general rule of thumb is to pause one second between syllables, saying "one, one thousand" to yourself.

3. As your students are able to consistently blend two-syllable words, you can begin to include words with more syllables.

Syllable Sort

1. As with the rhyming sort described in the rhyme work section, you will choose pictures of words with one, two, and three syllables. Use headers with numbers 1, 2, and 3. If you are worried your students may not recognize all of the numbers, you can put dots on the header cards or have key words like *cat, rabbit,* and *kangaroo.*

2. Have your students verbalize each picture and clap for the syllables. Then sort the pictures by the number of syllables they hear/clap in the words. *Zebra* would be placed in the two-syllable category with *rabbit.*

3. After the sorting is finished, have students say each word, count the syllables, and explain why they have each picture in the categories.

Mystery Bag

1. Get a bag. We have used paper bags with question marks written all over them. Then collect a variety of objects with names comprising multiple syllables, including only one syllable. If objects are not available, you could use picture cards.

2. Have students choose an object/picture from the mystery bag. Once an object is chosen, the student must clap the syllables.

3. You can extend the work by grouping all mystery objects/pictures into categories based on the number of syllables.

4. You can also modify the activity by having a student select an object without showing the group. The student has to present the word by syllables to the group. Then the group must put the syllable parts back together to make the word.

Racetrack Game

1. This is a variation of the racetrack game in the writing word activities. You can use the printable version in online Appendix B: Emergent Toolkit Activities. Create the game by putting pictures with various syllables. You can have words with many syllables, such as *hippopotamus* with five syllables. Then you will need a deck of pictures for play. See Figure 4.9.

2. Students begin play by choosing a picture card from the deck. Then they clap out the syllables and look to the racetrack to find the space that matches the same number of syllables. They move their marker to the spot. Continue play until someone gets to the finish.

3. You can encourage collaboration and continuous participation by having the group work together and move collectively around the racetrack. Children can take turns picking from the deck, and the group would clap the syllables in unison. Or they take turns picking from the deck and clapping out syllables while the group confirms their answer.

Instructional Strategy: Word Work

● Purpose: to build an awareness of words in spoken language.

As children move along their awareness of the phonological structure of language, they become quite adept at identifying rhyme and start to explore spoken words in

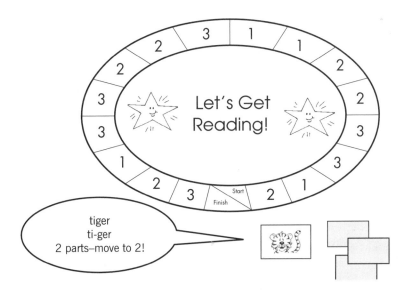

FIGURE 4.9. Syllable Racetrack Game.

sentences and phrases. The following activities are designed to facilitate an aware-ness of a spoken word. Remember, these activities are all oral without use of print. Each of the following activities is designed to encourage an awareness of words in spoken language. These activities are meant to compliment your concept of word in print work, working in tandem not only to build an awareness of spoken word but also of words in print.

Be the Word

1. As in the Be the Word strategy from the reading words activities, your students will "be the words." However, this activity does not have a connection to print. You will begin by having your students memorize a nursery rhyme or jingle.

2. Once memorization is confirmed, have students sit in a circle. Begin the recitation by saying the first word and standing up. Then the child sitting to your right will say the next word while standing up. Proceed around the circle with children saying the next word while standing up.

3. After going around the circle one time, start again. Simply begin the reci-tation at the point where you finished. Have all children standing and direct the next child to say the first word while sitting down. Proceed around the circle with children saying the next word while sitting down.

Head, Shoulders, Knees, and Toes

1. Like in the rhyming version, students say a word as they touch head, shoul-ders, knees, and toes. You will begin by presenting your students with a short sentence. Based on your students' abilities, you may choose very short sentences consisting of single-syllable words, such as "I like milk." Or you may choose short sentences with two-syllable words, such as "I can smell the yellow flower."

2. Model the first sentence for your students. Touch your head with the first word, shoulders with the second, and so on. If you have more than four words, simply move back up your body. For example, if working with the sentence, "I can smell the yellow flower," you would say "I" while touching your head, "can" while touching your shoulders, "smell" while touching your knees, "the" while touching your toes, "yellow" while touching your knees, and "flower" while touching your shoulders.

3. Orally present a sentence to your students to segment while touching. Stu-dents can do this in unison, or you can go around your group having students work with different sentences.

How Many Words?

1. Give each student a numbered chart like the one in Figure 4.10. A printable version ("How Many Words?") is provided in online Appendix B: Emergent Toolkit Activities. Each student will also need markers of some sort, such as unifix cubes or plastic chips. Orally present your students with a short sentence. As with the other activities, you would choose short sentences with single-syllable words or include two-syllable words. You may also choose to use a sentence from the text you are using to practice concept of a written word. In this case, you would be providing your students with oral practice before tying the work to print.

2. Model moving a marker into each numbered square as you say each word. Afterward, discuss how many words your sentence had. For example, if working with "I like milk," you would push a marker into the first square while saying "I," in the second square while saying "like," and in the third square while saying "milk." Then you would talk about how the sentence "I like milk" has three words.

3. Then give your students a new sentence to push markers for each word. The students can do this in unison or individually with the same sentence, or each student with a new sentence.

4. After your students push a marker per word, discuss how many words in the spoken sentence.

Instructional Strategy: Onset–Rime Work

- Purpose: to encourage an awareness of onset–rime in spoken words.

As children move to the end of the emergent stage and begin to move into the beginner stage, they need to start considering sounds within a syllable. This begins with the awareness of onset and rime, such as the /c/ and /at/ in *cat*. The following activities encourage students to segment and blend onset–rimes. In addition, these activities are all oral without a connection to print.

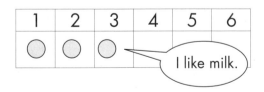

FIGURE 4.10. "How Many Words?" numbered chart.

Guess My Word

1. Collect pictures of single-syllable words.

2. Present your students with the target word, breaking it apart by onset–rime. As you break apart the onset and rime, pause for 1 second.

3. Ask your students to blend for the word. To provide assistance for later emergent readers, you will present them with two picture choices. They will match your clue to the picture. For example, you would say "c-at" while showing them a picture of a *cat* and a *cow*. The children will then need to work to blend the onset and rime, using the pictures to help support them.

Mystery Bag

1. Like the mystery bag in the syllable work activities, you begin with a bag and picture cards or objects. You need to collect pictures of single-syllable words. Make sure to include single-consonant onsets rather than those with blends. For example, choose c-at rather than cl-ap.

2. Students will pick a picture card out of the bag and segment it by onset–rime. As in the syllable version of the activity, they could also conceal the picture while saying it by onset–rime for the group to blend and say the word. Then the student can reveal the picture to check.

3. If students are not able to segment by onset–rime, you can use this activity as a blending game. You choose the mystery picture and segment it by onset–rime for the group. The group would blend the word, and you would reveal the picture for checking.

Word Knowledge Toolkit Part IV: Transferring Word Knowledge to Context

Instructional Strategy: Letter and Sound Hunts

- Purpose: to make the connection of the purpose of phonics/ spelling work to reading and writing.

A critical step to the letter–sound instruction detailed in the writing words section is helping students understand the application to their reading. A quick, easy, and, most importantly, effective way to accomplish this goal is to have your students look for examples of letters or sounds in the texts you are using for concept of word instruction. As students hunt for letters and/or sounds, you can reinforce how letter–sound knowledge is helpful while reading.

1. Keep notes about letters and sounds that have been taught to each small group. Target letters and sounds that are currently being taught as well as those that have been previously taught.

2. Preview texts used for tracking text activities to ensure plenty of instances where the target letters and sounds are used.

3. Have students turn to a specific page in books or line in text to hunt for the target letter and sound. Students can simply point to letters. Or you can supply them with engaging ways to point out letters, such as highlighting tape, Wikki Stix, viewfinders, and so on.

4. Make sure students are continually verbalizing the letter name and the letter sound as they point out their "finds."

Instructional Strategy: Targeted Word Hunts

● Purpose: to further build a concept of word in print.

Along with letter and sound hunts, students need to extend their concept of word activities in which they track text (see the reading words section). Tracking text during their "memorized reading" activities is a good first step; however, students need to build upon this activity by pointing out, or identifying, individual words in text. Students commonly use two strategies to identify words: (1) read back into the text and (2) use initial sounds. For example, you might ask students to identify *wall* in "Humpty Dumpty sat on a wall." The student might track the line again to "read back" to identify the word. Or the student might think about the text on the page and match the /w/ with the word starting with that sound—*wall*. It is important to encourage their use of these two strategies.

Targeted Word Hunt

1. Select texts for this tracking text activity using the guidelines on page 80. To further refine your selection, look for books with words beginning with sounds targeted during your initial sound sort activity.

2. Have your students turn to a specific page or attend to a specific line of text. Point to or highlight the target word and ask, "What word is this?"

3. Encourage your students to either read back in the text to help identify the word or use the initial sound.

4. Follow up after the word is identified by reinforcing the initial sound match of the target word.

For example, you might choose *My Monster and Me* (MCP Authors, 1996) for your tracking text work while you are teaching /m/. You would have your students turn to a specific page, such as "My monster munches a muffin." Then you would point to *muffin* and ask them to identify the word. Call your students' attention to the *m* starting *muffin*. Then reread the line while pointing to each word. Reinforce that *muffin* begins with /m/ and we see the letter *m*.

Instructional Strategy: Sentence Frames

- Purpose: to help facilitate letter–sound connections and provide models of sentence writing.

Your students also need to make connections to their writing. Picture Captions in the writing words section is an effective way to begin to make these connections. Sentence Frames can also encourage connections of letters and sounds while providing models of sentences. The sentences you use can be pulled from the texts you are using for your concept of word activities and tied to your initial sound work. Or they could be pulled from your read-alouds. Either way, Sentence Frames provide you with a supportive way to encourage your students to apply their letter–sound knowledge to writing.

1. Select a sentence to use for your sentence frame. Make sure it is short and engaging. Then choose a key word from the sentence to leave out. This blank space will become the target word for your students to write. For example, you could pull the repetitive sentence from *My Monster and Me* (MCP Authors, 1996), leaving out the final word. See Figure 4.11.

2. Point and read together the sentence and pause expectantly at the blank.

3. Help your students brainstorm options for the blank. If you want to encourage their use of a target sound, such as /m/, you could ask them to choose from their pictures from their initial sound sort targeting /m/.

4. Help students segment sounds in the words they are writing and make letter–sound connections. Encourage letter–sound connections but do not expect correct spellings. Helping students segment as many sounds as possible while making letter–sound connections is the goal, not correct spellings.

My monster munches a _____ .

FIGURE 4.11. Sentence frame for *My Monster and Me.*

_____ hibernate in the winter.

FIGURE 4.12. Sentence frame example.

Modifications

• Students may require more support. You can model segmenting words and making letter–sound connections. Then after modeling for the group, you can do examples as a group, inviting your students to help segment sounds and make letter connections.

• Sentence Frames can play double duty. For example, you can use Sentence Frames for tracking practice during concept of word activities. Or you may want to review key concepts or vocabulary from thematic units. After reading *Animals in Winter* (Bancroft, 1997), you may want to reinforce *hibernation* as a vocabulary term. So, your frame might be _____ hibernate in the winter. Students could use the read-aloud to brainstorm examples of animals that hibernate in the winter and then fill in their sentence frames. See Figure 4.12 where an emergent writer wrote "Bears hibernate in the winter" with the assistance of a teacher. Notice, the word is spelled phonetically and correct spelling was not expected.

Conclusion

Taking a developmental stance for instruction will allow you to target the needs of your students and ensure "just right" instruction. The TSI will help you identify the needs of your students, and additional assessments, such as letter–sound knowledge or concept of word, will help you fine-tune your instruction. At the same time, you will continue to focus on the milestones of the stage as you work toward those ultimate goals. Your instruction will fit within a balanced literacy framework, which ensures time for reading *and* writing alongside transferring these skills. This approach to word recognition instruction will move your emergent readers to the next stage—the stage of beginning readers.

CHAPTER 5

The Beginning Reader and Writer

BUILDING A BANK OF KNOWN WORDS

- What are the reading characteristics of the beginning reader?
- What are the writing/spelling characteristics of the beginning writer?
- How do the feature scores in the Tiered Spelling Inventory (TSI) guide your word knowledge instruction at this stage?
- What are the instructional milestones of this stage?
- How might you organize your literacy block for word knowledge at this stage?

Ms. Walker's first-grade class has 21 students. Some of her students are late in the emergent stage while others have moved into the transitional stage of reading and writing. The majority of her students are beginning readers and writers like Devonte. As students pile into the classroom this morning, Devonte checks in using the attendance roll, marks his lunch choice, and unpacks his backpack. Then he settles on the group rug with Ms. Walker and the rest of the class, ready for the morning message and calendar time. Ms. Walker transitions into her language arts 2-hour block with a whole-class read-aloud. Devonte particularly enjoys the read-aloud, especially today. The class has been learning about the Earth's cycles and changes in seasons. Today's read-aloud is *The Reason for the Seasons* (1996) by Gail Gibbons. Ms. Walker focuses on building content knowledge while also modeling the use of context to define unknown words.

Devonte moves through small-group rotations. Ms. Walker uses a traditional circle–seat–center format. When Devonte's group is with Ms. Walker for their small-group work, they concentrate on a combination of supported, guided reading and word knowledge activities. Today, Devonte's group is reading two Ready Readers: *The*

Lucky Duck (Clark, 1996) and *Rush, Rush, Rush* (Engles, 1996). Ms. Walker chose these books to help her students apply their target feature for this week, short *u*, and reinforce digraphs from previous lessons. They wrap up their day with *Be the Builder* as the students *build* words Ms. Walker orally presents. By the end of the activity, Devonte has the following *Be the Builder* sheet (see Figure 5.1). Notice how the activity provides a great deal of practice for Devonte to apply the /u/ in words like *duck* and *stuck*, as well as reinforce his use of digraphs in words like *rush* and *brush*. In addition, he has the opportunity to work on phoneme segmentation and blending, moving from *pug* to *plug*, *tuck* to *stuck*, and *muck* to *mush*.

Devonte moves to his center time, designed to promote targeted reading and writing practice. He chooses to write about the Earth's cycles. Specifically, he draws a picture of the Earth orbiting the Sun and writes about how the Earth's orbit of the Sun affects our seasons. You can see his writing sample in Figure 5.2. Devonte's writing is very consistent with the writing of other beginners. He uses a period to note the end of his overall piece but not individual sentences. Random uppercase letters find themselves throughout his writing, and reversals are noted with *B* in *orbits* and *D* in *and*. His spellings are phonetically regular, and he uses some spacing between words. He is also able to spell some high-frequency words, as well as content-driven words, due to his reference to the book *The Reason for the Seasons* (Gibbons, 1996). Last, we can read his piece given the context (i.e., Earth cycles), deciphering his phonetic spellings (e.g., SEZUNS for *seasons*).

The language arts block ends with Devonte's time at seatwork. Today, Devonte is playing a game his group played yesterday with Ms. Walker. He teams up with two other students to play Be a Star! This is a generic board game in which students move around the board selecting word cards as directed by their landing place. Devonte's group plays this game as a team rather than as individuals competing against one another. So, they move around the board together with only one playing piece. Upon selection, students take turns reading aloud each card. If the student cannot accurately read a word, he or she can get help from a friend. Once the players are to the end, they

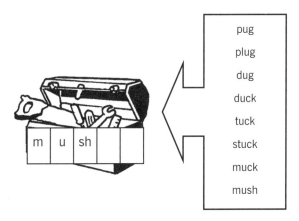

FIGURE 5.1. Devonte's *Be the Builder*.

FIGURE 5.2. Devonte's writing sample: The Earth orbiting the Sun.

count the cards they collected. Ms. Walker has challenged the students to have 25 words by the end of the game. The game includes one last step: the students must each write a sentence using at least three of the words. Devonte's sentence today used the following words from Be a Star!: *the, was, here.* See Figure 5.3 for his sentence: "The elephant was here."

This chapter is devoted to beginning readers like Devonte. We first outline the defining characteristics of the beginning reader, as well as the beginning writer

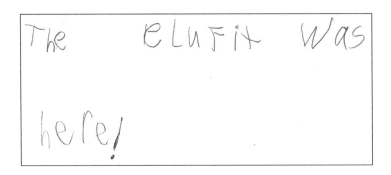

FIGURE 5.3. Devonte's *Be a Star!* sentence.

and speller. We then outline the common features of study for phonics and spelling instruction for the beginner stage. Next, we provide guidance on how word knowledge instruction fits within the language arts block for the beginning reader. Last, we present scheduling ideas and ways to monitor your students' word knowledge progress.

Characteristics of Beginning Readers and Writers

Devonte's literacy characteristics are consistent with those of a beginning reader (Bear et al., 2012; Ehri, 1997; Morris, 2005). In the spring semester of kindergarten, many students move into the beginner stage of reading and writing. Students tend to finish this stage in the spring semester of their first-grade year. However, you may have beginners at the start of kindergarten if they are exceeding grade-level expectations. Students who struggle learning to read and write may continue to be beginners as second graders or higher. Regardless of their age or grade level, beginners exhibit specific characteristics common in the stage. This stage is a stepping-stone to the next stage and is critical in laying the foundation on which to build.

Reading Characteristics: Building a Store of Known Words

The beginning reader and writer is *beginning* to accrue a store of known words (see Figure 5.4) but must still engage in word-by-word reading. We are reminded of a first grader who pushed his sleeves up, getting ready for the *work* of reading. The beginner labors through text. This labor is important to encourage, though. It builds the muscles necessary for real reading. To assist his efforts, the child will often fingerpoint while reading, and will always read aloud. On initial reading of a book, this work will produce a quite monotone rendition of the text. As he

Beginning Reading Characteristics	• Reads word by word. • Reads aloud. • Often fingerpoints while reading. • Reads in a monotone manner and with limited expression. • Has a limited bank of known words. • Begins to use code-based strategies when decoding.

FIGURE 5.4. Reading characteristics of the beginning reader.

repeatedly reads a book, our beginning reader can become more accurate and, therefore, more fluent and expressive.

The Common Core State Standards (CCSS) have thrown a monkey wrench into traditional descriptions of the text that beginning readers use. Specifically, the CCSS reference Lexiles (measures of readability that take the vocabulary and sentence length into account). However, these measures do not apply easily to the difficulty and supports of the texts beginning readers need. In fact, the Lexile map, available at *Lexile.com*, has a special designation, BR, to represent "beginning reader." That is because there is more to text description for beginning readers than meets the eye. There are a variety of systems available to help you measure beginning reader texts, such as Guided Reading levels (Fountas & Pinnell, 1996) and Developmental Reading Assessment (DRA) levels (Beaver & Carter, 2005). We will maintain the traditional language of text difficulty for these readers, as Lexiles do not apply. See Figure 5.5 for a conversion chart outlining common systems of measurement available today and how they relate to the more traditional descriptions of beginning reader texts. Specifically, we will compare traditional levels with Guided Reading, DRA, and Lexile levels.

Stage	Traditional Levels	Guided Reading	DRA	Lexile
Emergent	Readiness	A	A	BR
		A	1	
		B	2	
		B	3	
	Preprimer A	C	4	
Beginner	Preprimer B	D	6	
	Preprimer C	E	8	200–400
	Primer	F	10	
	Primer	G	12	
Transitional	Late First	H	14	
	Late First	I	16	
	Early Second	J	18	
	Early Second	K	20	300–600
	Late Second	L	24	
	Late Second	M	28	
	Early Third	N	32	

FIGURE 5.5. Beginning reader text conversion chart.

Texts for beginning readers range from Preprimer to Primer levels. Students at this stage enjoy the supportive nature of the Preprimers (late kindergarten to early first grade), a level comprising Preprimer A, Preprimer B, and Preprimer C. As they work with Preprimer A books, beginning readers benefit from the repetitive sentence structure and predictable word changes, cued by the illustrations. Beginners use the picture cues and initial sounds in words to help them read successfully. As they move to Preprimer B books, such as *Big Pig and Little Pig* by David McPhail (2000), they must rely more on their burgeoning decoding skills and building store of sight words due to the decrease of supports like repetitive sentences. Preprimer C books, such as *Big Egg* by Molly Coxe (1997), have limited support in the illustrations. Now the illustrations extend the story. The text is not repetitive and more text appears on each page.

Beginning readers then move into the Primers where they may find themselves involved in their first series, such as the *Biscuit* series by Alyssa Satin Capucilli (1996). Students may also begin to read for learning new information with nonfiction titles like *Octopus under the Sea* by Connie Roop (2001). Beginners at the Primer level also enjoy classic fiction titles like *More Spaghetti, I Say!* by Rita Golden Gelman (1993) or *Buzz Said the Bee* by Wendy Lewison (1992). Many publishers provide a multitude of options for beginning readers. Some popular publishers are Hello Reader!, Rookie Readers, and I Can Read.

Another text consideration for beginning readers is the type of text. Generally, we consider the criteria suggested by Hiebert (1999): literary quality (high-quality literature texts), high-frequency words (controlled vocabulary texts), and phonetically regular words (decodable texts). We suggest a balanced approach with these types of texts. Text choice decisions should be based on the reading needs of the beginner as well as your instructional purposes; how you use texts is especially important. If you are conducting a lesson to build your students' bank of high-frequency words, you need texts that provide multiple opportunities for your students to practice reading those words. In this case, a text with controlled vocabulary may be the best option. Likewise, if you are completing a lesson on word knowledge features (e.g., *ch, th, sh*), you will want to choose decodable books to give your students ample opportunities to use those features while decoding. Children need opportunities to solidify their word knowledge and flex their decoding muscles. Word knowledge has been self-taught in some studies (Cunningham, Perry, Stanovich, & Share, 2002; Share, 1995) and word-solving skills have been shown to improve (Menon & Hiebert, 2005) when students are provided many opportunities to practice decoding.

Children starting out in the beginner stage often tend to focus on salient features to help them read words. These features may or may not utilize the letters and sounds in the words. For example, they may attend to the two *t*'s in the middle of *little* or quotes in dialogue to remind them of *said*. Using this strategy is helpful at first; however, children will experience confusion when they encounter other words with similar characteristics. The child who uses quotes around dialogue as a cue for *said* will misread other words related to dialogue, such as *ask* and *says*. Beginners need teachers to guide them toward more strategic reading where they use code-based strategies flexibly and decisively. Code-based strategies require students to connect the letters in the words to the sounds they represent.

Writing and Spelling Characteristics: The Word-by-Word Life of the Beginner

You can learn much about a beginning reader by analyzing spellings (Bear et al., 2012; Ganske, 2014; Henderson, 1990; Morris, 2005; Read, 1971). Figure 5.6 summarizes the defining spelling and writing characteristics. Beginners start this stage with a limited awareness of individual sounds in words, or phonemes. At first, you'll notice your students omitting the medial vowel sound. Notice this omission in Figure 5.7. It is the result of early beginners' limited phoneme segmentation skills. They are not able to segment the medial vowel, so they are unable to represent it while spelling. As they move through the stage, their phoneme segmentation skills will advance, allowing them to segment and represent these medial vowels. At the beginning of the beginner stage, your students may be "using but confusing" some consonant sounds (Bear et al., 2012). Most consonant sounds will be firm by this point, but some may continue to be misrepresented, such as *D/T, B/P, K/G*. Remember these sounds from Chapter 2. They are the voiced and

Beginning Writing and Spelling Characteristics

- Spelling
  - "Uses but confuses" short vowel patterns, blends, and digraphs with a letter–name strategy.
  - Masters above features by the end of the stage.
- Writing
  - Begins to capitalize sentence and use ending punctuation; learns to construct sentences of complete thoughts but inconsistently uses spacing between words.
  - Has a limited number of automatically spelled words.
  - Writes short pieces due to their disfluency.
  - Continues to require conscious attention to navigate upper- and lowercase letters.

FIGURE 5.6. Writing and spelling characteristics of the beginning reader.

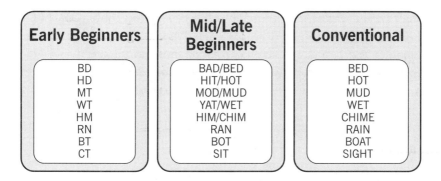

FIGURE 5.7. Comparing and contrasting early to mid/late beginners.

unvoiced paired sounds. These sounds may remain troublesome for students as they solidify their understandings. Other sounds commonly misrepresented are short vowels with some very predictable confusions, such as *A* for /ĕ/, *I* for /ŏ/, *O* for /ŭ/, and *E* for /ĭ/ (Bear et al., 2012).

Students at this stage will also often confuse consonant blends and digraphs. Their difficulty with blends also stems from their inability to segment fully. Students will often spell *flip* as FIP and *grab* as GAB. Some blends are particularly difficult. For example, affricate blends (e.g., *dr, tr*) are often confused because of the friction produced in your mouth. Try it yourself. Say *drive* and notice how the *dr* sounds like /j/. Now say *trick* and notice how the *tr* sounds like /ch/. Due to this, you may notice your students spelling *drive* as JIV and *trick* as CHIK. Another difficult blend is the preconsonantal nasal—the *m* or *n* prior to the final consonant (e.g., *sing, jump, honk*). Students who continue to have difficulty with preconsonantal nasals omit them rather than misrepresent them (e.g., SIG for *sing*, JOP for *jump*, HOCK for *honk*).

Beginning readers are often referred to as letter–name spellers (Bear et al., 2012). The team of University of Virginia researchers who coined this description was astute. Beginners use the names of letters to represent the sounds they segment in words. Consider the beginning speller who represents the /ĕ/ in *bed* as BAD. The /ĕ/ is most closely represented by the letter name *A*. Try it yourself. Say /ĕ/ and then the letter name *A*. Try the same thing with *mud*. Say /ŭ/ and then the letter name *O*. Think about the shape of your mouth and the sound. Both sounds are articulated in the back of your mouth, causing your mouth to make an "O" shape, and sound very similar. This same phenomenon explains HIT for *hot* and HIM for *chime*. The initial and final sounds in *hot* are represented correctly; however, the short vowel is not. Say the letter name *I* and /ŏ/. Again, we can easily see how the letter name *I* can influence the representation in a beginning reader's spelling.

If you are interested in knowing more about these spelling confusions and how to resolve them, we suggest you read *Words Their Way* (Bear et al., 2012). It is a text that we continue to learn from every time we reread it.

The misspellings of long vowel words—*chime, rain, boat*, and *sight*—are also very common. Beginners do not consider vowel teams (i.e., the silent letters used to represent long vowels). They have a very linear approach to spelling. They hear a sound and then put a letter down to represent that sound. These students do not consider the fact that some sounds require multiple letters to represent them. This explains why *chime* is missing the *e*-marker as a long vowel pattern. The letter name also explains the *H* for /ch/. Say the letter name—*H*. You will say /āch/. The beginner who does not already know about the digraph *CH* will use *H* because you hear /ch/ in the letter name. For these reasons, we can expect to have HIM as a reasonable beginning spelling for *chime* as in Figure 5.7.

Beginning writing is as disfluent as beginning reading for many of the same reasons. Beginning readers' disfluent reading is mostly due to their limited store of known words. Their writing is similarly disfluent because they cannot spell a large number of words without the need for painstakingly working through each sound. Not only are they stifled by their word bank but they are also orchestrating sentence construction and handwriting demands. The beginning writer must think about spacing between words, capitalization, punctuation, complete sentences, lingering letter formation issues, and spelling. Writing for the beginner is a labor-intensive task. Remember, though, that the labor is required for muscle building.

Beginning Readers' Word Knowledge Development: Common Features of Study

The major breakthrough for the beginner is increased accuracy and automaticity with short vowel sounds and with phonemic segmentation and blending. As beginners process more sounds in words, they are able to "anchor" to more parts of the word. With a better "anchor," they will be more likely to commit a word to their lexicon. Having a word in your lexicon means you can read and spell the word automatically—you no longer have to sound or stretch it out to read or spell it. Consider the child who still cannot consistently segment the medial vowel. Then think about *big, bag, bog, bug*, and *beg*. If your student is not "anchoring" the medial vowel, all five of these words would be represented as BG. Because of this, children in the beginner stage must participate in a systematic study of letters and sounds, including individual consonants and vowels, consonant digraphs, and consonant blends for spelling—the back end of the zone. As they move through the stage, you need to address more advanced features to support decoding—the front end of the zone.

Features of Focus for Spelling: Working at the Back End of the Zone

Figure 5.8 summarizes the orthographic features that children should examine at this stage of development for spelling. The selected features were informed by Bear et al. (2012) and Morris (2005). Key words to highlight target features are a critical piece of your explicit instruction. First, highlighting the target features using key words allows you to emphasize letter–sound connections. Second, use of key words also provides a consistent reference for you and your students. Third, key words encourage your students to begin practicing analogies. As you and your students study medial short vowels *a* and *e*, you will highlight the letter–sound connection by isolating the medial sound in *cat* and *bed*. You will also refer back to these words for analogous comparisons when students are unsure. For example, when spelling *task*, direct your students to say the word and compare with their key words: *task–cat* or *task–bed*. The orthographic features presented in Figure 5.8 also include key words to highlight each feature.

Short Vowel Word Families

We will begin instruction for early beginners with short vowel word families. The consistency of the medial vowel is a support for the early beginner. Students early in the stage benefit from this level of support, because they need to be able to read the words we use for instruction. As we ask them to read words from contrasting families, such as *AG* and *AT*, we take advantage of their ability to rhyme. To read the *AG* words, they simply need to adjust the initial sound with the rhyming chunk: *tag, bag, rag, sag, wag* and *cat, bat, hat, sat, pat, mat*. Short vowel word families are ending rimes. The rime unit of a single-syllable word is the vowel and everything that follows, thus the *at* in *cat* and the *ag* in *tag*. Note though, that we must quickly move students away from using the word family as a crutch to avoid processing the medial vowel (O'Connor, 2007). You will see that we only use the support of the families temporarily.

Initial Blends and Digraphs

Once your students are able to represent the medial vowels in words, whether or not they do so accurately, we can start to help them read and spell consonant blends and digraphs. If your students are not representing digraphs and are using letter–name representations or do not know them on a check of letter–sound knowledge, then you may want a very supportive contrast as in Figure 5.9. Notice how the student is spelling digraphs: HIN for *chin*, SIP for *ship*, and HAT for *that*. Our feature contrast would be chosen to teach digraph sounds in a very supportive manner. If, however, your students are confusing digraphs (e.g., CHIP for *ship* and

Short Vowel Word Families	
Short-*a* families	an (can) at (cat) ag (bag) ap (cap)
Short-*i* families	in (pin) it (sit) ig (pig) ip (lip)
Short-*o* families	op (top) ot (pot) og (dog)
Short-*u* families	un (sun) ut (nut) ug (bug)
Short-*e* families	et (net) eg (leg) ed (bed)
Across families	ot, et, at (pot, net, cat) ag, eg, ig (bag, leg, pig) op, ip, ap (top, lip, cap) ack, ick, ock (tack, sick, clock) ill, ell, all (hill, bell, tall)
Initial Blends and Diagraphs	
Digraphs	ch (chin) sh (ship) th (think)
l-blends	cl (clip) fl (flag) bl (blue) pl (play)
s-blends	sl (slide) sw (swing) sn (snake) st (stairs)
r-blends	gr (grape) cr (cross) dr (drive) tr (tree)
Short Vowels	
A (cat) I (pig) O (pot)	

(continued)

FIGURE 5.8. Beginning readers: Common features of study with key words.

U (bug) E (bed)		
Final Blends and Diagraphs		
Ending digraphs	ch (rich) sh (rash) th (math)	
Ending blends	sk, st, sh (desk, nest, cash) ck, ch, ct (tack, rich, act) ft, st, nt (lift, nest, ant)	
Preconsonantal nasal	ank, ink, unk (bank, sink, junk) amp, ump (lamp, jump) ang, ing, ung (fang, sing, lung)	

FIGURE 5.8. *(continued)*

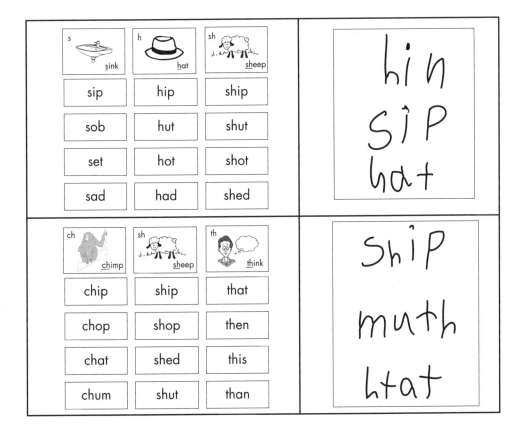

FIGURE 5.9. Digraph sorts to meet student needs.

MUTH for *much*), then your feature contrast would provide students with opportunities to compare digraph sounds in a less supportive manner.

Short Vowels

We work on short vowel word families early in the stage, and short vowels come up again for a second round of instruction to ensure mastery. The purpose of the short vowel word family study is to help your students "anchor" to the medial vowel. We work to help them segment medial vowels and begin to include them more consistently in their spellings. This anchor to the medial vowel also helps beginning readers commit new words to their store of words known by sight. Why would we bring short vowels back into our instruction? Through a study of medial short vowels, we move across word families and take away the support of the rime unit. Now instead of using the rimes *ET, AT,* and *OT* to help differentiate among words like *pet, pat,* and *pot,* your students will have to isolate medial short vowel sounds to differentiate among words like *mask, path, drag* and *nest, fleck, fret.* This review of the short vowel will often be quick; however, you may have students who struggle to make this transition.

Students at this stage use letter names to help them represent sounds that are unfamiliar or difficult. You'll observe your students, for example, spelling /ĕ/ with an A. Try it yourself. Say /ĕ/ and then the letter name A. Other vowels are equally similar: /ĭ/ and the letter name E, /ŏ/ and the letter name I, and /ŭ/ and the letter name O. Students experiencing difficulty with these sounds need to isolate contrasting medial vowels as they compare commonly confused short vowel sounds. See the sort targeting /ĕ/ and /ă/ (Figure 5.10).

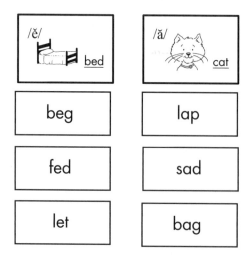

FIGURE 5.10. Sort contrasting /ĕ/ and /ă/.

Be careful with your word choice. Some consonants change the vowel sound. Consider the *a* in *cart, chalk, camp,* and *sank.* Then compare to the /ă/ in *cat* to the *a* in these words. Think about *bird, silk, limp,* and *pink.* Again, compare the /ĭ/ in *pig* to the *i* in these words. These four consonants, R, L, M, and N, impact the vowel sound across vowels, but so do others. The *w* in *hawk* impacts the sound of *a.* As is evident in these examples, sometimes the consonant works to control the vowel and change the sound, as in *cart, bird, fork, hurt,* and *germ.* Sometimes the vowel sound is not directly impacted, but the consonant poses a particular confusion for beginners. For example, the *l* in *elk* is difficult for a child who uses the letter–name strategy. As the child "sounds out," the vowel + consonant /ĕl/ matches the letter name L. Therefore, the child would most likely write LK, applying the letter name L to the /ĕl/. A good rule of thumb to remember is that vowels have a variety of sounds—long, short, and neither. For beginners, it is best to avoid the "neither" category until the short sounds are firm.

Final Blends and Digraphs

As your students build their phonemic segmentation skills, they will turn their attention to the ends of words. Digraphs (i.e., *sh, ch, th*) at the ends of words are relatively easy for the letter–name speller; your students can use what they know about digraphs to represent those sounds at the ends of words, such as *path* and *moth.* Your students also need to attend to consonant blends at the end of the word. We will focus on frequent ending blends, such as *lift, raft,* and *soft.* Common endings are:

-ft as in *lift*	*-st* as in *fast*
-sk as in *desk*	*-lf* as in *elf*
-lk as in *milk*	*-sp* as in *gasp*
-lp as in *help*	*-lt* as in *belt*

Students can contrast words ending with *FT* and those ending with *ST*, for example, as in Figure 5.11.

Preconsonantal Nasals

By the end of the stage, your students will need practice with difficult ending blends. Preconsonantal nasals are a subcategory of the ending blends in Figure 5.11 and perhaps includes the most common ending blends. They are included here as a separate feature because they are the most difficult to blend and segment. These blends include the *M* and *N* prior to the ending consonant, such as the *n*

-ft			-st		
		li<u>ft</u>			fa<u>st</u>
raft	left		last	fist	
shift	soft		must	cost	
tuft	gift		nest	list	

FIGURE 5.11. Contrasting ending blends: *FT* versus *ST*.

in *land* and the *m* in *camp*. Students learning about preconsonantal nasals need opportunities to segment the nasals, segmenting each sound in *camp*: /k-ă-m-p/. It is also helpful to think about highly frequent endings because the vowel changes when followed by a nasal. Consider the /ă/ in *cap* and the /ă/ in *camp*. Or consider the /ĭ/ in *wing* and *wig*. Lessons focusing on highly frequent endings can help your students have more accurate spellings of nasals. See Figure 5.12 listing these frequent nasal endings.

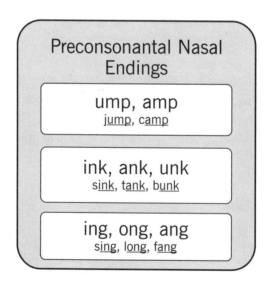

FIGURE 5.12. Highly frequent nasals.

Features of Focus for Decoding: Moving to the Front End of the Zone

Features at the front end of the zone of word knowledge development advance your beginning readers' decoding skills. As your beginners move into late Preprimer and Primer texts, you will notice a load on their decoding skills that involves vowel patterns. We are reminded of students reading books like *A Buzz Is Part of a Bee* by Carolyn Nunn (1990). In this book, students are confronted with words with vowel patterns in sentences like "A leaf is part of a tree" (p. 3). In this sentence, a student would benefit from knowledge about the vowel team *ea* in *leaf*. Without this knowledge, your student will take the linear approach of a typical beginner, saying /l-ĕ-ă-f/. If we consider teaching phonics features at the front end of the word knowledge zone, we can equip our students with the necessary feature knowledge for decoding. Books at the Preprimer C and up levels require students to have knowledge about vowel patterns, specifically vowel–consonant–*e*, *r*-controlled vowels, and vowel teams detailed in Figure 5.13.

Vowel–Consonant–*e*	aCe (cake) iCe (bike) oCe (bone) uCe (cube)
***R*-Controlled Vowels**	ar (car) or (horn) er (germ) ir (girl) ur (curl)
Vowel Teams ***Vowel Digraphs***	ai (rain) ay (tray) igh (light) ie (pie) iCC (kind) oa (boat) ow (snow) oCC (cold) ui (fruit) ue (glue) ew (chew) oo (stood/zoo) ee (sheep) ea (peach)
Vowel Teams ***Vowel Diphthongs***	oi (oil) oy (boy) ou (cloud) ow (cow)

FIGURE 5.13. Beginning readers: Features of study at the front end of the zone.

Vowel–Consonant–e

The most common, and subsequently most useful, vowel pattern for beginners is the vowel–consonant–e pattern. This feature will help your students as they work to become more and more strategic as decoders. Even when we think about learning high-frequency words, this feature is a major help. For example, consider *make, place, take, made, write, name, came, same, while*, and *those*. These words all come from the first 200 words on the high-frequency words list in Chapter 6 (Figure 6.15).

R-Controlled Vowels

Many words in the texts read by beginners have *r*-controlled vowel patterns. Having knowledge of this vowel pattern is essential for the beginner to successfully decode while reading. Fry (2004) analyzed a corpus of 17,000 words in an effort to determine the frequency of spelling patterns. He found that for vowels, the *r*-controlled vowel was one of the most frequent in this corpus. Fry recommended teaching the *r*-controlled vowel feature early. Taken with our own experience in texts written for beginning readers, we also believe in the utility of the *r*-controlled vowel pattern in words like *her, short, for, after, ever, large*, and *first*. Armed with this knowledge, your beginners reading "Sam is one smart dog" in *My Dog Talks* by Gail Herman (1995) will decode *smart* with a greater likelihood of success.

Vowel Teams

The vowel patterns that make up this feature include vowel digraphs (e.g., *ea* in *team* and *oa* in *road*) as well as vowel diphthongs (e.g., *oi* in *point* and *ow* in *frown*). This feature will also contribute to your students' greater decoding success; they will encounter words with this feature in the texts they read. In addition, learning more about this feature will help your beginners better learn the high-frequency words that are so crucial at this stage. Consider words like *each, about, look, how, down, know, took*, and *good*. All of these words are in the first 200 high-frequency words from Chapter 6 (Figure 6.15). Or consider your beginning readers in the Primer-level text *A Bug, a Bear, and a Boy* by David McPhail (1998) when confronted with the sentence, "The boy eats from a bowl" (p. 6). When you have instructed your beginners at the front end of the zone and addressed vowel teams, they can use the OW vowel team knowledge to help them decode *bowl* even if this would still be a difficult word for them to spell.

   The features of study for beginners previously outlined, including those from Figures 5.12 and 5.13, range from the back end to the front end of the word knowledge zone. Using the TSI, you will be able to identify the needs your students have for the back end of the zone. As your students move into late Preprimer texts and above, you will observe in books and/or in your students a need for instructing toward the front end of the zone to address those features necessary for successful decoding. Chapter 6 is devoted to activities to teach across the zone.

Common Core Alignment

The features we have described detail what children in the beginner stage should *know* about the written English system. The next Word Knowledge Toolkit section describes activities that promote what children should *be able to do* with this spelling-system knowledge (e.g., manipulating sounds in words helps promote children's ability to segment spoken single-syllable words into their complete sequence of individual sounds). Figure 5.14 identifies the CCSS standards detailing what children *should know and be able to do*, which are targeted in this chapter.

Phonological Awareness
- Isolate and produce the initial, medial vowel, and final sounds (phonemes) in three-phoneme (consonant–vowel–consonant, or CVC) words.
- Distinguish long from short vowel sounds in spoken single-syllable words.
- Orally produce single-syllable words by blending sounds (phonemes), including consonant blends.
- Add or substitute individual sounds (phonemes) in simple, one-syllable words to make new words.
- Segment spoken single-syllable words into their complete sequence of individual sounds (phonemes).

Phonics and Word Recognition
- Read common high-frequency words by sight.
- Know the spelling–sound correspondences for common consonant digraphs.
- Decode regularly spelled one-syllable words.
- Read words with inflectional endings.
- Recognize and read grade-appropriate, irregularly spelled words.

Spelling
- Spell simple words phonetically, drawing on knowledge of sound–letter relationships.
- Conventional spelling for words with common spelling patterns.

FIGURE 5.14. CCSS for beginning readers (skills spanning the kindergarten and first-grade years).

Beginning Readers and Writers:
A Balanced Literacy Diet

Word study, or decoding and spelling, is one essential component of a balanced, comprehensive four-part literacy diet, but it is only one part. Figure 5.15 illustrates the components of the diet along with the approximate "portion sizes" for the components. As you can see, your beginning readers should spend a large amount of time in appropriate and engaging reading and writing activities. They also need significant opportunities to expand their burgeoning word knowledge. Last, they continue to benefit from experiences with rich oral and written language throughout the day.

Notice in the figure how the percentages for each portion of the literacy diet have changed from the emergent reader and writer stage. You will notice a slightly larger percentage of time devoted to contextual reading and writing. The percentages are flexible and meant as suggestions. They are intended to provide you with general guidelines for each component's portion allotment of the literacy block; you may want to modify these amounts according to different children's needs at different times of the year. Chapter 6 will present instructional strategies to use during the word knowledge portion of the literacy diet.

Your focus of instruction during the word knowledge portion of the diet will depend on the end of the zone you are targeting. Sometimes you will address student needs in the back end of the zone, using the TSI to identify needs for spelling instruction. Other times, you will target decoding and phonetic features in the books you are using to identify features of study at the front end of the zone.

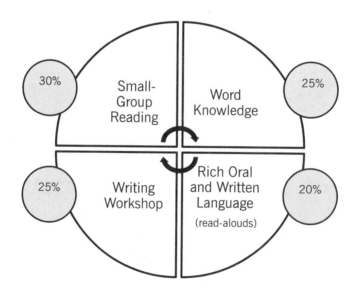

FIGURE 5.15. A balanced literacy diet for beginning readers.

Connecting decoding work to texts is critical; therefore, you will often teach features at the front end of the zone for decoding before reading. For example, students may require help with the vowel–consonant–*e* feature to successfully decode in a book you are using during small-group reading. With this in mind, your word knowledge instruction will most likely constitute the word knowledge portion of the diet but can also be included in small-group reading and writing workshop.

Beginner Milestones

As you consider a balance across the components of the toolkit, you also must keep the milestones for this stage in mind. The success of your instruction will not solely depend on your balance across the toolkit; it also depends on your attention to these milestones. The initial step is using assessment to determine what your students already know and where you should target your instruction. You will also think about your assessment data relative to the milestones, or where your beginners need to be at the end of the stage. Throughout the stage, a beginner must:

- Use letter–sound correspondence when writing, representing all phonemes in single-syllable words.
- Use decoding strategies to read unfamiliar words, including those with vowel patterns.
- Build a bank of words known by sight, including high-frequency words.

As you plan word knowledge instruction, these ultimate milestones should be considered so that your instruction does not become a bank of activities. Instead, your instruction is targeted, always working toward the milestones of the stage. These milestones should be met in the spring semester of the first-grade year. Students should finish their first-grade year in the next stage as transitional readers.

Daily and Weekly Schedules

Let's return to Devonte and Ms. Walker's first-grade classroom from the beginning of this chapter. Her literacy block consists of 120 minutes devoted to both whole-class and small-group work. We will look closely at how she structures this 120-minute block, and how she incorporates the four components of literacy while considering the portion sizes of the balanced literacy diet:

1. *Small-group reading instruction* (75 minutes). Ms. Walker meets with three small reading and word knowledge groups per day for approximately 25

minutes each. She organizes these flexible groups according to her students' literacy strengths and needs. This small-group time is devoted to two components: (a) word study instruction and (b) supported reading practice. Students not meeting with Ms. Walker are either working at centers or doing seatwork. The center and seat activities are extensions of the classroom instruction, such as the science objectives noted at the beginning of the chapter.

2. *Word study* (10 minutes of the small groups' 25 minutes). See Figure 5.16 for a description.

3. *Writing workshop* (30 minutes). Ms. Walker organizes her writing workshop in the following two parts: (a) whole-class modeling and (b) individual writing time while Ms. Walker conferences with students. Every other week, the class gathers for author's chair sharing.

4. *Read-aloud* (15 minutes). Ms. Walker begins the language arts block with read-alouds for a variety of purposes. Sometimes her goals revolve around narrative structure and early comprehension strategies. At other times her goals include informational texts to extend the content-area instruction.

Throughout the week, Ms. Walker works to include activities that are teacher guided and independently focused. Additionally, she ensures that she includes activities across all four areas of the Word Knowledge Toolkit. Her ultimate goal is to make sure her students read, write, manipulate features in words, and transfer their word knowledge to reading and writing contexts. Figure 5.16 illustrates word knowledge activities her students might complete during a typical week. Each of these activities is detailed in Chapter 6. The words included in each of these activities are derived from her analysis of each group's progress through features we have identified for you in this chapter.

Ms. Walker has planned instruction with the milestones of the beginner stage as a guide. Additionally, her decisions about including activities across the Word Knowledge Toolkit are also noteworthy:

	Monday	Tuesday	Wednesday	Thursday	Friday
Teacher Guided	Double-Duty Sort	Push and Say	Show Me!	Dictated Sentences	Writing Sort (as final assessment)
During Reading and Writing	Strategic Reading and Spelling				
Independent Practice	Writing Sort	Sentence Building	Bingo	Mix It Up! Word Hunt	Writing Sort with Buddy

FIGURE 5.16. Weekly word knowledge schedule in Ms. Walker's class.

- *Reading words*—Double-Duty Sort, Strategic Reading, Sentence Building, Bingo
- *Writing words*—Writing Sort (multiple times during the week), Strategic Spelling
- *Manipulating words*—Push and Say, Show Me!, Mix It Up!
- *Transferring words*—Dictated Sentences, Word Hunt

Working across the word knowledge zone is also evident in Ms. Walker's daily and weekly schedule. Her attention to transferring words during teacher-directed and independent work is complemented with activities across the literacy block and throughout the day.

- During writing workshop, Ms. Walker models, provides guided practice, and encourages independent use of strategic spelling techniques.
- During small-group reading instruction, Ms. Walker models, provides guided practice, and encourages independent use of strategic reading techniques.
- Morning message also includes a level of modeling and guided practice as Ms. Walker and the class construct their messages.

Alternative Schedule

The toolkit can be incorporated into any language arts block. For example, you may have a district- or school-mandated reading basal. The following is a sample schedule for Mr. Ramos, a first-grade teacher who uses a basal program. Notice how Mr. Ramos uses the basal to introduce core literacy strategies/skills for whole-class instruction during shared reading, while still organizing his literacy block according to the four components of the balanced literacy diet:

1. *Shared reading/interactive read-aloud* (20 minutes). On Mondays, Mr. Ramos introduces the key reading strategies/focus skills of the week (e.g., predicting) with the core basal during a shared reading time. Depending on the needs of his students and instructional goals for these lessons, he sometimes opts for an interactive read-aloud format, in which he engages his students with higher-level questions and rich discussion. This format is particularly powerful when he uses this time to read aloud from a rich-language text at a higher level than his students can read themselves.

2. *Small-group reading instruction* (60 minutes). Mr. Ramos usually meets with three small reading groups per day for approximately 20 minutes each. Importantly, his students continue to work all week with the same reading strategy/skill (e.g., prediction) that he introduced during shared reading on Monday. In this way, all of his students are provided additional opportunities and support

to practice this reading strategy, but in texts and contexts that are appropriate to their ability and needs. Students who Mr. Ramos is not meeting with usually spend this time (a) rereading familiar texts for fluency as a follow-up from a previous small-group session and/or (b) reading their independent reading text, which Mr. Ramos allows students to choose from a selection of appropriate, engaging books. Mr. Ramos also incorporates strategy instruction to build his students' decoding skills.

3. *Word study* (15 minutes). Figure 5.17 illustrates word study activities Mr. Ramos asks his students to work on during a typical week.

4. *Writing workshop* (25 minutes). Mr. Ramos uses whole-class mini-lessons, small-group instruction, and individual conferences in a writing workshop format to teach writing.

Mr. Ramos has incorporated activities throughout his week with the milestones of the beginner stage as a guide. Throughout the week, he ensures students are transferring their word knowledge to their reading and writing. He has also included activities across the Word Knowledge Toolkit:

- *Reading words*—Double-Duty Sort, Fast Reads, Strategic Reading
- *Writing words*—Writing Sort (multiple times during the week), Strategic Spelling, Tic-Tac-Toe
- *Manipulating words*—Sound Blending, Show Me!
- *Transferring words*—Word Hunt

When Will Your Students Be Ready to Move to the Next Stage?

As you use the activities detailed in Chapter 6, you will begin to see your students applying the targeted skills. You can use the assessments offered in this book to

	Monday	Tuesday	Wednesday	Thursday	Friday
In Class	Double-Duty Sort	Sound Blending	Show Me!	Fast Reads	Writing Sort (as final assessment)
During Reading and Writing	Strategic Reading and Spelling				
Homework/ Independent Work	Tic-Tac-Toe	Word Hunts in Reading	Writing Sort		

FIGURE 5.17. Weekly word study schedule in Mr. Ramos's class.

help you assess the beginning reader milestones: (1) use letter–sound correspondence when writing, representing all phonemes in single-syllable words; (2) use decoding strategies to read unfamiliar words, including vowel patterns; and (3) build a bank of sight words, including high-frequency words. These foundational skills indicate movement into the next stage—the transitional reading stage. See Figure 5.18, which helps you to use your assessment data to gauge these milestones.

We suggest administering the beginner tier of the TSI at least three times in a year in order to monitor your students' progress. Additionally, we suggest you administer cumulative spelling checks in the interim to ensure maintenance; we generally find once every 4–6 weeks adequate. You will find the information from the Informal Decoding Inventory (in online Appendix A) helpful as you consider growth in decoding skills. You should also use the High-Frequency Word Assessment in the online Appendix A: Assessments (*www.guilford.com/hayes4-forms*) to help monitor your students' growing bank of known words. Taken together, these assessments provide you with multiple pieces of evidence about your students' ability to:

- *Demonstrate* their understanding.
- Show *maintenance* and *transfer* of these understandings.

Transferring word knowledge to contextual reading and writing is the ultimate goal of your instruction. Observations of your students' application to reading can be measured using the Informal Decoding Inventory. You could also turn to running records of their reading, looking for examples of decoding efforts relative to the strategies and features you have taught. To help you systematically observe the transfer to writing, we have created a Writing Observation Guide for beginning readers (see Figure 5.19 and online Appendix A: Assessments). You can use this guide with writing samples as well as observe student performance on activities

Milestone	Assessment Evidence
• Using letter–sound correspondence when writing, representing all phonemes in single-syllable words	• TSI: Score of 18 or higher • Cumulative spell checks with over 90% accuracy • Beginning Writer Observation Guide
• Using decoding strategies to read unfamiliar words, including vowel patterns	• IDI real words • Short Vowels 8–10 • Consonant Blends/Digraphs 8–10 • IDI nonwords • *R*-Controlled Vowels 2–7 (or higher) • *V*–Consonant–e 2–7 (or higher)
• Building a bank of words known by sight, including high-frequency words	• High-Frequency Word Assessment

FIGURE 5.18. Beginner-stage milestones and assessment evidence.

Writing Observation Guide: Beginning Reader

Dates	10/30	11/7	11/14	11/20	11/29	12/12
• *Short Vowel Families* o Short *a*						
o Short *i*						
o Short *o*						
o Short *u*						
o Short *e*						
• *Initial and Final Consonant Digraphs* o CH	✓	✓		✓	✓	✓
o SH		✓	✓	✓	✓	
o TH	✓		✓	✓	✓	✓
• *Initial Consonant Blends* o *l*-blends			✓	✓	✓	✓
o *s*-blends			✓	✓	✓	✓
o *r*-blends						
• *Short Vowels* o *a*						
o *e*						
o *i*						
o *o*						
o *u*						
• *Final Consonant Blends* o *sk, ck, ft*, for example						
o Preconsonantal nasals						

FIGURE 5.19. Beginning Writer Observation Guide.

from the toolkit (e.g., dictated sentences as noted above). We suggest you look for multiple pieces of evidence, 4–6 points, so you can be confident in your students' transfer of your word knowledge instruction. You'll notice the guide in Figure 5.19 allows for 6 points of evidence.

The guide in Figure 5.19 has been filled in by a teacher in preparation for quarterly report cards (see shaded cells). The teacher compiled toolkit activities, such as dictated sentences, and writing samples. After looking through each piece of evidence, the teacher noted the dates and checked each feature as evidence was noted. The student has demonstrated multiple instances of transfer for a number of the features studied throughout the grading period, specifically consonant blends and digraphs. Seeking a confluence of evidence, the teacher consults results from weekly and cumulative spell checks. The teacher can now confidently report that the student has a firm understanding of these targeted features: digraphs, *l*-blends, and *s*-blends. The teacher made a note about the *r*-blend category, recording specific affricate errors (e.g., *tr* in *trap* and *dr* in *drum*). With this in mind, the teacher makes the decision to focus on affricates, in particular, in the coming weeks.

These assessments and observations are offered to allow you to compile a variety of evidence to monitor your students' growth. With this information, you can confidently make decisions about students who need more instruction versus those who are ready to move forward. Using the milestones for the beginner stage, you can interpret the assessment results and make decisions about students who are moving into the next stage of word knowledge development—the transitional stage.

Conclusion

The skills acquired in the beginning reader stage lay the foundation for the next stage. Beginning readers are building a bank of known words that will enable them to develop some level of fluency in text. They are expanding their repertoire of decoding strategies and becoming more adept at identifying unknown words while reading. Beginning writers and spellers are solidifying their knowledge of short vowels, consonant blends, and consonant digraphs. They are moving toward the ability to segment at the phoneme level, allowing them to accurately represent blends in words such as *fast* and *drip*. Their written pieces are expanding but are relatively short because of their limited writing fluency. The Beginner Tier of the TSI provides you with information about their word knowledge. A comprehensive literacy diet provides beginning readers ample opportunities to practice their growing skills during reading and writing tasks. The activities in Chapter 6 allow you to strategically plan instruction that will help your students reach the milestones of the stage and move to the transitional stage.

CHAPTER 6

The Beginning Reader's Toolkit

ACTIVITIES AND STUDENT STRATEGIES

GUIDING QUESTIONS

- What are the four categories of the Word Knowledge Toolkit for Beginning Readers that promote deep word learning?
- What activities promote students' transfer of word knowledge to contextual reading and writing?
- What activities in the Word Knowledge Toolkit help beginning readers build a bank of words known by sight?
- What activities in the Word Knowledge Toolkit develop letter–sound correspondence and encourage students to represent all phonemes in single-syllable words?
- What activities in the Word Knowledge Toolkit teach decoding strategies beginners can use to read unfamiliar words?
- How do you know when your beginning readers have moved beyond the beginning reader stage to the transitional stage?

We suggest a "toolkit" approach to instruction rather than a variety of random activities. The activities we choose may have a specific purpose individually; however, a toolkit approach allows us to strategically choose our activities in order to meet instructional needs across word knowledge elements. Your strategic approach to word knowledge instruction should include *tools* developed for a specific purpose. Having completed your TSI (Tiered Spelling Inventory) from Chapter 2, you are able to identify the strengths and instructional needs of your students. Your instructional strategies, or *tools*, should be chosen to meet those needs and your instructional objectives. The toolkit comprises these four categories:

- *Reading words*—decoding practice.
- *Writing words*—spelling application.
- *Manipulating words*—word analysis.
- *Transferring words*—connect to context.

As you plan your instruction, you will work to incorporate activities from all four categories across your instructional week. However, make sure your week begins with a heavy dose of reading, writing, and manipulating words. The week should end with more attention to "transferring words."

Each strategy in the toolkit is presented with an instructional purpose, which is a subset of the overall purpose of the category. The instructional purpose will help you choose the right tools for your teaching objectives. The categories of the toolkit will help you focus on reading and writing words, as well as providing multiple opportunities for your students to manipulate words. Last, the toolkit offers activities for your students to apply their word knowledge in context. To this end, you should choose activities from each of the four categories of the toolkit (see Figure 6.1) over the course of your instructional week to ensure you are developing a firm understanding of how words work, which will ultimately help your students read and write words accurately and automatically. When choosing word knowledge activities, make sure your work takes place not only as isolated skills work but also during guided application:

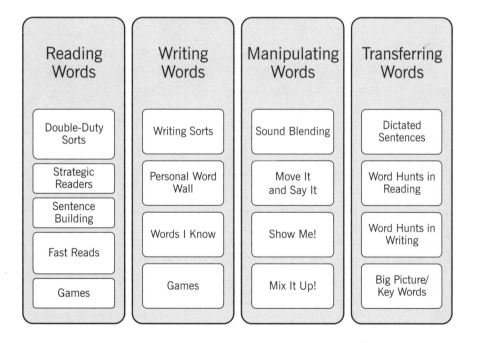

FIGURE 6.1. Word Knowledge Toolkit for beginning readers.

1. *During word study time*, make sure that each week you choose activities from the first three columns so that students are (1) reading, (2) writing/spelling, and (3) manipulating letters and sounds.

2. *During contextual reading and writing time*, make sure you are also providing opportunities for and coaching students to transfer their word knowledge to context.

This chapter is devoted to the activities that help you build your instruction guided by the toolkit. The bulk of the chapter describes the activities suggested above to give your students practice reading words, writing words, manipulating words, and transferring words. Use the Common Features of Study Chart (see Figure 5.8 in Chapter 5) and the Beginner Feature Sorting suggestions in online Appendix B: Toolkit Activities (*www.guilford.com/hayes4-forms*) to help you choose patterns and words for these activities that continually move your students' word knowledge forward—the goal of beginning reading instruction is to create transitional readers. We conclude the chapter with ideas about how to challenge your beginning readers with the front end of the zone as you build their understanding of vowel patterns necessary for successful decoding and ultimate word recognition.

Word Knowledge Toolkit Part I: Reading Words

The activities in this toolkit section provide a variety of ways to have your students repeatedly read words in meaningful ways. At the beginning stage of word knowledge, a major focus is on building a store of known words to help students be more accurate and automatic with word identification. The following activities will target these important word learning goals.

Instructional Strategy: Double-Duty Sorts

- Purpose: to compare, contrast, and categorize words by common orthographic features and sounds.

Beginning readers must attend to the sounds in words alongside their corresponding spellings (Bear et al., 2012). The Double-Duty Sort provides your students with activities to compare, contrast, and categorize words first by their sound features and then by their orthographic features. Sorts will become a core instructional activity for both your early and later beginning readers as you help them form generalizations to apply while reading unfamiliar words (Gillet & Kita, 1979). You will begin with sorting by sounds using pictures to encourage your students to distinguish between the sounds. Once you have worked through the sounds, then you will direct them to apply that work to reading words. Many sorting contrasts appropriate for beginning readers are available in online Appendix B: Toolkit Activities. We have divided the Double-Duty Sort into (1) sorting for sound and (2) sorting for spelling.

Sorting for Sound

1. Tell your students that you are going to sort pictures into a certain number of categories (usually two to four). Your students' job is to listen to the target sounds in the words. For example, your early beginners may be sorting by ending rime (e.g., *cat, hat, bat* into the /ăt/ category) and your later beginners may be sorting by medial short vowel (e.g., *pot, cost, lock* into the /ŏ/ category). The sort in Figure 6.2 targets initial digraphs. Use the keyword pictures (*chin, ship, think*) to help focus the discussion. You would begin this sound sort by saying:

> "Today we're going to listen for the beginning sounds in some words. Our first sound is the /ch/ at the beginning of *ch-ch-chin*. [Place the *chin* keyword card in front of the group.] We are also going to listen to the /sh/ at the beginning of *shhhhhhip*. [Place the *ship* keyword card in front of the group.] Our last category is the /th/ at the beginning of *thhhhhhink*. [Place the *think* keyword card in front of the group.]"

2. You will start by beginning the sound sort while thinking aloud.

> "I'm going to sort this first picture: *cheese*. First, I need to think about how *cheese* starts. I hear /ch/ at the beginning of *cheese*. Let me see where it belongs. Does it begin like *think*? *Thhhhhhink–ch-ch-cheese*. No. I'm going to try *ship*. *Shhhhhip–ch-ch-cheese*. No. Let me check *chin*. *Ch-ch-chin–ch-ch-cheese*. Yes. *Chin* and *cheese* both begin with /ch/. Now it's your turn. Here's our next picture: *shhhhhhop*. Ready, guys? What's the first sound you hear in *shhhhhhop*? Now let's think about the category. *Shhhhop–ch-ch-chin*? *Shhhhhhop–ship*? *Shhhhhhop–think*?"

3. Sort at least three pictures into each column, asking the students to name each picture aloud. After they say each picture, have them repeat the target sound. See Figure 6.2 for an example of a sound sort targeting the /ch/, /sh/, and /th/ digraphs. Notice the keyword pictures: *chin, ship,* and *think*. Notice some of the pictures contain words with long and *r*-controlled vowels. Since we are using them only as pictures and for their initial sounds, these are appropriate options. We would not, however, use the same words for the word sort. For example, *cheese, sheep,* and *thorn* would not be used in the word sort.

4. After sorting pictures in each column, ask your students to be *sound* sleuths:

"Let's say all of the pictures in *chin*'s group. *Chain, chips, cheese.* What is their beginning sound? Let's remember the key question good sound sleuths always ask:

    'How do these words *sound* the same?' "

Make sure that you require students to justify and explain their thinking about the words. The following questions will help guide them if needed:

"What, specifically, do *sheep, shop,* and *shirt* have in common? What part of the word are we listening for?"

"Tell us how they *sound* the same."

"Why is it important for us to think about words with sounds that are the same? How can it help us?"

The type of discussion that these questions can generate will promote deeper processing of the word parts and stronger knowledge of words.

Sorting for Reading

1. Now you will introduce the letter match (pattern) to the target sounds (Figure 6.3). As you bring out the pattern cards, review each category again.

"Words beginning with the /ch/ like *chin, cheese, chips,* and *chain* begin with *CH.* /ch/ is spelled *CH.* [Remove the picture cards as you bring out the *CH* pattern card.] *Let's think about chin.* Let's find the *CH* in *chin.* [Point out the word *chin* on the pattern card. You can highlight it for extra emphasis.]"

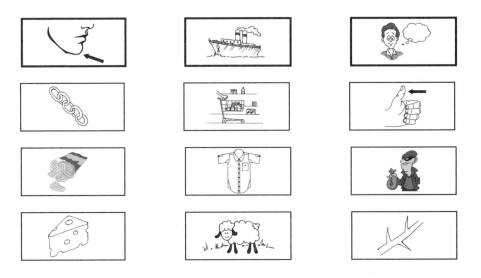

FIGURE 6.2. Completed sound sort.

FIGURE 6.3. Digraph pattern sort introduction.

Proceed with the other introductions in the same way. See Figure 6.4 to see how this sort will look after you have gone through the pattern introductions.

2. You will start by beginning the word sort while thinking aloud.

"I'm going to sort this first word: *chop*. First, I need to think about how *chop* starts. I hear /ch/ at the beginning of *chop*, and I can see the *CH* pattern at the beginning. So, I know it *sounds* right—/ch/, and I know it *looks* right—*CH*. [Point to the *CH* in *chop* as you talk about how it *looks*.] Now it's your turn. Here's our next word. [Place a word in front of the group—*shut*.] Ready, guys? What's this word? What two letters do you see? What does *SH* say? [Students say "Shut."] Yes, *shut*. Now which category? [Students place *SHUT* in the *SH* category.] *Why did you put it there? How does it sound* at the beginning? How does it *look* at the beginning? Just like *ship*."

3. Sort at least three words into each column, asking the students to read each word aloud. After they read each word, have them repeat the target sound. See Figure 6.4 for an example of a word sort targeting the /ch/, /sh/, and /th/ digraphs. Notice the keywords: *chin, ship*, and *think*.

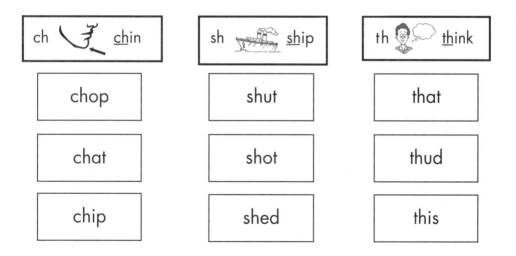

FIGURE 6.4. Completed word sort.

4. After sorting at least three words in each column, ask your students to be *word* sleuths:

> "Let's look at our *chin* category and read each word. *Chop, chat, chip.* What do all of these words have in common? Let's remember our three key questions good word sleuths always ask:
>
> 'How do these words *look* the same?'
> 'How do these words *sound* the same?'
> '*Where* is the pattern in the word (beginning, middle, or end)?'"

Make sure that you require students to justify and explain their thinking about the words. The following questions will help you guide this discussion if needed:

> "What, specifically do *this* and *that* have in common?"
> "Show me the parts that *look* the same."
> "Tell me how they *sound* the same."
> "Underline the pattern in each word."

The type of discussion that these questions can generate will promote deeper processing of the word parts and stronger knowledge of word patterns.

Modifications

- To provide less explicit instruction and scaffolding, follow the procedures for a Guess My Category Word Sort described in Chapter 8 (p. 198).

- There may be times you want your students to do the exploration and make generalizations. An open sort allows your students to do this. Rather than provide them with the introduction of the target sound with the keyword picture card, for example, supply them with the keyword picture cards along with the other picture cards. Tell your students to consider the pictures and sort them into like categories. A word of caution: Give your students some direction:

> "I want you to think about these pictures and sort them into three categories. Here's your hint: Think about how they sound at the beginning."

Giving your students this quick "hint" allows you to have a focused sort that will lead to your ultimate goal. After the sort is complete, ask them to justify their categories, using the questions provided in Step 4.

Instructional Strategy: Strategic Readers

- Purpose: to encourage students to be strategic when decoding unknown words while reading.

Building strategic readers requires an initial, crucial step. You must design your instruction for success. Students need to imagine that they can complete tasks successfully in order to begin to see themselves as strategic learners in charge of their own learning. If we are to build this sense of "I can do it," then we must have opportunities for students to participate in a learning experience with success. As Walpole and McKenna (2009) note, "Supporting novice readers in applying phonics strategies when they encounter unknown words is one of the keys to developing automaticity and independence" (p. 52). By completing the TSI and the IDI (Informal Decoding Inventory), as well as monitoring students as we observe them reading, we are arranging for this success. We need to also think about what strategic readers do. To this end, we will focus on strategic decoding for beginners highlighting code-based strategies, those strategies that direct them to analyzing the sounds in words. Our responses to the students should be very targeted, building and reinforcing the strategic, code-based work (Scanlon et al., 2010). As Clark (2004) cautions, we need to teach strategies that encourage children to attend to analyzing sounds and spelling patterns in words and to use meaning-based cues *only* as a check of whether their decoding was successful.

Impress upon students that they should be flexible and strategic as they choose and use their strategies. Regardless of the strategy, students must always check to make sure their word makes sense. Checking, or monitoring, to ensure their reading makes sense is presented as a highlighted strategy. Beginners must learn to monitor their reading for two reasons:

1. Monitor while reading to cue them when things do not make sense and they must "fix up."
2. Monitor while decoding to make sure their strategy use makes sense in the context of the sentence.

See Figure 6.5 for an example of the code-based strategies to emphasize with your students. The strategies can be reproduced and displayed in your classroom for a quick reference (see online Appendix B: Toolkit Activities). Your code-based strategies will shift across the stage. Your early beginners will often benefit from saying the first sound and checking with the final sound. Their limited word knowledge can sometimes hamper their efforts to "sound out" entire words. Quickly, though, beginners should be taught, and encouraged, to "say the sounds"—beginners must ultimately *fully* analyze words. To this end, you will teach strategies and then add to or modify them to reflect the skill of the developing reader. Online Appendix B has a Decoding Strategy Quick Reference to reflect these changes, with Figure 6.5 as one example.

You will begin by introducing and modeling strategies one at a time and build the bank of strategies your students can utilize. Strategic readers are flexible and do not rely on only one strategy; therefore, we need to provide students with the most helpful strategies for them at their stage of development. In your introduction, you should explain (1) what the strategy is, (2) how to use the strategy, and

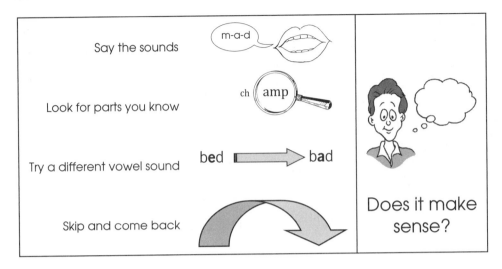

FIGURE 6.5. Strategy quick reference.

(3) when you would want to use the strategy. You will also provide an activity that illustrates the strategy. The following example highlights the *first sound/check ending* strategy used with *early* beginners. You might say:

> "Sometimes we come to words we don't know when we read. So, we need to have steps to help us figure these words out. The first thing we should do is think about the first sound. Thinking about the first sound can give us some ideas about what the word might be. Let's look at this sentence: 'The _____ is in the sky.' What word could go in this blank? [Field the group for options like *moon, sun, balloon,* etc.] You guys are right. Any of these options will work. They all make sense. But we have to look at the sounds in the word. [Reveal the first sound—*M.*] Now what word might work in the blank? Yes, *moon.* The *moon* is in the sky. [Show the word as you point and read the sentence.]"

As you introduce new strategies, you will extend the instruction to include checking with the last sound and then considering all sounds in the word. For example, with *moon* above, you would have students check the ending sound to confirm their thinking. *Moon* should end with *N* and the word does end with *N*.

1. Think aloud while using the strategy in a book to make sure your students understand how to apply the strategy while reading. You should choose a page from a shared reading with a word that lends itself to your target strategy. Then you will think aloud while applying the strategies. While thinking aloud, make sure to (a) identify the strategy and refer to the strategy toolkit, (b) explain how

you are using the strategy, and (c) tell why you have chosen the strategy. The following example, looking for "parts you know," is appropriate for mid/late beginners.

> "[Turn to your target page in *Biscuit Goes to School* by Alyssa Satin Capucilli (2002).] I was reading this page and got to a word I wasn't sure about. Here's my sentence: 'Is Biscuit going to the _____?' I'm going to use my strategy toolkit to help with this last word. When I look at this word, I see a part I know. I see *on* in the middle of the word. So, I'm going to sound it out: /p-on-d/. Oh, this is *pond*. Let's see. Does this make sense? Is Biscuit going to the pond? Makes sense in the sentence. I'm going to read on to make sure it makes sense in the story."

2. Provide your students with targeted guided practice. This practice should be brief and focused on the strategy. For example, if you are teaching mid/late beginners about changing the vowel sound, you would provide them with a series of short sentences with one word in each that exemplifies the strategy. This particular strategy helps students decode words they encounter with features they have not mastered yet, such as long vowel patterns. Knowing they can "flip" a short vowel to a long vowel will be extremely helpful. You might use this series of sentences:

He is a <u>kind</u> man.

I can <u>wind</u> up the toy.

She is a <u>wild</u> cat.

I put it on the <u>post</u>.

I <u>told</u> you to go.

Notice each of these sentences is simple in construction and contains easily recognizable words aside from the target, underlined words. We use the term *flip it* to indicate changing a vowel sound. You would support your students as they read the sentence up to the underlined word. For this example, your students will "sound out" the word. This would result in /k-ĭ-n-d/. Ask your students if that is a real word that makes sense in the sentence. Since the answer will be no, tell your students to "flip" the vowel. After your introduction, modeling, and think-aloud, your students will be ready to change the sound from short to long: /k-ī-n-d/. Now ask if they have a real word that makes sense in the sentence: He is a kind man.

3. Last, give your students plenty of opportunities to independently practice using the strategies. As you observe students using strategies, you should name their strategy and reflect upon its success. Be careful not to stop students too often to reflect on strategy use. You can talk about their strategy use "in the moment" of the reading, but you can also reinforce strategy use after reading. Remember, ultimately you want to reinforce flexible, decisive use of strategies.

"I noticed Devonte using one of our strategies from the toolkit today. He was reading *The Lucky Duck* [Clark, 1996]. Here's the sentence. [Turn to the page and point to the sentence as you read.] One wet, wet day a duck got stuck. Guess what? Devonte got 'stuck' on this word. [Point to *stuck*.] He stopped when he got here and chose this tool: Look for parts you know. He saw -*uck* and noticed it was also in *duck*. He said, 'Uck . . . duck . . . st-uck . . . stuck.' Then he made sure it made sense. A duck got stuck. Great work, Devonte. You were a strategic reader."

Modifications

• Sometimes beginners are able to blend all of the sounds but are unaware of a word part they need to be successful at decoding a particular word. For example, a beginner is reading and comes upon the unfamiliar word *crouch*. The beginner could blend the sounds if presented orally, but this same beginner is unaware of the *OU* vowel pattern. As you scaffold their decoding attempts, you can simply say, "The *OU* in that word says /ou/." Then the student can flex those decoding muscles and fully analyze the word. An important point to make here: Even though the student did not have the necessary word knowledge to successfully decode on his or her own, the teacher did not supply the word. The teacher provided some assistance, but the student did the heavy lifting of the decoding.

• Flipping the vowel is a helpful strategy when beginners are starting to learn about decoding long vowels; however, it is also a helpful strategy with early beginners as they practice negotiating short vowels. Consider the child who is still confusing short *e* and *a*. That child may be reading a story about a little boy who has a *pet* rabbit. Confusing the short *e*, the child says *pat rabbit*. If the child struggles with the word and is unable to self-correct, scaffold the attempt by saying, "Flip your vowel." In this case, you are flipping short vowel sounds.

• An important component to decoding strategy instruction is your scaffolding "in the moment" as you observe a student struggling to read a word. A quick reference for how to respond to students when they struggle can be found in online Appendix B: Toolkit Activities "What to Do When a Reader Needs Help with Words." We offer the following guidelines based on the work of Johnston et al. (2009), Morris (2005), and Clark (2004):

   o First, do nothing. Allow the child to try decoding. If you always correct students, they will not become independent, strategic readers.
   o If the child's attempt does not make sense, allow the child to read to the end of the sentence to see if their word makes sense. If the child doesn't catch the mistake, simply ask if it makes sense and remind them of this strategy.

o If the child misreads and goes back to self-correct without your prompting, name their good work to reinforce the strategy by saying, "Good job thinking about what you just read and going back to fix that word. That's what a strategic reader does." Even if the child has correctly identified the word, it is good to ask if it makes sense from time to time just to reinforce always monitoring.

o If the child remains stuck on a word, you can prompt with some general questions:

"What could you do here?"
"Do you see a part you know?"
"Does the word look like another word you know?"
"What part is giving you trouble?"
"Reread the sentence and see if that helps."
"Decode the parts you know, and I'll help with the rest."
"Think of the first sound and read on. See if that helps."
"Skip that word, read on, and come back to see if that helps."

Instructional Strategy: Sentence Building

● Purpose: to build a bank of known words.

Your students require contextualized practice reading words and must move beyond the isolated word-level work most often associated with word recognition activities. This activity is adapted from the sentence-building activity presented by Scanlon et al. (2010). Be sure your students can identify several words before using this activity. Most of the words in this activity will be high-frequency words, but you could also include more meaningful words for student engagement. The main goal of the activity is to provide repeated practice with high-frequency words in the context of a sentence. You will use and reuse your target words in different sentences. For example, if your target words are *my, is, have, the,* and *was,* then you could use these four sentences:

I love my mom.

Do you have my toy?

The toy was fun.

My mom was here.

1. Create your target sentences using your target words. Write your sentences on a sentence strip or print them on paper. Work with one sentence at a time. Chorally read the sentence with your students, encouraging them to point while reading. Have them read the sentence multiple times.

2. Have your students cut their sentences into individual words. If you had the sentence "My mom was here," then your students would end up with:

3. Have the students mix up their words. We usually give students a laminated 8½″ × 11″ piece of construction paper, which will serve as their work space (see Figure 6.6). Have your students mix up the words on their work space.

Think aloud reconstructing the sentences for at least one sentence.

"I remember my sentence said: 'My mom was here.' So, the first word is *my*. The first sound in *my* is /m/. I know you spell /m/ with *m*. I'm going to look for a word that begins with *m*. I see *mom* and *my*. [Bring these two words front and center to focus your think-aloud.] So, I know *my* ends with /ī/. This means *mom* can't be it, because it ends with *m*. Plus, I know this word. It is *mom*. So *my* is it. Plus, I see it begins with a capital letter. A sentence begins with a capital letter. Okay. The sentence is 'My mom was here' . . . so I need *mom*. I already have that. [Bring *my* and *mom* up to the top of your work space.] Next is *was*. My mom was here. *Was* begins with /w/, so I need to find a word beginning with W. [Bring *was* up to continue building your sentence.] The last word is *here*: My mom was here. So, *here* begins with /h/. This last word begins with H, so it must be *here*. Also, I see a period at the end of that word. I remember sentences can end with periods. So, here's my sentence: 'My mom was here.' [Point and read aloud.] [See Figure 6.7.]"

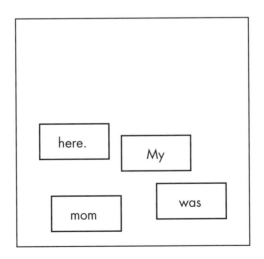

FIGURE 6.6. Work space.

Provide your students with guided practice. Begin by reading and rereading the sentence chorally. Once each child can easily and accurately read, while pointing, have them cut apart their sentences. Students will then mix up their words before building on their individual work spaces. After reading, make sure to follow up with your students. Point out the construction of the sentences and highlight target words: (1) begin with a capital, (2) end with punctuation, and (3) point out target words. Your target words might be chosen to reinforce the initial sound, words from the interactive word wall (see page 152), or words with phonics/spelling features.

Modifications

• Students who can recognize more words may not need this level of support. Therefore, you can give them individual words written on cards to form complete sentences. Your students will be able to practice constructing complete sentences that make sense.

• You could include the high-frequency words you are working on as well as exemplar words for the phonics and spelling features you are studying. For example, if you are teaching preconsonantal nasals and have completed lessons focusing on the -ank and -unk endings, then you could include *trunk* and *sunk* in your sentence.

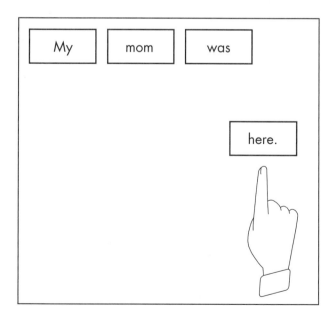

FIGURE 6.7. Sentence building.

Instructional Strategy: Fast Reads

● Purpose: to build word-level automaticity with a core set of high-frequency and decodable words.

Building automaticity is critical to the beginning reader. Specifically, we must build automaticity of a set of core high-frequency words. While automaticity in text becomes a focus at the next stage, the beginning reader needs to develop a certain level of automaticity of these core high-frequency words, in addition to those decodable words with the features they are studying. To build automaticity, we need to provide multiple opportunities for our students to read words. A key to these multiple reads is that they should be "repeated" reads. Having a variety of materials on which your students can repeatedly practice reading words is critical to the primary classroom. We have used Fast Reads for this purpose. See Figure 6.8 for a mixed short vowel word family Fast Read. This activity is an extension activity after the supportive sorting and introductory activities detailed in the reading words and writing words components of the toolkit. The Fast Read is less supportive to your students because we do not have the assistance of the columns. Notice the practice box at the top with the key word for each family.

1. Present students their own copy of the Fast Read with words that exemplify the features you are teaching for word study. Talk to your students about how it is helpful when reading and writing to think about these features. Have your students point to the key words in the practice box. Ask students to explain the features to you. We use questions about the sounds and letters for the features, as well as the key words. What do they sound like? What do they look like? What's the key word? For the example in Figure 6.8, you would ask about /ĕt/ and the letters that are used to represent /ĕt/, which we hear at the end of *jet*.

> "This fast read will help you practice the ending of *jet*. What's the ending? /ĕt/—yes. At the end of *jet*, we hear /ĕt/. *How do we spell /ĕt/? That's right—ET*. We can think about *jet* when we are spelling other words like *bet* and *set*. You know what? You can also think about *jet* when you are reading. Like the first word we see here. [Point to *let* on the first line.] I can see *ET* in that word. So, I know *ET* says /ĕt/ like in *jet*, so this word is *l-et. LET*."

2. Once you have primed your students for the features coming up, have them read through the Fast Read chorally with you taking the lead. Have your students point to each word as they read and help them maintain your pace as you all read together. You can echo read line by line if your students need that level of support.

3. After your students have had some guided practice with you, have them read their Fast Reads independently. As they read, move around the group and monitor their reading.

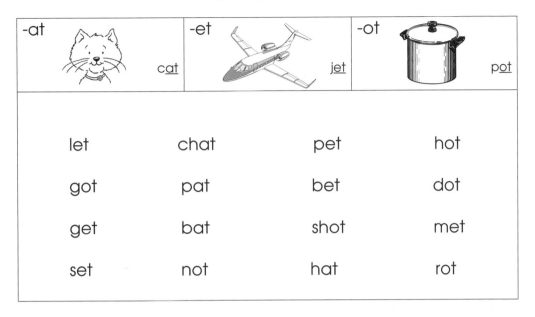

-at		-et		-ot	
	cat		jet		pot
let	chat	pet		hot	
got	pat	bet		dot	
get	bat	shot		met	
set	not	hat		rot	

FIGURE 6.8. Short vowel word family Fast Read.

4. Before wrapping up the activity, have your students talk about the target features using the questions from Step 1. Ask students to read example words of each feature by mining the words in the Fast Read.

Modifications

• Your students can read their Fast Reads to each other. Fast Reads can also be practiced in centers or during seatwork after you have had them practice in your small groups. If you have recording capabilities, your students can even record their Fast Read readings.

• If you have students motivated by timing themselves, they could time their Fast Reads to chart their decrease in time over multiple reads.

• Students can also search their Fast Reads for examples of the features of study. See Word Hunts in the transferring words section.

• Fast Reads do not have to be limited to words and features studied during word knowledge instruction. You could also choose to practice high-frequency words. Your students need to begin collecting a store of these words they are able to read quickly and accurately, so providing them with this practice can be helpful. Note: This type of decontextualized practice must be accompanied by bringing their study and attention back to contextualized reading and writing.

Instructional Strategy: Games with a Reading Focus

● Purpose: to promote accurate and automatic
  word recognition.

Beginning readers require multiple opportunities to practice reading words. These opportunities must be engaging in order to maintain student focus. Games are a perfect match. They provide repeated practice in a fun, engaging format. The activities in this section are all games that can be modified to fit your students' needs as well as a variety of classroom situations. Each can be customized with the words and patterns that a group is learning. We recommend that you initially play all of these games during teacher-guided practice to ensure students understand procedures. Then you will be able to move these games into centers and independent activities.

Tic-Tac-Toe

1. This game is an excellent review and practice format when studying short vowel word families or when you are trying to get your students to utilize rimes (e.g., *-at*, *-et*, *-ot*, *-it*, *-ut*). Provide students with a Tic-Tac-Toe board. See Figure 6.9. The board should be set up with rimes in each square; be sure to use rimes you have already introduced. You can also have your students simply make a Tic-Tac-Toe board on a piece of paper and direct them to the rimes they will put in each square.

2. Rather than *X* or *O*, students will choose a letter to put in front of the rime to make a whole word. To keep up with who has taken over which squares, they can use different colored crayons or markers.

3. In order to mark a square, students must make a real word by putting their letter with the rime. They must then pronounce the word they have made. For example, look at Figure 6.9. The student put *T* with *-ag* to make *tag*. Play continues as with any Tic-Tac-Toe game. Students take turns adding their letters and pronouncing the words until someone gets three in a row. Remember, it is always fun to get in a block. That is what happened with *tag*.

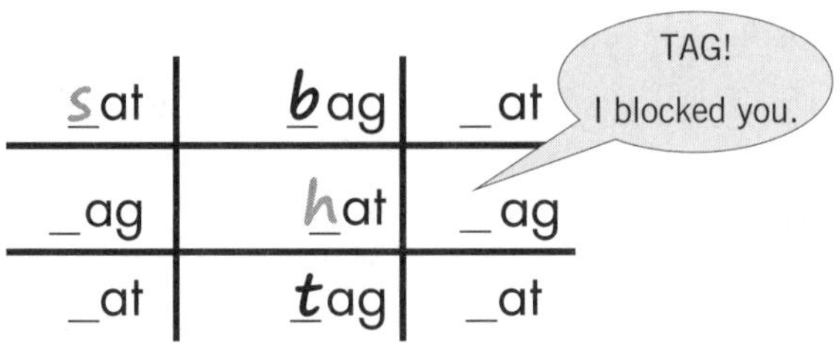

FIGURE 6.9. Tic-Tac-Toe.

Sentence Bingo

1. To play Sentence Bingo, you will need to create two things: Bingo playing cards and sentence strips for your students to use to draw. We suggest that your Bingo playing cards have at the most 16 cells, sometimes allowing for only straight across and others for diagonal. You want your games to be fast paced, and too many cells can make the game lengthy and take up too much of your valuable instructional time. Your card and sentence strips might look something like the nine-cell card in Figure 6.10.

2. Your students will pick a sentence strip from a collection in a Baggie or envelope. Once a strip is chosen, the student must read the sentence aloud and then repeat the underlined word. For example, if the student had the sentence "*That* cat is on a mat," then the student would repeat *that*. This is the word your student will look for on the Bingo card. When the student finds the target word, he or she will place a marker on the spot.

3. Students continue play, taking turns selecting sentence strips, reading, and marking their spots. In the Bingo card in Figure 6.10, the students can look for three in a row straight across or diagonally. You can choose to have your students complete the game as a team, collectively working toward filling in the entire card. Notice this game is targeting high-frequency words. You can also make Sentence Bingo with decodable words to practice your target word knowledge features. If you want to practice short-*e* words, you could have sentences like:

> The bell is on the bed.
>
> That check is red.
>
> Did you beg for a nest?

These sentences are short and simple. They provide your students with contextual practice without posing too much challenge. Even if you are focusing on decodable words, you will be including many high-frequency words. You should be cautious in your choices and include high-frequency words you have studied as often as possible. These sentences can work overtime, providing practice with both decodable and high-frequency words.

<<< B I N G O >>>		
was	that	from
are	or	can
all	have	do

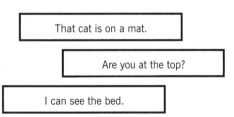

FIGURE 6.10. Sentence Bingo.

Concentration

1. As with Sentence Bingo, Concentration can be played to have repeated practice with decodable words targeting the features of study or high-frequency words. Make your cards for play, using card stock so you cannot see the print when the cards are turned over. We suggest having no more than 10 pairs, or 20 cards. You can make your pairs a variety of ways to match as seen in Figure 6.11. Students play as with traditional Concentration, looking for matches as they turn over two cards at a time. If students make a match, still direct them to take turns to encourage play for everyone.

2. As they make a match or at the end of the game, have students record their matches. They can write each word from all of their matches. This extension of recording their matches allows for one quick, additional practice with the words.

Parking Lot

1. This is an easy, spur-of-the-moment game and is adapted from Scanlon et al. (2010). Draw parking lots on pieces of paper with two rows of five or six spaces, one parking lot for each student. Then write target words in each parking space, making sure words are right-side up for students to read and each parking lot has the same words but in different spaces. Like the other games, these words can either be decodable words with target features or high-frequency words.

2. Distribute a parking lot to each child and a toy car.

3. Tell students where to park their cars. For example, you might say, "Park your car on the word *where*." Randomly ask students to identify their words by asking, "What space is your car in?" Once they have parked their cars, tell them they need to "back up" and get ready to park again. Make sure to have them park for each word and even park for some words multiple times. You can modify play

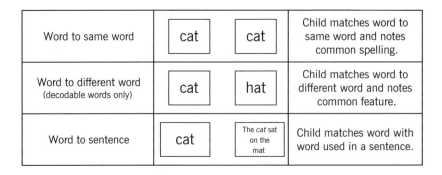

Word to same word	cat	cat	Child matches word to same word and notes common spelling.
Word to different word (decodable words only)	cat	hat	Child matches word to different word and notes common feature.
Word to sentence	cat	The *cat* sat on the mat	Child matches word with word used in a sentence.

FIGURE 6.11. Concentration pairs.

where	good	after	very	there	most
much	let	when	too	say	our

pack	much	moth	that	fled	list
must	flop	brick	best	trip	blast

FIGURE 6.12. Parking lots for high-frequency words and decodable words.

for decodable words by saying, "Park your car on a word with the short *a*, /ă/." Then have students read their words to you. See Figure 6.12.

4. After everyone has parked for each word, have them read their entire parking lots to one another.

Generic Game Board

1. Go to online Appendix B: Toolkit Activities for a variety of generic game boards. These game boards can be easily used for a variety of purposes. Notice the boards have numbers on each space. These numbers indicate how many cards to pick up. You can use them for review and repetitive practice of decodable words or high-frequency words. All students need to play are the game board, a spinner or dice, game pieces, and word cards.

2. Make cards with your words, either decodable or high frequency. Generally speaking, 35–40 words are plenty. Play will move too quickly if your spinner or dice goes beyond 3.

3. Students will take turns spinning or rolling to see how many spaces they will move. Then they move to that space and pick cards off the top of the deck according to the number on the space: if the space has a 3, they pick up three cards. As cards are picked, students must read aloud each word.

4. The game continues until each player makes it to the end. Students can then count their cards to see who collected the most words. If you have used decodable words to target features of study, you could have students collect all of their words to complete a big sort by feature. See the game in Figure 6.13. The students completed play and then did a sort by initial blends.

Modifications

Games can be played in their normal competitive nature. However, you can tweak the format to move away from individuals competing and move toward pairs or

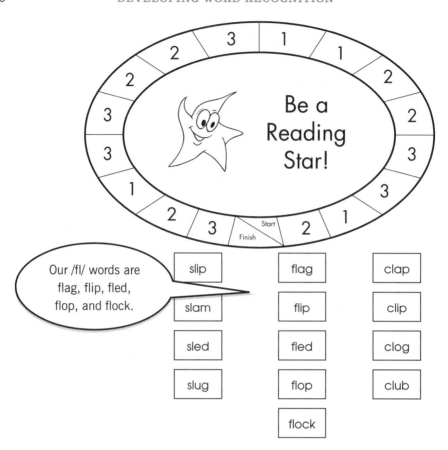

FIGURE 6.13. Generic game board.

groups working together. For example, rather than having each student take a turn to move around the board, you could have each student in a group take a turn moving a group pawn around the board and collect as many words as they can. This way, with each turn, every student is interested and participating rather than passively waiting a turn.

Word Knowledge Toolkit Part II: Writing Words

As discussed in Chapter 1, your students will find spelling words more difficult than reading words. It follows that your students must have multiple opportunities to practice writing the words during the week. The following activities provide students opportunities to spell their words in supported contexts. In addition, the activities will help you include repeated practice throughout the week with targeted, engaging activities.

Instructional Strategy: Writing Sort

● Purpose: to spell words correctly while simultaneously categorizing them in the appropriate column by common spelling patterns.

Writing sorts require students to (1) spell words correctly and (2) categorize words in the appropriate column (Bear et al., 2012). These two tasks help your students move from memorizing *how* to spell words and begin to think about *why* the words are spelled that way. Writing sorts can serve as an instructional activity while you support your students with their strategic spelling. Providing your students with guided practice while writing is critical because these are the opportunities where you can observe your students' level of mastery of the features.

1. Present your students with a blank chart to use for recording their words similar to the one in Figure 6.14. Your students can write the headers on the chart or you can give them a chart with the headers already in place. Earlier in the stage, your students will probably benefit from having headers already provided; later in the stage, your students may be able to handle putting their own headers on the chart. Regardless, before beginning the activity, either review the headers if you have placed them on the chart already or review the headers as you have your students write the headers in.

2. Call out a word and have students repeat the word. Then have them compare the target word to each category.

"Okay. Here's our word: *met*. What word? Yes, *met*. Which category does *met* go in? Is it /ăt/ like *cat*, /ĕt/ like *jet*, or /ŏt/ like *pot*? *Cat–met*? *Jet–met*? *Pot–met*? That's it. *Jet–met*. They both have /ĕt/ at the end: *Jet–met*. Let's write *met*. What's our first sound? Yes, /m/. How do we write /m/? M. Good. Now. What's next? /ĕt/. Good. How do we spell /ĕt/ in *jet* and *met*? *Et*. Yes."

3. Continue with each word in this same manner: guiding students as they compare and contrast categories and helping them spell each word.

Modifications

● You should use a set of steps for strategic spelling that will emphasize your features. For example, let's go through the steps for considering medial short vowels like in the word *shed*. Notice how the steps specifically focus the students on short *a* versus short *e*, two sounds that are particularly difficult for some students to differentiate.

"First, say the word aloud. *Shed*. Write down your first sound: /sh/."
"Second, say the vowel sound in the middle. /ĕ/."

-at cat	-et jet	-ot pot
hat	*met* *bet*	*dot*

FIGURE 6.14. Partially completed writing sort.

"Third, think . . . is it short *a* /ă/ or short *e* /ĕ/? Think about your key
    words: *shed–cat*? *Shed–bed*? Yes. *Shed–bed.*
"Last, write down your last sound: /d/."

• Writing sorts can also be used as an assessment. Calling out words from
your categories and directing students to write them in the appropriate column
without looking at their word cards turns this activity into a spelling test. The
Blind Writing Sorts in Chapter 8 are essentially spelling assessments.

• Writing sorts can also be done in pairs, with one student calling out the
words first (playing the teacher) and the other student spelling the words. After 5
words, roles are reversed. You can provide a completed writing sort for them to
check their work.

• If the child has no partner to work with (e.g., doing homework alone), the
student can do an individual writing sort. The student places all the word cards
in a pile. The student picks a card, looks at the word, and then writes the word in
the correct column. Students should be directed to put their word card above their
written word to check spelling before moving to the next word. The student continues in this way until all the words have been spelled and categorized.

Instructional Strategy: Interactive Word Wall

• Purpose: to provide support while writing, as well as to provide
    repeated practice with highly frequent words used in writing.

Word walls are common in the primary classroom and are typically devoted to
high-frequency words. High-frequency words are important to include in your

daily instruction, because they comprise most of the words in our texts, especially the beginner books found in the primary grades. The 25 most common words account for one-third of the words in beginning texts, the 100 most common words account for one-half of the words in those texts, and the first 300 account for 65% of the words found in texts (Fry & Kress, 2006). These facts certainly make a striking argument for the need of high-frequency word practice. Figure 6.15 presents 200 high-frequency words in sets of frequency with the first 20 words as the most frequently occurring words. We consulted a variety of lists for comparison: (1) Fry's *1000 Instant Words* (1996), (2) Dolch words (1936), and (3) word lists from *Word Matters* (Fountas & Pinnell, 1996). A few critical factors were considered in choosing the 200 words below:

- Words not on all three consulted lists were eliminated.
- We chose words commonly found in current Preprimer and Primer texts.
- We chose words students are likely to need in their own writing.
- We used our own experience working with students in our reading centers and in schools.

These lists can serve as a springboard for your selection of words to target. However, you can also consider other factors. For example, you should also pull words from your instructional materials. If you have chosen a book with *from* on every page, then you should teach that word to prepare your students for the reading even if you are still working on words from List 1. The lists are not meant to be selective to the point of exclusion. There are words your students will be motivated to learn, such as *love, mom,* and *happy*. These words are not on any of the lists, but they are words you could incorporate into your instruction occasionally to engage and interest your students. The following guidelines can be used as you plan your interactive word wall instruction.

1. Assess your students. Begin with the first 20 words and build from there. You can use the High-Frequency Word Assessment provided in online Appendix A: Assessments. To administer this assessment, show your students the "student" lists while you record their accuracy on your record sheet. We usually use the 5-second rule of thumb; if they have not identified the word within 5 seconds, then move to the next word. You can also use an activity called Shop a Word (Flanigan & Lanzetti, 2005/2006). The following maps out the procedures for the activity:

- Identify the high-frequency words to target.
- Make cards for each word (one set per student).
- Place the sets in a pocket chart.
- Have students "shop for words" twice a week at the end of their reading group.

List 1	List 2	List 3	List 4	List 5
the	that	each	many	write
of	was	were	would	first
and	are	there	two	call
a	with	use	into	find
to	they	what	day	down
in	no	how	look	though
is	one	their	more	come
you	up	will	has	made
it	but	by	see	may
he	if	when	go	part
for	all	her	way	over
on	from	your	could	new
as	so	out	people	take
I	me	about	my	only
at	can	then	than	little
be	said	them	been	who
or	this	some	other	know
had	have	make	now	place
not	do	like	did	got
an	she	him	get	live

List 6	List 7	List 8	List 9	List 10
year	let	must	found	always
work	right	big	still	together
below	too	even	learn	often
back	any	such	should	until
give	same	because	every	children
most	tell	here	between	began
very	boy	why	own	took
after	follow	ask	keep	once
thing	came	went	never	without
our	want	read	thought	enough
just	show	need	under	almost
name	also	different	saw	above
good	us	around	seen	before
man	three	move	while	sometime
think	small	try	along	soon
say	put	kind	might	those
where	end	again	something	ever
help	does	off	seem	become
through	another	play	next	usually
much	large	away	begin	however

FIGURE 6.15. High-frequency word lists.

- Have students bring their words to you after they shop. If they can read them, the words go in their word bank. If they cannot, then the words go back on the chart.
- The words collected in their word banks can be practiced using activities in this chapter to develop automaticity with the words. For example, word bank words can be used with the generic game boards or in the parking lot activity.

2. Having assessed your students' recognition of these words, create a collection of words to begin your instruction. We recommend including a variety of words in your word wall. You will, of course, include high-frequency words. However, you should also include decodable words from your word knowledge instruction. Including these words not only provides more repetitions of practicing the words but it also helps demonstrate to your students specific application of these words into their writing. You will also want to include words of interest to further engage and motivate your students. These words are not all "created equal"; therefore, we use these considerations:

- 70% high-frequency words.
- 20% decodable words.
- 10% interesting words.

3. We find it most helpful to teach words in preparation for a new book reading. As you preview books for your small-group reading instruction, you should pay attention to high-frequency words that may not be already known. To introduce these words before reading:

- Write the word for students to see as you say the word aloud.
- Tell your students the word is coming up in their reading. Also tell your students that the word is very common, and they will see the word in many books.
- Discuss the phonetic regularities of the word. For example, three out of the four sounds in *from* are phonetically regular with the *O* as the only deviation.
- Have students read the word.
- Have students write the word and then read the word again.
- Turning through the book, point out the word. Have students read the word again. Introducing *from* might sound something like this:

   "We are going to learn to read a word that you will see in our book today. The word is *from*. It is a word that comes up a lot in books and a word you will want to use in your writing, too. It is a very useful word to know! I'm going to write the word. The first sound in *from* is /f/, so I'm going to write *F*. The next sound I hear is /r/, so I'm going to write *R*. After that, I hear /u/. In this word, you use *O* for that sound. Last, I hear /m/, so I need to write *M*. You can see that all of the sounds in the word are ones you know. The only tricky one is the *O*. Let's say the sound: /f r ŭ m/. What's the word? *from*. [As you talk through the spelling, make sure to point out how you are spelling the word. Display the word for the students to see and leave visible as you move to the book.] *Look at this page in our new book. Who can find the word from?* Yes, *from*. [Point out the word in the book. Then bring the word you wrote back up and ask them to read the word again.]"

(*Note*: This procedure and "teacher talk" is similar to the introduction suggested by Walpole and McKenna, 2009).

- Revisit the word during and after reading.
- Make sure to include the word in writing activities, such as the Dictated Sentence activity in the transferring words section.

4. Practice the words in a variety of ways, using the games in the reading words section. Be sure to include activities that include reading the words but also writing the words. Remember these words should be read accurately, but they also must be read automatically. These words should be read "by sight," meaning they are read immediately without a need for decoding. Therefore, multiple opportunities for practice are essential. Students can also build words from the word wall with letter tiles or write words, making sure to name the letters as they build or write. See Figure 6.16. This activity has students build words with tiles in the middle column and write words in the far right column. The far left column is provided for the teacher to write target words for which the students need additional

The Word	Build It!	Write It!
went	w e n t	*went*
are	a r e	
they		
from		
why		

FIGURE 6.16. Word wall additional practice.

practice. See online Appendix B: Toolkit Activities for a printable form ("Build It" Form) for this activity.

5. Encourage your students to use the word wall. You can easily do this by playing a game we call "What Word Am I Thinking?" This game is a simple guessing game. Anyone can offer clues, such as "I'm thinking of a word beginning with Y and is 365 days." Quick interactions such as this have one purpose: to get your students to use the word wall. You should also model use of the word wall. While writing, model using the word wall to accurately write a word. For example, while writing the morning message "Did you give Ms. Davis your ticket?" model using the word wall to write the word *give*:

> "I want to write: 'Did you give Ms. Davis your ticket?' I'm unsure about how to spell *give*. But I know that is one of our word wall words. I'll look under G. [Read down the G list.] There it is: *G-I-V-E—give.*"

Modifications

• You may want to get a measure of known words by assessing individual students. We have found the activity Your Pile–My Pile (Scanlon et al., 2010) to be a quick, effective way to measure known words. This activity is also known as Pick Up (Johnston et al., 2009).

  o Tell students that you will show them words on word cards. Words they know right away will go into a pile. Words they do not know will go into another pile. Tell them that any word not known right away will go in that second pile, as well as words you might help them read accurately. Let them know that words in this second pile need more practice.

  o Show words one at a time. Place words that are automatically and accurately recognized in a pile. This pile is "your" pile, or the pile for the student. Any word that is inaccurate or is not automatic should be placed in another pile. This second pile is "my" pile—those words needing more practice. Once a word is missed, read it aloud for the child and then have the child repeat while looking at the word.

  o Make a note of the words the student knew both accurately and automatically. These words will be used for the game at least one more time to ensure they are words known by sight.

  o Once you have gone through all words and you have two piles, move to "my" pile and begin again. Continue with the same procedure until all words are in the student's pile.

• We often think of a word wall as one displayed on the wall in the primary classroom. You may want to have personal word walls for your students. These may be built and used by individual students or they may be built for a small group. Personal word walls allow you to differentiate this work based on the needs of your students. Online Appendix B: Toolkit Activities provides a printable template for personal word walls. We often find it easy to glue these word wall sheets inside folders, making them sturdier and easier to use. See Figure 6.17.

Instructional Strategy: Words I Know

- Purpose: to introduce children to spelling unfamiliar words through the use of analogy.

Words I Know is an efficient, beneficial activity that provides your students with ample opportunity to practice writing words while using analogies with rimes (e.g., the *AT* in *cat, sat, chat*). This activity is similar to the work of Gaskins (2005). The rimes included in Figure 6.18 are among the 37 most frequent rimes that enable your students to read 500 of the most commonly used words in primary-grade texts (Adams, 1990; Wylie & Durrell, 1970). We have only included short vowel rimes because students at this stage need to solidify their knowledge of these particular vowel sounds.

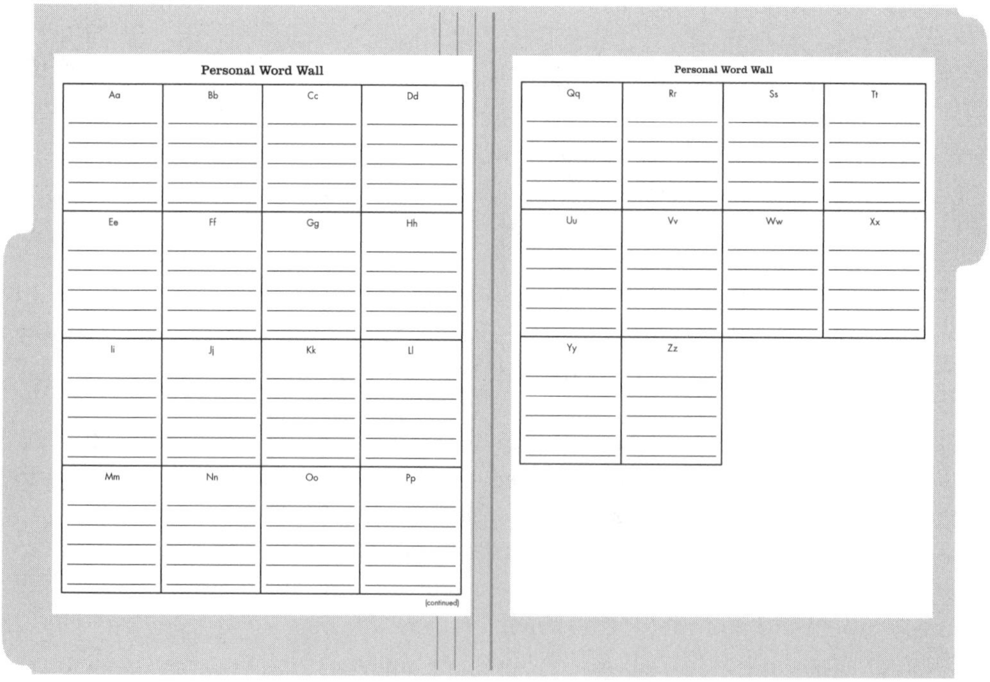

FIGURE 6.17. Personal word wall.

1. Make copies of the Words I Know form in online Appendix B: Toolkit Activities. Choose your target rime based on your features of study. For example, if you are studying short-*e* words, then you would choose short-*e* rimes. Or if you are studying short vowel word families -*at* and -*an*, then you would choose those two rimes. We suggest making booklets of 15 or so pages for continued use and review.

2. Give each student a paper copy of a booklet. Notice the first line on the page is If I know _____, then I know. This line allows you to gear the work to your target rimes.

3. Introduce the rime by writing it down on a dry-erase board and telling the students what it says. Then talk to them about how knowing this "chunk" will help them read and write many words.

> "The chunk we are going to work on today is /ămp/. It is spelled *a-m-p*. /ămp/. This chunk is used a lot in words you read and words you write. So, it is helpful to know it. Everyone, how do we spell /ămp/? *a-m-p*. Everyone get out your booklets. Write /ămp/ in your first blank. [Direct them to the blank.] Read with me: 'If I know amp, then I know . . .' "

4. Now you will direct your students to write words with this rime: *lamp, camp, damp, champ, ramp, stamp, clamp, cramp*. You can either dictate the words or give students "clues" to the words. For example, you would say: "I'm thinking of a word beginning with /cl/ and ending with /ămp/. Invite a student to provide the word: *clamp*. Then have the group write the word. As they are directed to write a word, say: "If I know *amp*, then I know clamp."

5. After writing the entire list, have the students read the page. "If I know *amp*, then I know *lamp, camp, damp, champ, ramp, stamp, clamp*, and *cramp*. To extend the work, have your students highlight, underline, or circle the target rime—in this case *amp*. See Figure 6.19, the Words I Know sheet.

at	it	ot	ut	et
an	in	op	ug	eg
ap	ig	og	up	ed
ag	ip	ock	uck	eck
ack	ick		ump	est
ash	ill		unk	ell
amp	ing			
ank	ink			

FIGURE 6.18. Frequently occurring rimes.

If I know _____ , then I know . . .

FIGURE 6.19. Words I Know.

Instructional Strategy: Games for Writing Words

- Purpose: to provide multiple opportunities for students to write words, ultimately building their accuracy and automaticity.

Games provide your beginning writers with fun, engaging opportunities to practice writing words. Primary classrooms are filled with games; however, many of these games involve *reading* words but not *writing* them. You can take any game offered in the reading words activities above and modify it to include a writing component. To illustrate, we have provided two modified games below: Sentence Bingo and Generic Game Board. However, any game can be adjusted to include writing. A word of caution: writing adds time to the game, especially for beginning writers. Therefore, you may want to consider ways to make your games efficient and allow for plenty of writing opportunities.

Sentence Bingo

1. After completing the Bingo game or while playing the game, have students write/record all words they collected on their Bingo cards.

2. You could use sticky notes for markers, having the student write the target word on the sticky note before marking the spot. This modification requires students to read the target word in a sentence, identify the word on the Bingo card, and then write the word.

3. Have students collect all words marked and write a sentence using two or more of the words. Then they can read aloud and share their sentences with the group.

Generic Game Board

1. After play, have students write/record the words on the word cards they collected. If your students played with decodable words, they could write the words in a writing sort rather than sorting the word cards. Do not have them write during play because that can slow down play and you can lose engagement across the group.

2. Have students take their individual collections and write a sentence using two or more of the words. Then they can read aloud and share their sentences with the group.

Word Knowledge Toolkit Part III: Manipulating Words

In addition to reading and writing words, students need to explicitly focus on the individual sounds in the words. The third part of your instructional Word Study Toolkit provides opportunities for students to manipulate words. Specifically, the activities are designed to blend sounds, segment sounds, and manipulate or change sounds. Chapter 1 talked about synthesizing sounds in words or "building words up" and analyzing words or "breaking words down." By working with individual sounds, or phonemes, children not only deepen their knowledge of *specific words* but they further develop their ability to segment sounds in words. The ability to segment blends found at the beginning and ending of words, as well as medial vowel sounds, is known as full phonemic segmentation. Having full phonemic segmentation will allow your students to process words more fully and will help build their knowledge about how words work.

Instructional Strategy: Sound Blending

- Purpose: given a target word presented sound-by-sound, to blend the sounds together to make a whole word.

Students need practice blending sounds to make whole words. Many activities have been designed for this purpose (e.g., "troll talk" from Adams, Foorman, Lundberg, & Beeler, 1998). When beginners are decoding an unknown word, they must say the sounds, hold them in memory, and blend all sounds together. This particular activity is completely oral and should be practiced with your early beginners to help them engage in activities where they must blend sounds. All other activities in this section include a connection to print where students segment and blend using letter connections. Connecting to letters is especially effective; therefore, you should always consider additional activities like those in the next activities along with the blending activities here. We will introduce I Spy and Puppet Sound Blending. In either activity, you can use pictures to provide support.

I Spy Sound Blending

1. Collect pictures representative of the words to be blended. Be thoughtful in your collection. As you are beginning with this activity, especially with early beginners, you should concentrate on two-sound words and move to three- and four-sound words. Remember, this activity is completely oral, so no word will be written for students to see. Figure 6.20 provides options for each.

2. Lay out three picture options for your students with one picture as your target. For example, you might put *hay, knee,* and *tie* down with *knee* as your target. Say: "I spy with my little eye: /n/ /ē/. You have to put the sounds together to find out which picture I spy. /n/ /ē/." We generally pause 1 second between sounds. Be careful not to add a schwa to sounds, particularly stop consonants. Be careful to say /b/ rather than /buh/. Also, do not elongate continuant consonants. Say the sound and pause 1 second before saying the next sound. Be careful to say /m/ rather than /mmmmmmmmmm/.

3. Once the word is provided, have students chorally segment and blend the word again with you. To make segmenting more concrete, hold up fingers as you segment. We generally hold up fingers, keeping fingers apart. Then when you blend, put your fingers together. This quick motion provides a visual for separate sounds and blend for one word.

4. Collect the pictures and lay out three new pictures for I Spy. Follow Steps 2 and 3 for continued work.

Two Sounds	Three Sounds	Four Sounds
sea	cat	clap
two	bed	stuck
key	pig	flag
day	pot	clock
bee	sun	desk
hay	ship	grape
knee	play	plug
zoo	snow*	gift
toe*	tack	sleep
mow*	rock	broom
tie	clay	nest

*Avoid adding /w/ when pronouncing long o; do not say /s n ō w/.

FIGURE 6.20. Sound blending suggestions.

5. If you notice students having trouble, think back to your picture choices. Do you need to use only two-sound words rather than words with more sounds? If you were focusing on words like *gift* and *clock*, then you may need to move to *cat* and *pot* or *sea* and *toe*, avoiding blends. Or do you need to use continuous sounds and avoid the harder stop sounds? For example, it is easier for students to blend /sssssssssssssssē/ than /bē/.

Puppet Sound Blending

1. Make sure to have a puppet with a mouth you can move. We have found making a sock puppet works well, and students love them.

2. Tell your students your friend [give your puppet a name] likes to play a game. The puppet likes to say words one part at a time. The students must then blend the parts together to make the whole word. Follow the same guidelines as in I Spy above. Pause 1 second between sounds. Avoid adding a schwa to your sounds.

3. If students have difficulty, first add the picture support detailed in I Spy above. Lay out three picture options to help support your students. Or consider your choice of words to blend. Perhaps you need fewer sounds or you need continuant sounds rather than stop sounds.

Instructional Strategy: Move It and Say It

- Purpose: given a target word, to segment the word into individual sounds, or phonemes.

Many children find it easier to blend than segment. Practicing blending activities can make the transition to segmentation tasks easier. Notice how these sound blending activities provide a model of segmenting words. Move It and Say It is a supportive first step for your students as they begin segmentation activities. This activity is based on the work of Ball and Blachman (1991), who found phonemic awareness training in kindergarten positively influenced later reading and spelling skills. We have taken this original work, adapting it to include a connection to print with letters (Blachman, 1994). These activities are especially helpful to your students as they spell unknown words. To successfully spell words, they must segment sounds in words, match the sounds to letters, and get the letters on the page.

1. Identify a sequence of words to Move It and Say It based on the features you are studying. For example, if you are studying short-*o* word families, then you could include *pot, hop, log, chop, fog, hot, shot, mop, hog*, and *dot*. Ten to 12 words are usually enough for this activity.

2. Provide your students with letter tiles or magnetic letters. We have found giving them a work space is helpful. A laminated piece of construction paper for

letter tiles or a baking tin for magnetic letters will work nicely. We suggest only providing your students with the letters necessary for completing the activity. Avoid having more than 12–15 letters. For example, the short-*o* family words above would only need the following letters: *P, O, T, H, L, G, C, F, S, M, D*—11 letters. Some teachers like to put consonants in one color and vowels in another color. That is fine but not critical. The focus here is the segmentation in the "move" and the blending in the "say."

3. Have students put letters at the bottom of their work space, leaving the top for making words. See Figure 6.21 for an example.

4. Call out your first word for your students to make at the top of their work space. If students need more support, you can have them make *DOT* by telling them to bring up their *d*, then their *o*, then their *t*. If students need this level of support, move from word to word but direct them to letter changes. For example, you would move from *dot* to *hot* to *pot*, *pop* to *mop* to *chop* to *hop*, then to *hog* to *fog* to *log*. With this sequence, all you need to do between words is direct your students to move one letter away to replace with another:

> "Now that we moved and said *DOT*, I want you to take away your *D* and put your *H* at the beginning. Let's move and say this word."

5. Now that a word is made, have your students "move and say" the word (see Figure 6.22). You will need to do this chorally for multiple times before your students will be able to do this alone. To "move and say," your students will move a letter forward while saying its sound. Once all letters have been moved, then the students will blend those sounds to say the word: /d/ /ŏ/ /t/—*dot*. You can follow up by asking how many sounds are in the word.

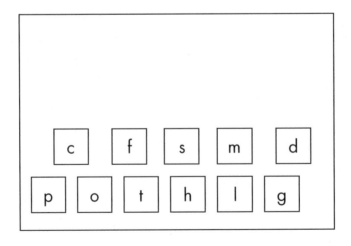

FIGURE 6.21. Sound blending work space.

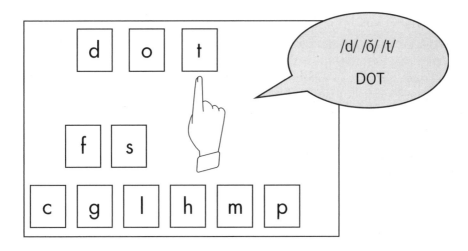

FIGURE 6.22. Sound blending example.

Modifications

• If your students are having difficulty, then use Elkonin boxes (Elkonin, 1971). Elkonin boxes are simply boxes your students use to "move" their tiles. These boxes help make the "separation" of sounds more concrete for students. Consider *chop* in Figure 6.23. By "moving" into the boxes, you can clearly illustrate for your students that *CH* makes one sound (it's in one box) but is two letters. For this reason, we always keep letters of digraphs on separate tiles rather than on one only.

• If your students are easily able to complete the Move It and Say It activities, consider:

   o Having students make the words at the top of their work space without your assistance. You may need to help them segment the words chorally prior to them making the words. If so, hold up your fingers, separating them, as you say each sound chorally with your students. Talk about how many fingers you have up to help them think about how many sounds they need to represent.

   o Move immediately to Show Me! pockets and Mix It Up! next.

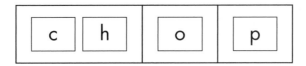

FIGURE 6.23. Elkonin boxes.

Instructional Strategy: Show Me! Pockets

• Purpose: to focus students' attention on the target features
  of a given word by building words.

Show Me! pockets takes the work of the sound blending and Move It and Say It activities to the next level. During the Show Me! activity, your students will build their own words in a fun, engaging game format. The activity puts the load of making the words on the students. Students must orchestrate segmenting sounds, making the letter connection to the sound, and then choosing the letters for their Show Me! pockets. Therefore, this activity is often implemented after much practice blending and segmenting with the previous activities.

1. Choose a set of words you will ask your students to spell in the Show Me! pockets activity. These words should mirror the features you are studying. If you were studying *l*-blends, you could choose the following words: *flip, clap, plug, bled, flop, flag, club, plum, glad*, and *slip*.

2. Make your Show Me! pockets. These are easy to make. Fold a piece of card stock not quite in half, leaving about 2 inches extra on one side. Fold that 2-inch lip up to make a pocket. Staple the ends of the pocket. We have found that stapling on the pocket to make slots for your letter tiles is helpful so that your tiles won't slip around. See Figure 6.24 with arrows pointing to spots where you would staple.

3. Make your letter tiles. These tiles should be rectangles with the letters positioned at the top to leave blank space where the tile will be stuck in the Show Me! pocket. See Figure 6.24 to see where the student is making *flop* in the Show Me! pocket. As with the Move It and Say It activity, only give your students the letter cards they will need to make the words you have chosen to work with for the activity.

4. Explain to students that you will be telling them words to make in their pockets. They are to keep their work to themselves until you say, "Show me!"

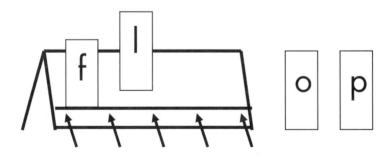

FIGURE 6.24. Show Me! pockets.

Give them their first word, such as *flop*. Observe your students as they build their words. Assist as needed. When you see all students are done, say, "Show me!" Your students will then turn their pockets around. Check their work. Your students will like turning their pockets for the big reveal.

5. After everyone's pockets have been revealed, have your students turn their pockets back around and either chorally or individually say each sound and then blend for the whole word.

6. Direct them to take their tiles out and get ready for the new word.

Instructional Strategy: Mix It Up!

- Purpose: to focus students' attention on specific parts of a given word by mixing up the letters and asking the students to spell the word again.

The "Mix It Up!" game is a fast-paced, game-like activity that helps focus your students' attention on certain parts of a word. This focus should guide the choice of words used for this activity. For example, if you are targeting initial blends in words, then you will want students to build words with and without initial blends. Having students build words that *do* as well as words that *don't* will let them practice distinguishing between words with and without initial blends, such as *cap* and *clap*. An added bonus of the activity is the extra practice segmenting and blending individual sounds in words.

1. Each student is provided with a set of letter tiles on a magnetic board or individual work space. We often use letter tiles printed on card stock with a laminated piece of construction paper as a work space.

2. Tell students which word they will spell first, directing them to "stretch out" using their fingers to count the sounds. See Figure 6.25. After students have determined the number of sounds, chorally "sound out" the word as everyone, including you, counts on their fingers.

3. Ask students to spell a word with the tiles while calling attention to the number of sounds (e.g., "Use your tiles to spell the word *pat*. Remember *pat* has three sounds.").

4. As students build their words, direct them to move and say each sound in the word to check their spelling. The big focus here is to talk about how many sounds you hear and make sure they are representing each sound.

> "You all thought about the three sounds in *pat* and *pushed* /p/ /ă/ /t/. [As you say each sound, you will "move" your letters to demonstrate.]"

5. Direct students to collect their letter tiles to clear their space. Then direct them to spell a new word: *path*. Follow the same procedure, moving from Step 2 to Step 4.

> "Okay, everyone. Sound out *path*. How many sounds do you hear in *path*? [Monitor students as they "sound out" and count with their fingers.] Now let's do this together. Hands up. Ready? /p/ /ă/ /th/. [Hold up your fingers along with the group.] How many sounds do we have? Yes, three again. Now let's spell *path*. [Monitor students as they spell with their letter tiles.] Now let's move it and say it. Ready? [Monitor students as they move and say. Make sure they are each *moving* only once while *saying* /th/.] How many sounds in *path*? Yes, three. How many letters did you need to use to spell *path*? Yes, four. Why? *Pat* had only three sounds just like *path*. But *path* has more letters. [Encourage students to articulate that the /th/ sound has two letters: *TH*. This discussion reinforces the *TH* digraph.]"

6. After this initial demonstration and careful, supported beginning to the activity, you can move forward at a faster pace.

- Have students "sound out" target word, thinking about the number of sounds they hear in the word.
- After "sounding out," students spell the target word with letter tiles.
- Have the group move it and say the target word.
- Move to the next word.

FIGURE 6.25. Mix It Up!

Modifications

- If your students have difficulty during the activity, simply step back to the more supported demonstration phase, Steps 2–5.

- If your students need more challenge, do not have them collect letter tiles between making words. You can challenge them to change one part of the target word to spell a new word. Tell them to spell a word and then change the word by adding or taking away a sound to make the new word. For example, you could have them spell *pat* and direct them to change *pat* to *path* while keeping *pat* in front of them. The students would need to decide which part of the word they are changing, the beginning, the middle, or the end. Then they would need to decide what the change is. In this example, they are changing the ending /t/ to make it /th/ simply by adding *H*. You can still follow up by having them move and say to reinforce their segmentation skills.

Word Knowledge Toolkit Part IV: Transferring Word Knowledge to Context

The ultimate goal of word study is not more word study; the ultimate goal of word knowledge instruction is to help our students become better readers, writers, and thinkers. This is why we need to explicitly support our children's attempts to transfer their word knowledge into contextual reading and writing. Unfortunately, as we discussed in Chapter 1, this type of knowledge transfer is often the "missing link" in word study instruction. The following activities, within the context of the principles of word study transfer discussed in Chapter 1, will support your students' attempts to apply word knowledge into their reading and writing.

Instructional Strategy: Dictated Sentences

- Purpose: to apply word knowledge instruction to sentence writing.

Dictated sentences allow you to have your students write words following target features in the context of a sentence, rather than a set of isolated words. These sentences are also helpful because you can incorporate words with previously studied features. An added strength of the dictated sentence is that it offers the opportunity to write highly frequent words from your word wall. As you can see, a carefully constructed dictated sentence can give you quite a large payoff.

1. Consider your target feature and construct a short, simple sentence with at least two words exemplifying your target feature. Incorporate a word with a

previously studied feature as long as you can easily do so without creating a much longer sentence. Also, consider your word wall words.

2. Once you have constructed a sentence, model writing it for your students. While writing, you can model using the word wall as well as using any big-picture graphics to reference your target feature and key word. For example, the dictated sentence "The black ship has a clock" might be modeled this way:

> "The sentence is 'The black ship has a clock.' [Hold up a finger for each word as you say the sentence.] This sentence has six words. So, I will need to be sure to have six words. My first word is *the*. I know that one right away. *THE*. [Write *THE*.] My next word is The *black*. Okay. *Black*. This word starts with one of our features for this week. The *BL* like at the beginning of *BLUE*. Yes. I hear a *B* and *L*. /b/. [Write *BL*.] Now I need /a/ and /k/. But I know /ak/ is spelled *ACK* like in *BACK*. [Write *ACK* to finish *BLACK*.] My next word is *SHIP*. I remember /sh/ and our key word is *SHIP*. Let me look back at that big picture. Yes, *SHIP*. [Write *SHIP*.] Now I have The black ship . . . has. I know that word is on the word wall. Starts with /h/ -*H*. I'll check my spelling on the word wall by looking at the *H* group. There it is: *HAS*. Got it. [Write *HAS* on your paper so all students can see it.] *My next word: The black ship has a . . . oh, that's definitely one I know right away.* [Write *A*.] My last word: The black ship has a *clock*. *CLOCK*. That begins with one of our features, and it is our key word: *clock* begins with *CL*. Let me look back at my big picture. [Write *CLOCK*.] Now I just need to remember: Sentences begin with a capital letter and end with a period. [Make sure to check for a capital and a period.]"

3. After many opportunities to observe you writing dictated sentences, then your students are ready to write their own. Repeat the sentence as many times as necessary. Call your students' attention to the word wall and big pictures as references when needed. Always remember to reread the sentences when finished to check their work.

Modifications

• You may find some students need extra support getting each word written down. After saying the sentence aloud and counting up how many words are in the sentence, you can write lines for each word. You should provide plenty of space between the lines to emphasize spacing between words. Then direct your students to write each word in the corresponding blank.

• You could have your students immediately hunt for target words or features directly after writing the dictated sentence for further emphasis.

Instructional Strategy: Word Hunts in Reading

- Purpose: to promote the transfer of word knowledge to students' contextual reading.

Students should search for exemplars of words from word knowledge instruction in their reading. This practice helps illustrate the utility of this work and how it applies to their reading. Without this practice, students may not make the connection between your small-group work and reading words in books. Through a word hunt, your students will search in previously read texts so students can focus on the hunt rather than the story. A word hunt in reading does not need to take a great deal of time. However, to ensure success, you should first make sure you have plenty of exemplars in the book. You may have students search an entire book or focus on target pages that you have already previewed. The key is maximizing the chance of success.

1. Select a previously read text that has multiple examples of the target feature(s). Make sure the book has already been used. Decodable books are often good choices for beginners. For example, the Ready Reader *Ted's Red Sled* is an excellent choice for a student hunting for words with short *e* (Pernick, 1996).

2. Beginners will need a great deal of support to have success with a word hunt. Model for them many times to ensure they understand the task. With *Ted's Red Sled*, you would read aloud the page: "So Ted went back to bed." In this sentence, you would point out *Ted* and *bed*. As you find a new word, you will record it on paper, a dry-erase board, or elsewhere.

3. Students who are new to word hunts or are early beginners may need to hunt for words page by page. Other students may be ready to hunt through an entire book. Monitor your students as they hunt through text, making sure they are thinking about both the sound and the pattern match. For example, beginners have the tendency to identify words like *what* and *was* as good short-*a* options. While they have the right pattern (the letter *a*) for a short-*a* hunt, they do not have the correct sound. The *W* preceding the *A* changes its sound. Therefore, students could identify these words as "oddballs" but not as short-*a* examples. We almost always include an oddball category in word hunts because of the variety of words they will find in their reading.

4. A critical final step to hunting for words in reading is reflecting after the hunt. You will need to either check in with individual students to verify their written hunts, or invite students to share back as you record the found words for the group to see and explain.

Modifications

- If you have text copies of your books, then your students can hunt on the text copy, highlighting examples as they read. A text copy is a typed-up version of a book without the assistance of illustrations/pictures. Simply type up each page as a line of text as in Figure 6.26. Students can hunt for words in the text copy based on features of study, but the text copy in Figure 6.26 is best suited for a hunt of high-frequency words like *said* and *see*.

- Students can work in pairs or small groups as they hunt through text. Make sure they record the words they find. Also, make sure the pairs or groups report back to the main group about the words they find.

- Your small groups can go on word hunts during centers or seatwork. Just make sure you have them search through previously read books, and they record the words they find so you can monitor their work. You could also provide self-checks with a "word hunt guide" you provide for the book. A word hunt guide is a previously completed word hunt for a book your students can use to check their hunts after completion.

Instructional Strategy: Word Hunts in Dictated Sentences

- Purpose: to promote the transfer of word knowledge to students' contextual writing utilizing the Dictated Sentences activity.

Word hunts in writing not only encourage your students to think about applying their word knowledge to their spelling while writing, but also encourage beginners to start employing the editing process to some degree. Editing for a beginner is a teacher-supported activity. Beginning readers and writers are not able to participate in self-editing; the task is simply too overwhelming for them. Having them do targeted word hunts in their writing is a way to get their feet wet.

"I can see the little cat," said the pig.
"I can see the little bat," said the cow.
"I can see the little dog," said the chick.
"I can see the little frog," said the goat.
"I can see the little flea," said the duck.
"I can see the little bee," said the sheep.
Eek!

FIGURE 6.26. Text copy.

1. Choose a piece of writing where you have at least two or three spelling errors appropriate to point out to your student based on the features you have covered so far in the year. Have your big pictures available to refer to as necessary.

2. Plan to either conference individually with students or meet with them in small groups. Beginners will need you to heavily support this activity. Begin with modeling the process, making sure the writing piece is clearly visible to the student(s). Select a specific feature to "hunt" for and begin by modeling this search. The first step is to say the target feature and point out visually with the big picture. Then model reading aloud only one sentence, reflecting on words with the target feature within the sentence. Once a word is located, refer to the big picture to highlight the spelling. Then model checking the writing to ensure a correct spelling. It is helpful to first pinpoint a word that is spelled correctly. Then model checking an error with the correction as a follow-up. You can also hunt for words from your word wall to reinforce highly frequent words.

3. After you have provided plenty of opportunities for your students to observe you hunting for correctly and incorrectly spelled words, students can "hunt" in their own writing. However, you will need to make this a very controlled activity in order for it to be beneficial for your beginners. We suggest using Dictated Sentences with beginners for one critical reason: you know there are instances of the target features. You will need to direct your students by each sentence. For example, consider the sentence in Figure 6.27 offered up by a first grader. It reads: "I like to pet my baby chick." This sentence was a dictated sentence from a previous activity in the week. The student had previously studied digraphs and short vowel word families to include -*et* and -*ick*. In addition, the teacher expected correct spellings of some highly frequent words from the word wall, specifically *I*, *to*, and *my*. Last, the student was most recently in a focused study of short *e* and *i*.

FIGURE 6.27. First grader's Word Hunt in Writing.

With this knowledge, the teacher directed the student to hunt for the target word wall words to check their spellings. The student misspells the highly frequent word *like* (spelled as LICK), and the teacher directs the student to use the word wall. Then the teacher had the student hunt for short-*e* and -*i* words. The first step reinforced the student's correct spellings of the word wall words, and the second step demonstrated the student's accurate use of short *e* (*pet*) and *i* (*chick*).

Instructional Strategy: Seeing the "Big Picture" and Using Key Words

• Purpose: to promote the transfer of word knowledge to students' contextual reading and writing.

The graphic organizers we are most familiar with are found in social studies and science. However, we can use these same organizers to visually present our features of phonics and spelling work. This "big picture" helps students "see" how these features relate to one another and can work as quick references. See Figure 6.28 for a big-picture graphic organizer for digraphs. These graphic organizers will change over time as you introduce and practice new features. Notice how the big picture offers key words for digraphs found in both the initial and final position of words. The following activity illustrates how you can use the big picture and the key words to assist your students as they read and write unfamiliar words.

1. Introduce the big picture when you introduce your sort. Make sure it is large enough so you can display it in your room. Your main goal is to help your students see how the features fit together as you fold the organizer into your instruction.

2. Use consistent key words for each feature, which can be found in Figure 5.8 in Chapter 5 as well as in Beginner Feature Sorting lists in online Appendix B: Toolkit Activities. See Figure 6.28: *CH* with *ch*in and ri*ch*, *SH* with *sh*ip and wi*sh*, and *TH* with *th*ink and ma*th*. These key words will be used to help students when reading and spelling by analogy. In addition, you want to use key words that are known words so that your students can refer to these *known* words while trying to spell *new* words with the same features. Let's consider the following example of using the big picture and key words as an instruction to spelling *new* words.

> "We are going to think about the beginning sounds in words. Today, we are going to focus on three sounds. First, we will think about the /ch/ at the beginning of the word *chin*. Let's listen at the beginning of *chin*. What is the first sound we hear? /ch/. Yes, that's right. So, when we are trying to spell words with the /ch/ sound, we can use what we know about *chin*. How do we spell the /ch/ at the beginning of *chin*? You got it. *CH*. [Refer your students to the big picture and point out the *CH* feature with *chin*.] Using the *CH* that we know is at the beginning of *chin* will help us spell

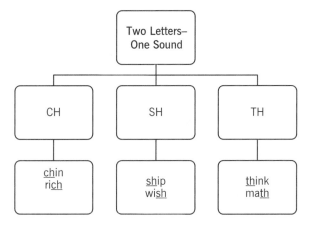

FIGURE 6.28. Big-picture graphic organizer digraphs.

other words like *chat* and *chick*. So, if you can't remember what letters make the /ch/ sound, you can come back to this big picture and our key word *chin*.

3. Refer to the big picture and key words during contextual reading and writing. You can help your students be more strategic in their spelling. For example:

"Let's think about the word *shed*. If I didn't know how to spell this word, I would need to first think about my first sound. What's the first sound? /sh/. Yes! Now I'm going to look back at my big picture. Where is my feature /sh/? Yes, it is /sh/ like at the beginning of *ship*. So, *ship* and *shed* begin alike. So, I use *SH* for /sh/ in *ship*, and I use *SH* for the /sh/ at the beginning of *shed*."

Conclusion

When you teach with a developmental stance, you are ensuring that you are meeting the needs of your students within the word knowledge zone. The TSI is designed to allow you to identify your students' needs at the back end of the zone—meeting their spelling needs. At the same time, your students may be facing features in text necessitating an instructional eye toward the front end of the zone—meeting their decoding needs. This work also fits within a balanced framework that allots time for reading *and* writing words, as well as encouraging transfer of these skills. Taken together, this approach will produce strategic readers and writers, catapulting your beginning readers to the next reader stage—the transitional stage of reading.

CHAPTER 7

The Transitional Reader and Writer

BUILDING AUTOMATIC WORD KNOWLEDGE FOR FLUENCY

GUIDING QUESTIONS
• •

- What are the reading characteristics of children in the transitional stage?
- What are the spelling and writing characteristics of children in the transitional stage?
- How do the feature scores from the Tiered Spelling Inventory (TSI) guide you in your word knowledge instruction at the transitional stage?
- What are the three main instructional milestones for the transitional stage?
- How might you organize your literacy block for word knowledge instruction at this stage?

It's a Wednesday morning in early January, and Ms. Kurosawa is working with a small reading group in her second-grade classroom. The group has been reading *Cam Jansen and the Mystery of the Babe Ruth Baseball* (Adler, 2004) for the past week. Before the group begins Chapter 3, she asks her students to summarize what has happened so far in the story. After affirming student answers, probing for deeper thinking, and clarifying a misconception about the story events, she asks the group to make predictions for the upcoming chapter. Once students have shared and justified their predictions, they begin silently reading to the next preplanned stopping point.

As she normally does during this silent reading time, Ms. Kurosawa begins checking in individually with the children in the group. She first moves next to Alex and asks him to whisper read to her. As he reads, Ms. Kurosawa is reminded of the significant progress in reading fluency and word recognition Alex has made since September. Because Alex's comprehension has always been strong, he regularly used context clues to help him decode unknown words—sometimes context was helpful, other times it wasn't. However, Alex's fluency was not nearly as strong as his comprehension. In the beginning of the year, he often read in a monotone, choppy, word-by-word manner. But now, by the middle of the school year, he can read more fluently, often reading entire phrases together, pausing appropriately at commas and periods, and reading with more smoothness, expression, and speed.

While whisper reading, Alex stumbles on a two-syllable word—*complain*. Because the context is not very helpful in this sentence, Alex stops and looks up at Ms. Kurosawa for help. She gently nudges him, "What do good readers do when they come across a difficult word?" Alex answers hesitantly, "Look for words or word parts I already know?" Ms. Kurosawa says, "That's right. Do you see any parts you know? Look at all parts of the word." Alex says, "Well, there is the *-ain* pattern, like in our key word, *rain*. So that must be *pl-ain*—*plain*!" Ms. Kurosawa says, "Good thinking. What part of the word is left?" Alex covers up the *plain*, so he can focus on the beginning of the word and answers "*com, com-plain, complain*!" Alex proceeds to reread the sentence to see if *complain* makes sense, and, deciding that it does, continues reading.

As Ms. Kurosawa moves to the next child, she smiles to herself as she thinks of how Alex's improvements in reading fluency have been fueled by his growth in word recognition. Again, at the beginning of the year, Alex might have tried sounding out a word like *complain* letter by letter, as in *c-o-m-p-l-a-i-n*. This type of word analysis, processing and "remembering" eight different letter sounds one by one, takes a large amount of cognitive attention, leaving little "brainpower" left for comprehension. In addition, letter-by-letter decoding won't work for most long vowel pattern words like *plain* in which the *AI* long vowel pattern must be processed as a single unit in order for the reader to automatically recognize that it is a long vowel. In fact, as they move through the stage, children will begin to process larger chunks, such as the high-frequency *-ain* ending.

However, instead of having to decode and remember eight different letters, Alex's new level of word knowledge equips him to process the word *complain* in only three familiar parts, or "chunks"—*com-pl-ain*—a much easier cognitive task. As Ms. Kurosawa knows, recognizing three known letter patterns is much easier than sounding out letter by letter, particularly with all of the long vowel pattern and multisyllabic words that Alex will be encountering in his reading and using in his writing in second grade. Alex's much stronger, more efficient level of word knowledge allows him to more automatically recognize increasingly sophisticated words and word patterns, in turn supporting more rapid and fluent oral reading. Put simply, stronger word knowledge supports improved fluency.

This chapter focuses on transitional readers like Alex. First, we highlight the defining reading and spelling characteristics of children in this stage of development. Next, we describe the common features of study for phonics and spelling instruction at the transitional stage and discuss how word knowledge instruction fits within the language arts block for transitional readers. Finally, we end the chapter by presenting ideas for scheduling and ways to monitor your students' word knowledge progress.

Characteristics of Transitional Readers and Writers

Bear et al. (2012) have identified children such as Alex as transitional readers and writers. We embrace this term because this stage serves as a bridge between the beginner stage of reading, where reading and writing are difficult processes requiring a large amount of conscious attention, and the more advanced stages, where children can read nearly everything they encounter with adequate fluency. Like all transitional readers, Alex is in the process of building his automatic word recognition and his reading fluency. Like a fledgling bird flying for longer and longer periods of time, Alex will be able to read longer and longer chunks of text with practice and support as he progresses through this stage. This reading stamina will sustain him as he encounters increasingly sophisticated words and texts.

Reading Characteristics: Becoming a Fluent Reader

The transitional reader and writer is building word knowledge automaticity and reading and writing fluency (see Figure 7.1). One of the most important "skills" that transitional students acquire is the ability to decode and recognize words in chunks, or letter patterns, decoding by analogy instead of having to process each

Transitional Reading Characteristics	• Reads at approximately the late first-grade to early third-grade level. • Begins to read in phrasal units. • Improves prosody, intonation, expression. • Stops word-by-word reading and fingerpointing. • Increases reading rate, nearing 100 words per minute by end of stage. • Reads silently, with silent reading predominating as child moves along this stage. • Decodes nearly all single-syllable words and many multisyllabic words in context accurately and automatically. • Decodes and recognizes "chunks" or patterns of words as single units (e.g., -ake of cake is processed as a single orthographic unit).

FIGURE 7.1. Reading characteristics of the transitional reader.

unfamiliar word they encounter letter by letter as they did as beginning readers. According to Ehri (1997), these students have moved from the full alphabetic phase to the consolidated alphabetic phase. This level of word knowledge represents a quantum leap forward in processing efficiency, as the *c-o-m-p-l-a-i-n* versus *com-pl-ain* example from Alex's vignette above makes clear. This more efficient decoding will lead to improved automatic word knowledge and rapid growth in sight-word vocabulary.

Because students can read individual words more quickly and efficiently, their reading fluency in context also improves, an important instructional milestone at this stage. Instead of the word-by-word, monotone reading characteristic of the beginner stage, transitional readers begin to read in phrasal units, pausing appropriately at natural phrase boundaries as well as at commas and periods. They read with increased expression, intonation, and smoothness as their reading rates increase, nearing 100 words per minute by the end of this stage (Bear, 1992). Because they have so automatically internalized specific sight words and more sophisticated word patterns, they are able to read silently and no longer need to fingerpoint read to "hold themselves up" as they march across the page.

Texts for transitional readers range from early chapter books, such as *Hi! Fly Guy* by Tedd Arnold (2006) at the beginning of this stage to more complex texts such as *Flat Stanley: His Original Adventure!* by Jeff Brown (2009). Transitional readers may become engrossed in a book series, such as *Detective Camp* (Roy, 2006) from the *A to Z Mysteries* series, *Rumble in the Jungle* (Stilton, 2011) from the *Geronimo Stilton* series, or *Henry and Mudge and the Wild Goose Chase* (Rylant, 2003) from the *Henry and Mudge* series. Because series of books have consistent sets of characters and similar plot structures, they are supportive vehicles for students at this stage. It is also important to provide transitional readers equal access to different genres, including informational texts, as their ability to dig in to increasingly sophisticated concepts increases. See Figure 7.2 for a summary of text levels across commonly used leveling systems.

Writing and Spelling Characteristics: Becoming a Fluent Writer

Just as children at the transitional level can *decode* words in chunks or letter units, they can also spell words that contain common chunks, or orthographic patterns, with increasing accuracy and fluency. See Figure 7.3 for the writing and spelling characteristics of transitional students. Long vowels are a central focus of spelling at this stage, with students examining common long vowel patterns such as the *aCe* in *cave*, the *ea* in *team*, the *igh* in *sight*, and the *oa* in *float*. This ability to internalize common spelling patterns represents a more abstract level of word knowledge than the letter-by-letter understanding of beginning readers.

It is important to note that, as we discussed in Chapter 1, transitional readers' ability to decode words will outstrip their ability to spell words. The spelling–reading

Stage	Traditional Levels	Guided Reading	DRA	Lexile
Emergent	Readiness	A	A	BR
			1	
		B	2	
			3	
	Preprimer A	C	4	
Beginner	Preprimer B	D	6	
	Preprimer C	E	8	
	Primer	F	10	200–400
		G	12	
Transitional	Late First	H	14	
		I	16	
	Early Second	J	18	
		K	20	300–600
	Late Second	L	24	
		M	28	
	Early Third	N	32	

FIGURE 7.2. Transitional reader text conversion chart.

Transitional Writing and Spelling Characteristics

- Spelling
  - Demonstrates solid control of short vowel patterns, blends, and digraphs from the beginner stage.
  - "Uses but confuses" common long vowel patterns, complex consonants, and abstract vowels.
  - Masters above features by end of stage.
  - Improves spelling fluency, requiring less conscious attention while writing.
- Writing
  - Increases length of written pieces.
  - Improves writing quality, including more attention to complex ideas, vocabulary choice, and depth of written pieces.

FIGURE 7.3. Writing and spelling characteristics of the transitional reader.

slant should be taken into account during instruction. For example, while working on spelling the *oo* long vowel pattern in words like *mood*, transitional readers will be able to decode this same pattern *while reading* multisyllabic words such as *poodle* and *cartoon*. We discuss this type of more advanced decoding instruction later in this chapter under the subheading "Features of Focus for Decoding: Moving to the Front End of the Zone."

At the beginning of the transitional stage, your students may be "using but confusing" common long vowel patterns, spelling words such as *rain* as RANE, *sweep* as SWEAP, or *sight* as SITE (Bear et al., 2012). Notice that these misspellings, while not conventionally correct, are more sophisticated than the misspellings of these same words by a beginning reader (see Figure 7.4 for a comparison of letter–name and within-word misspellings). For example, why does RANE in Figure 7.4, a transitional reader misspelling of *rain*, represent a more sophisticated word knowledge than RAN, a beginning reader misspelling of this same word? The transitional reader realizes that he or she must mark the long-*a* vowel sound with a silent letter. Although the student chooses the wrong pattern for this particular word (the *aCe* pattern rather than the *ai* pattern found in *rain*), the choice of an allowable English spelling pattern for a long-*a* sound demonstrates thinking in chunks, or patterns, rather than simply by individual letters and sounds. See *Words Their Way* (Bear et al., 2012) for a more detailed description of this within-word pattern stage of development.

By the end of this stage, transitional readers will be accurately and automatically spelling (1) common long vowel pattern words like the *oo* in *moon* and the *ui* in *suit*, (2) complex consonants like the *tch* in *patch*, (3) *r*-controlled vowels like the *are* in *dare*, and (4) abstract vowel patterns like the *ou* in *cloud* and the *aught* in *caught*. Of course, students will only make progress through this stage, and in their literacy skills, if they are given ample time and opportunity to actually apply these skills in contextual reading and writing; they need to see words many times in meaningful contexts in order to correctly link a spelling to a word's meaning.

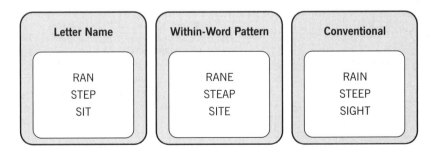

FIGURE 7.4. Comparing and contrasting letter–name, within-word, and conventional long vowel spellings.

See the balanced literacy diet later in this chapter for specific recommendations of instructional time for contextual reading and writing at the transitional stage.

Students' increased spelling fluency supports their increased writing quality. As spelling requires less conscious attention at this stage, students' minds are freed up to focus on longer written pieces with increasingly sophisticated plots, more complex characters, and more variety in vocabulary choice. Students at this stage also begin to explore a greater variety of genres, including informational text and poetry. They can also begin to learn the basic components of text-based argument targeted in the Common Core State Standards (CCSS).

Transitional Readers' Word Knowledge Development: Common Features of Study

The major breakthrough in word knowledge development for transitional readers is the ability to process letter patterns in chunks, as opposed to the letter-by-letter approach. Because of this, children in the transitional stage are able to profitably examine vowel *patterns* that are more abstract than the single-syllable consonant-vowel-consonant (CVC) short vowel patterns learned by beginning readers. These orthographic patterns include common long vowel patterns, ambiguous/abstract vowel patterns, complex consonants, *r*-controlled vowels, and homophones and homographs. Figure 7.5 summarizes the orthographic features that children should learn at this stage of development. We selected these patterns for study based on work by Bear et al. (2012) and Morris (2005).

Common Long Vowel Patterns

Common long vowel patterns are one of the primary features mastered during this stage. Children begin with long vowel vowel–consonant–*e* (VCe) patterns such as *cave, slide, home,* and *cube.* As they move through this stage, students also work to master many other common long vowel patterns such as the *ai* in *rain,* the *ay* in *clay,* the *ea* in *dream,* the *igh* in *flight,* the *oa* in *boat,* and the *ow* in *stow.* One of the central concepts we want students to grasp at this stage is that, in English, *we usually mark long vowels with a silent vowel marker.* These silent vowel markers include:

- The "silent *e*" found in VCe words like *cake.*
- A silent vowel paired with a sounded vowel, commonly known as "vowel teams," as in the *ai* in *rain* and the *oa* in *boat.*
- A silent consonant paired with a vowel, such as the *y* in *clay* and the *w* in *stow.*

Common Long Vowel Patterns	
Long *a*	aCe (made) ai (rain) ay (day)
Long *e*	ee (seem) ea (bean) e (me)
Long *i*	iCe (bite) igh (sight) y (dry)
Long *o*	oCe (bone) oa (soap) ow (low)
Long *u*	uCe (cube) oo (moon) ew (dew)
Short vs. Long *R*-Controlled Vowel Patterns	
a	ar (car) are (dare) air (fair)
e	er (her) ear (clear) eer (steer) ear (heard)
i	ir (dirt) ire (fire)
o	or (corn) ore (store) our (court) oar (roar)
u	ur (hurt) ure (pure)
Abstract Vowel Patterns	
ow (how) and ou (house) oi (boil) and oy (toy) oo (book) and oo (moon)	
Complex Consonant Patterns	
tch (patch) and ch (reach) dge (fudge) and ge (huge) str (string), spl (splat), spr (spring), shr (shriek), thr (through), and squ (squeak)	

FIGURE 7.5. Transitional readers—Orthographic Features of Study chart.

Long *R*-Controlled Vowels

At this stage, we want to build on children's knowledge of *r*-controlled vowels from the beginning reader stage, moving on to an exploration of how the *r* also influences long vowels in addition to the short vowels learned in the beginner stage. If you compare the long *a* sounds in the words *fade* and *fare*, you can hear (and feel) the difference in the long *a* sounds. The *r* that follows the vowel *a* subtly changes the long *a* sound. When examining these long *r*-controlled vowels, we provide opportunities for children to compare and contrast these new patterns with the known short *r*-controlled vowel patterns examined in the beginner stage as demonstrated in the sort in Figure 7.6.

Abstract Vowels and Diphthongs

Our university students are often surprised when they learn that there are vowel sounds in English that are neither long nor short. We refer to these sounds/patterns as *abstract vowels*, and usually teach them after common long vowel patterns, later in this stage. Abstract vowel teams include the vowel sounds found in *taught* and *stood*. In addition, we pay close attention to a subcategory called *diphthongs*. This type of abstract vowel are those patterns that actually include two vowel sounds, also known as vowel "glides," in which we glide from one vowel sound to the next vowel sound. Diphthongs examined at this stage include vowel teams such as the *oi* in *soil* and the *ou* in *hound*. Notice how these vowel teams come later in the sequence after long vowel teams have been taught.

Complex Consonants

By the end of the beginner stage, students will have solid control of most consonants, blends, and digraphs. However, there are more *complex consonant patterns*

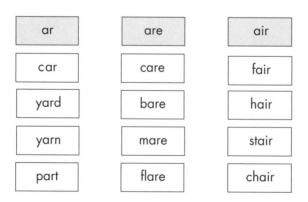

FIGURE 7.6. AR/ARE/AIR word sort.

that students will still need to master during the transitional stage. These patterns include initial three-letter blends and digraphs such as *str* (*strap*), *spl* (*split*), *shr* (*shrink*), *thr* (*through*), and *squ* (*squawk*). We teach these features near the end of this stage because the words that contain these complex consonant patterns include many different vowel patterns.

In addition to the triplets mentioned above, we also teach complex consonant patterns found at the end of words. For example, contrasting the *tch* versus *ch* patterns (see Figure 7.7) yields an important orthographic concept for students. Far from being random, there is a pattern here, as there is in so many words in English: words ending in *tch* are usually preceded by a short vowel, while words ending in *ch* are usually preceded by a long vowel. This is the kind of incredibly useful pattern that helps students spell, decode, and store words more effectively and efficiently.

Homophones and Homographs

Homophones are words that *sound* the same, but are spelled differently and have different meanings, such as *rain/reign/rein*, *beat/beet*, *threw/through*, and *peek/peak/pique*. Homographs are words that are *spelled* the same, but have different meanings (and may or may not have different pronunciations) such as *bear* (the animal) and *bear* (to carry), or *sow* (to plant a seed) and *sow* (a female pig). While homophones and homographs will be encountered by beginning readers, children need to learn many of these words during the transitional stage because they occur so frequently in transitional-stage texts.

Importantly, these types of words provide an excellent opportunity to expand children's vocabularies and introduce them to the use of context clues and dictionaries, including online dictionaries, to find word meanings. For example, most second-grade students will know the meaning of the word *rain*, but how many know or could effortlessly use the related words *reign* or *rein* in oral language? A number of the instructional strategies in the next section, such as Hot Seat, can be modified to focus on the meaning of words as well as the spelling.

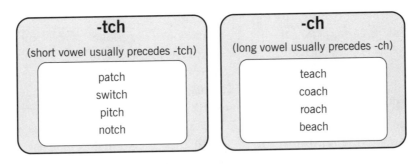

FIGURE 7.7. *tch/ch* word sort.

Features of Focus for Decoding: Moving to the Front End of the Zone

As your students progress through the transitional stage, they will come across an increasing number of multisyllabic words in the texts they are reading. Whether they are reading *Henry and Mudge and the Big Sleepover* by Cynthia Rylant (2007) near the beginning of this stage, or the classic *How to Eat Fried Worms* by Thomas Rockwell (1973) near the end of this stage, they will encounter words like *suppose, pillow, recoiling*, and *furtively*. You will notice that these multisyllabic words contain some of the same spelling patterns that they are already studying in single-syllable words: (1) *suppose* contains the o–consonant–*e* pattern in single-syllable words like *bone*, (2) *pillow* contains the *ow* pattern in single-syllable words like *snow*, (3) *recoiling* contains the *oi* pattern in single-syllable words like *oil*, and (4) *furtively* contains the *r*-controlled pattern in words like *fur* and *hurt*. It is important to teach your students that these very same spelling patterns occur in the stressed syllables of multisyllabic words.

We should directly and explicitly teach our transitional readers how to leverage their knowledge of single-syllable patterns and apply it to those same patterns they notice in multisyllabic words *while reading*. We want to emphasize that we will not be testing our transitional students on the *spelling* of these multisyllabic words; however, we do want them to begin to apply them while *reading* multisyllabic words. Figure 7.8 highlights some high-utility features to teach transitional students for their decoding knowledge at the front end of the word knowledge instructional zone in multisyllabic words.

Directly teaching the features of study for children at the transitional stage outlined in Figure 7.5 will support your students in forming a solid foundation in word knowledge at this stage. From this solid foundation, your transitional readers can begin to work at the cutting edge of their word knowledge by applying what they know about the spellings of single-syllable words to multisyllabic words while reading. Chapter 8 is devoted to activities to teach across the zone. For example, the two-step sort is a particularly powerful activity that supports students in making the leap from single-syllable to multisyllabic words for reading at the front end of the zone (see pp. 200–201 in Chapter 8).

While it is important to directly teach your transitional readers the common vowel patterns found in multisyllabic words (summarized in Figure 7.8), this is not enough. It is also important to directly teach your students how to analyze these multisyllabic words into their constituent syllables—how to determine "where" the syllable breaks are found. In Chapter 8, "The Transitional Reader's Toolkit," we introduce a streamlined four-step strategy that transitional readers can use to decode multisyllabic words (see pp. 204–206). We want to emphasize that this ability to decode and store multisyllabic words while reading is foundational for children at this stage and, as we discuss later, is one of the three instructional milestones for transitional stage readers.

Common Long Vowel Patterns in Stressed Syllables of Multisyllabic Words	
Long-*a* patterns	aCe (graceful) ai (exclaim) ay (player)
Long-*e* patterns	ee (asleep) ea (defeat)
Long-*i*	iCe (advice) igh (slightly)
Long-*o*	oCe (homestead) oa (approach) ow (below)
Long-*u*	uCe (dispute) oo (balloon) ew (mildew)
Short vs. Long *R*-Controlled Vowel Patterns	
a	ar (carpet) are (careful) air (repair)
e	er (serpent) ear (fearless) ear (nearly)
i	ir (thirty) ire (desire)
o	or (cornfield) ore (storey) our (resource) oar (hoarder)
u	ur (sturdy) ure (insure)
Abstract Vowel Patterns	
ow (chowder) and ou (mountain) oi (boiler) and oy (royal)	

FIGURE 7.8. Transitional readers—features of study at the front end of the zone.

Common Core Alignment

The preceding Common Features of Study section describes what children at the transitional stage should *know* about the spelling system (e.g., common long vowel patterns). Chapter 8, "The Transitional Reader's Toolkit," describes activities that promote what children should *be able to do* with this spelling-system knowledge (e.g., word sorting promotes children's ability to distinguish between long and short vowel words). Figure 7.9 identifies the CCSS standards detailing

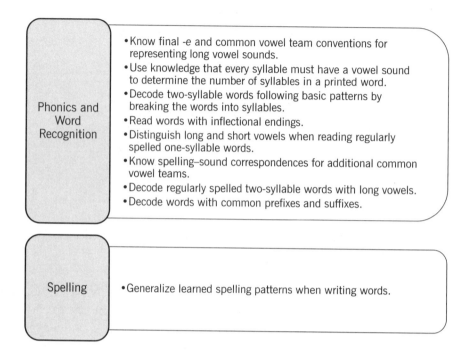

Phonics and Word Recognition

- Know final -e and common vowel team conventions for representing long vowel sounds.
- Use knowledge that every syllable must have a vowel sound to determine the number of syllables in a printed word.
- Decode two-syllable words following basic patterns by breaking the words into syllables.
- Read words with inflectional endings.
- Distinguish long and short vowels when reading regularly spelled one-syllable words.
- Know spelling–sound correspondences for additional common vowel teams.
- Decode regularly spelled two-syllable words with long vowels.
- Decode words with common prefixes and suffixes.

Spelling

- Generalize learned spelling patterns when writing words.

FIGURE 7.9. CCSS for transitional readers (skills spanning grades 1–2).

what children *should know and be able to do* that are targeted in these transitional stage chapters.

Transitional Readers and Writers: A Balanced Literacy Diet

As we have mentioned throughout this book, word study is one essential component of a balanced, comprehensive four-part literacy diet. Figure 7.10 illustrates both the components of the diet and the approximate "portion sizes" for each component. Put simply, children at the transitional stage should (1) spend a large amount of time in appropriate and engaging reading and writing activities; (2) should have many experiences with rich oral and written language throughout the day; and (3) should have a smaller, but still essential part of their instruction focused on building their word knowledge.

Notice in Figure 7.10 how the percentages for each portion of the literacy diet have changed from the beginning reader and writer stage, which we introduced in Chapter 5 (Figure 5.15). Specifically, in Figure 7.10 there is a slightly larger percentage of time focused on contextual reading and writing to reflect the ability of

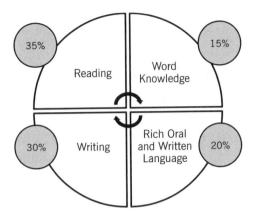

FIGURE 7.10. A balanced literacy diet for transitional readers.

children at the transitional stage to read and write independently for longer, more sustained periods of time. Remember that these percentages are not set in stone, but rather are intended to provide you with a general sense of how much of your allotted literacy block to spend on each component of instruction; you may want to modify these amounts based on various children's needs at different times of the year.

For word knowledge instruction, remember to use the TSI to help you decide where to target instruction for the back end of the word knowledge zone. This back end of the zone of instruction will help students solidify and consolidate their word knowledge, providing a firm footing for further growth in reading and spelling. At other times, you will want to help students tackle the more difficult, multisyllabic words they are encountering in their reading—features found at the front end of their zone. We strongly recommend that this front-end-of-the-zone word work be connected to the texts students are reading. For example, you may want to directly teach your students how to use their knowledge of long vowel *a* patterns to tackle multisyllabic words with that same long vowel *a* pattern (e.g., the *ai* pattern in *maintain*) before reading a text that contains related words that follow this pattern (e.g., *sustain* and *retain*).

Transitional Milestones

In teaching, it is always important to keep your "big-idea" instructional goals in mind. For word knowledge instruction, these instructional goals are the word knowledge milestones that transitional readers must reach to enable further growth as readers and writers. By the end of this stage, the transitional reader and writer should be able to:

- Chunk common long and abstract vowel patterns while reading and writing.
- Use decoding strategies to read unfamiliar words, including multisyllabic words in context.
- Increase automaticity of word knowledge to enable fluent, expressive, meaningful reading.

As you plan word knowledge instruction, keep these ultimate milestones in mind so that your word study instruction does not devolve into a set of disconnected, purposeless activities. Rather, keep your instruction focused, always working toward the ultimate milestones on the transitional reader path.

Daily and Weekly Schedules

As we conclude this chapter, let's return to Ms. Kurosawa and her second-grade classroom from the beginning of this chapter to see how she fits word study into her 120-minute literacy block. Importantly, Ms. Kurosawa organizes her literacy instruction by honoring the four components and commensurate portion sizes of the balanced literacy diet:

1. *Small-group reading instruction* (45 minutes). Ms. Kurosawa usually meets with two small reading groups per day for approximately 20 minutes each. She organizes these flexible groups according to her students' literacy strengths and needs. Students she is not meeting with usually spend this time (1) reading their small-group texts in preparation for their next meeting, or rereading familiar texts for fluency as a follow-up from a previous small-group session; and/or (2) reading their independent reading text, which Ms. Kurosawa allows students to choose from a selection of appropriate, engaging books.

2. *Word study* (15 minutes). See Figure 7.11 for a description.

3. *Writing workshop* (35 minutes). Ms. Kurosawa usually organizes her writing workshop in the following three parts: (1) whole-class mini-lesson, (2) individual writing time while Ms. Kurosawa conferences with students, and (3) whole-class author's chair during which students share their writing with the class.

4. *Read-aloud* (25 minutes). Ms. Kurosawa uses this time to read aloud rich language texts, both narrative and informational, to her class; engage in critical and creative thinking; and introduce and model reading strategies.

How do the students in Ms. Kurosawa's class spend their daily 15 minutes of word study instruction across a week? Figure 7.11 illustrates word study activities her students might complete during a typical week. Each of these activities is described in Chapter 8.

Notice how Ms. Kurosawa has judiciously chosen word study activities from each of the first three parts of the instructional Word Knowledge Toolkit to ensure that students are building strong, flexible word knowledge:

- *Reading words*—Guess My Category, Concentration, and Speed Sort.
- *Writing words*—Writing Sort (both as Monday homework activity and a Friday assessment), Give Me a Clue!
- *Manipulating words*—Building Words—Reading/Spelling.

However, Ms. Kurosawa also knows that word study instruction alone is not enough; she needs to explicitly coach and support her students in their attempts to transfer this word knowledge into contextual reading and writing. This is why she makes sure to choose the activities from the fourth part of the Word Knowledge Toolkit—transferring word knowledge. Importantly, these activities will be incorporated into reading and writing instruction during the week:

- During writing workshop, Ms. Kurosawa provides her students time to conduct word hunts as part of the editing phase of the writing process (see the word hunt activity in Chapter 8). Specifically, she works with students to create editing charts that target the exact spelling features they have examined during word study instruction, thus building the bridge between word study and writing for her students.

- During small-group reading instruction, usually at the beginning or end of a session, Ms. Kurosawa makes sure to pull a few multisyllabic words from the text and models and coaches the students in decoding the words by syllable and/or morpheme either before or after the reading.

This schedule sample incorporates a teacher-led language arts block with trade books as the core reading materials. You may be in a district or school using a basal reading program. To see an example of how the Word Knowledge Toolkit

	Monday	Tuesday	Wednesday	Thursday	Friday
In Class	Guess My Category	Building Words—Reading/Spelling	Give Me a Clue!	Speed Sort	Writing Sort (as final assessment)
Homework	Writing Sort		Concentration		

FIGURE 7.11. Weekly word study schedule in Ms. Kurosawa's class.

can be incorporated within a basal reading program, refer to Chapter 5 (p. 125). In this example, Mr. Ramos, a first-grade teacher, uses the toolkit within his basal reading program.

When Will Your Students Be Ready to Move to the Next Stage?

As you teach your students the skills they need to progress through the transitional stage, you will begin to see their ability to read and spell single-syllable words become more accurate and automatic, particularly their ability to process long vowel pattern words. In addition, you will also see improved accuracy and automaticity in their *reading* (but not necessarily *spelling*) of multisyllabic words in context. The assessments we discuss in this book can help you determine when your students are reaching the three major transitional reader milestones we discussed above: (1) chunk common long vowel and abstract vowel patterns while reading and writing; (2) use decoding strategies to read unfamiliar words, including multisyllabic words; and (3) increase automaticity of word knowledge. Figure 7.12 highlights assessments you can use to determine when your students are reaching these transitional milestones.

We recommended administering the Transitional Tier of the TSI at least three times in a year for progress monitoring purposes. You can also administer cumulative spelling checks to check for maintenance of spelling skills in between these

Milestone	Assessment Evidence
Using common long vowel and abstract vowel patterns in spelling	• TSI: Correct score of 18 or higher on transitional tier • Cumulative spell checks with 90% or better accuracy • Transitional Writing Observation Guide

Using decoding strategies to read unfamiliar words, including multisyllabic words	• IDI real words
	  o Compound Words 8–10
	  o Closed Syllables 8–10
	  o Open Syllables 8–10
	  o *V*–Consonant–*e* 8–10
	  o *R*–Controlled Vowels 8–10
	  o Vowel Teams 8–10
	• IDI nonwords
	  o Compound Words 6–10
	  o Closed Syllables 6–10
	  o Open Syllables 6–10
	  o *V*–Consonant–*e* 6–10
	  o *R*–Controlled Vowels 6–10
	  o Vowel Teams 6–10

FIGURE 7.12. Transitional stage milestones and assessment evidence.

TSI administrations; we usually give these cumulative spell checks once every 4–6 weeks. The Informal Decoding Inventory (IDI) is another important assessment to help you gauge your students' growth in decoding skills. These different assessments provide you with different pieces of information to assess your students' ability to:

- *Demonstrate* their understanding.
- Show *maintenance* and *transfer* of these understandings.

In addition to the assessments described above, you will also want to determine whether your students are transferring their word knowledge skills into contextual reading and writing. To analyze transfer to contextual reading, you can perform a miscue analysis from an informal reading inventory or a running record (Leslie & Caldwell, 2011). In this case, you would scan a number of passages or texts the child has read, looking for target words that follow the orthographic features your children are learning (e.g., if the student has studied the *ou* and *ow* abstract vowel patterns, you might find the words *round, surround*, and *plow* in a passage). From this set of target words, you would identify words that were either (1) correctly read or (2) not correctly read.

To analyze word knowledge skill transfer to writing, we have created an informal observation guide to help you systematically observe your students' contextual writing (see Figure 7.13 and a printable version of the Writing Observation Guide: Transitional Reader in online Appendix A: Assessments; *www.guilford. com/hayes4-forms*). The guide is designed to help you look for evidence of your students' application of the following features in their contextual writing: long vowel patterns, *r*-controlled vowels, abstract vowel patterns, and complex consonants. In the sample writing guide, the teacher is focusing on the other long vowel patterns (see shaded cells in Figure 7.13) because that is what this particular student, Sasha, has been learning during word knowledge instruction. We usually look for at least four writing samples across a number of weeks before we feel confident that a feature has been mastered in context. In the Figure 7.13 example, it appears that Sasha has mastered the long-*a* and long-*e* vowel patterns (five and four writing samples, respectively, in which Sasha has spelled words containing these features correctly). We would want at least one more piece of evidence for the long-*i* vowel patterns since we already have three pieces of evidence that Sasha has spelled these long-*i* features correctly. Sasha is still working toward transferring her word knowledge of long-*o* and long-*u* vowel patterns into her writing.

All the assessments we have described provide you with direct evidence of your students' word knowledge skills. You can use this information, in conjunction with informal observations of their ability to apply these skills in contextual reading and writing, to help you determine which students need additional instruction in certain skills, and to identify students ready to move on to the next stage.

Writing Observation Guide: Transitional Reader

Dates	9/16	10/4	10/23	11/14	12/11
• *Long Vowels with E-Marker*					
• *R-Controlled Vowels* o ar, are, air					
o er, ear, eer					
o ir, ire					
o or, ore, our, oar					
o ur, ure					
• *Other Long Vowel Patterns* o aCe, ai, ay	✓	✓	✓	✓	✓
o ee, ea, e		✓	✓	✓	✓
o iCe, igh, y			✓	✓	✓
o oCe, oa, ow					
o uCe, oo, ew			✓		✓
• *Abstract Vowel Patterns* o ow, ou					
o oi, oy					
o oo					
• *Complex Consonant* o tch/ch, dge/ge					
o Three-letter blends					

FIGURE 7.13. Sample transitional writing observation guide for Sasha.

Excellent books describing more advanced stages of literacy development, outside the scope of this book, include the following:

- *Words Their Way: Word Study for Phonics, Vocabulary, and Spelling Instruction* (5th ed.) by Bear et al. (2012).
- *Word Journeys: Assessment-Guided Phonics, Spelling, and Vocabulary Instruction* by Ganske (2014).
- *How to Plan Differentiated Reading Instruction: Resources for Grades K–3* by Walpole and McKenna (2009).
- *Differentiated Reading Instruction in Grades 4 and 5: Strategies and Resources* by Walpole et al. (2011).

We hope that your transitional students will make such excellent progress that you will need to consult these additional resources quickly.

Conclusion

In this chapter, we have discussed the defining characteristics of transitional-stage readers and writers, identified the target features of word knowledge instruction at this stage, and highlighted the three major instructional milestones of focus. In addition, we have emphasized the critical importance of word knowledge being part of a comprehensive, balanced approach to literacy instruction that includes substantial amounts of meaningful reading in appropriate texts and purposeful writing in context. In Chapter 8, "The Transitional Reader's Toolkit," we describe word knowledge activities that focus on reading words, writing words, manipulating words, and transferring word knowledge back into context for transitional-stage children. As you read the next chapter, keep in mind that these activities and strategies are not ends unto themselves; rather, their purpose is to support your students in becoming more skilled and strategic readers, writers, and thinkers.

CHAPTER 8

• • • • • • • • • • •

The Transitional Reader's Toolkit

ACTIVITIES AND STUDENT STRATEGIES

GUIDING QUESTIONS

• What are the four categories of the Word Knowledge Toolkit that promote deep and flexible word learning?

• Which activities promote students' transfer of word knowledge into contextual reading and writing?

• Which activities help students build automaticity in word recognition?

• Which activities target the important transitional stage milestone of decoding multisyllabic words?

This chapter describes teacher activities and student strategies to support transitional readers' word recognition development. Like the emergent and beginning readers' toolkits in previous chapters, the transitional reader's toolkit consists of the following four categories of activities:

• *Reading words*—decoding practice.
• *Writing words*—spelling application.
• *Manipulating words*—word analysis.
• *Transferring words*—connect to context.

Over the course of a week, choose activities from each of the four parts of the toolkit (see Figure 8.1) to ensure that your students are developing solid word knowledge that promotes reading and writing words accurately and automatically and the ability to think about words deeply and flexibly. These activities will also provide multiple opportunities for your students to apply this word knowledge in

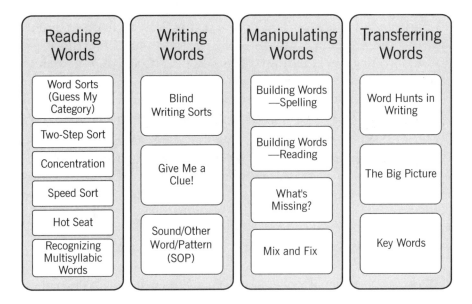

FIGURE 8.1. Word Knowledge Toolkit for transitional readers.

context. The ultimate goal of this word knowledge instruction should result in your students not only (1) "knowing" many more words but also (2) knowing how words work, and (3) being motivated to learn about more new words.

Before moving on to the activities and strategies in the toolkit, it is helpful to keep the following two points in mind to ensure that the word work we do with our students is always purposeful and mindful:

• Remember to work at both ends of the word knowledge instructional zone, solidifying word knowledge skills at the back end of the zone (spelling), but also taking time to focus on your students' decoding skills (particularly with multisyllabic words for transitional readers) at the front end of the zone.

• Remember that we don't do these activities just to fill up our word work time. We do these toolkit activities with the three major transitional reader milestones in mind as our ultimate goals:

  o Chunk common long and abstract vowel patterns while reading and writing.
  o Use decoding strategies to read unfamiliar words, including multisyllabic words in context.
  o Increase automaticity of word knowledge to enable fluent, expressive, meaningful reading.

When choosing word study activities:

1. *During word study time*, make sure that each week you choose activities from the first three columns so that students are (a) reading, (b) writing/spelling, and (c) manipulating words during word study time (Columns 1, 2, and 3 from Figure 8.1). Use the Orthographic Features of Study chart (Figure 7.5 in Chapter 7) and the Transitional Feature Sorting lists in online Appendix B: Toolkit Activities (*www.guilford.com/hayes4-forms*) to help you choose patterns and words for these activities to ensure that your students' word knowledge is continually improving.

2. *During contextual reading and writing time*, make sure you are also providing opportunities for and coaching students to transfer their word knowledge to context (Column 4 from Figure 8.1).

Word Knowledge Toolkit Part I: Reading Words

Section 1 of the instructional toolkit includes activities that provide multiple opportunities for children to read words. At the transitional stage of word knowledge, reading accuracy is not enough; students also need to build (1) word recognition automaticity and (2) multisyllabic word recognition ability to tackle the longer and more sophisticated words they will encounter in texts at the late first-grade level and higher. The following activities will target these important word learning goals.

Instructional Strategy: Guess My Category Word Sort

- Purpose: to compare, contrast, and categorize words by common orthographic features.

Word sorting is a powerful core instructional activity that provides students multiple opportunities to compare, contrast, and categorize words according to common orthographic features and to form generalizations students can apply to unfamiliar words they encounter in their reading (Gillet & Kita, 1979). The Guess My Category word sort is a type of word sort activity that provides students a middle level of scaffolding (see modifications below for variations with more and less support; Flanigan et al., 2011).

1. Tell your students that you are going to sort some words into a number of categories (usually two to four categories). Your students' job is to figure out your categories.

2. Sort at least two words into each column, asking students to say each word aloud with you as you read it, and to read down the entire column each time you put a new word in the column. This will increase the chances of students "seeing" and/or "hearing" the common patterns across the words. See Figure 8.2 for an example of a short *a*, *aCe*, *ai*, *ay* sort at this stage.

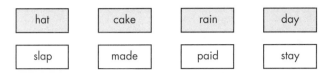

FIGURE 8.2. First step in Guess My Category sort.

3. After sorting two words in each column, ask your students to think about the words:

> "Who can tell me what the words in this column have in common? How about this column? Why do you think I sorted them this way? Let's remember our three key questions we always ask:
>
> 'How do these words *look* the same?'
> 'How do these words *sound* the same?'
> '*Where* is the pattern in the word (beginning, middle, or end)?' "

4. As students share their hypotheses about the word patterns, guide them to recognize the pattern and/or rule with a few more words in each column. Make sure that you require students to justify and explain their thinking about the words:

> "What, specifically do *rain* and *paid* have in common?"
> "Show me the parts that *look* the same."
> "Tell us how they *sound* the same."
> "Frame the pattern with your hands."

The type of discussion that these questions can generate will promote deeper processing of the word parts and stronger knowledge of word patterns.

5. By the end of the sort, make sure your students have a solid understanding of the pattern and/or rule. Ask them to sort their own sets of the words before they leave the group so that you can check for accuracy and, at this stage, increasing automaticity with the sort as the week progresses. Also, ask your students to articulate the pattern and/or rule in their own words.

See Figure 8.3 below for an example of a completed sort.

Modifications

• To provide more explicit instruction and scaffolding, follow the procedures for a closed sort described in Chapter 6 (pp. 132–136).

• To provide less explicit instruction and scaffolding, follow procedures for an open sort also described in Chapter 6 (p. 136).

FIGURE 8.3. Completed sort (short *a*, *aCe*, *ai*, *ay*).

Instructional Strategy: Two-Step Sorts

- Purpose: to work at the front end of the zone while solidifying features at the back end.

A "two-step" sort is another variety of sort that is unique in that it allows students to work at both ends of the word knowledge zone in the same activity. See Figure 8.4 for an example of how the short *a*, *aCe*, *ai*, *ay* sort illustrated in Figure 8.3 can be made into a two-step sort by adding two to three multisyllabic words in each column. Notice how these multisyllabic words at the bottom of the columns contain *the same exact long vowel patterns* that the students are examining in the single-syllable words at the top of the columns. It is important to only include two-syllable words for which the vowel pattern your students are examining is in the accented syllable. Consider the two words *compl<u>ai</u>n* and *mount<u>ai</u>n*. In *complain*, the *ai* pattern is sounded because it is in the accented syllable (the second syllable of this word). However, you will notice that the *ai* in *mountain* does not have the long *a* sound because it is in the unaccented syllable. A few tips with two-step sorts:

- When creating a two-step sort, make sure the multisyllabic words contain the same patterns that are found in the single-syllable words (e.g., the *ai* in *rain* and *maintain*).

- When first introducing a two-step sort, introduce the single-syllable words earlier in the sort and the multisyllabic words later in the sort. In this way, students can use the single-syllable words as a guide for decoding the more difficult multisyllabic words.

- Make sure that these multisyllabic words are for reading. Do not test your students on the spelling of these multisyllabic words.

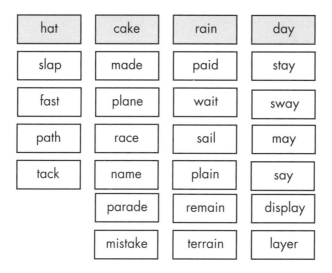

FIGURE 8.4. Completed "Two-Step" sort (short *a*, *aCe*, *ai*, *ay*).

Instructional Strategy: Concentration

● Purpose: to read and match pairs of words by identifying the common word patterns.

This age-old parlor game, also known as "Memory," is a perfect follow-up activity to an initial word sort because children must take their word knowledge to the next level by reading words and identifying word patterns, but *without the support of the columns that you would have in a sort*. The competitive nature of this game also provides a motivating format for word learning.

1. Have students studying the same patterns pair up in groups of two. Only one "deck" of word sort cards is needed per pair.

2. Students lay 16 of the word cards face down in a four-by-four array.

3. Student 1 turns two cards over and must read them correctly aloud. If the two cards are words that fall under the same category/pattern header (e.g., *cake* and *made* are both *aCe* words and would be a match), the student must "prove it" by identifying the pattern (e.g., "*Cake* and *made* are a match because they are both *aCe* words that say the long *a* sound."). Student 1 then takes this pair of cards off the board and gets a point. See Figure 8.5 for an example of a Concentration game at this step.

4. If Student 1 turns two cards over, reads them, and discovers that they are *not* a match (e.g., *cake* and *raid* are not a match because, although both are long

a patterns, they are different long *a* patterns—*aCe* vs. *ai*), he or she must put the cards back in their place, face down.

5. After Student 1's turn, Student 2 picks two cards, turns them over, and reads them. Student 2 can use his or her "memory" of the previous cards turned over to help pick two cards that are a match.

6. The game continues until all cards are off the board. The winner is the student with the most pairs of matches.

Instructional Strategy: Speed Sort

- Purpose: to build word-level automaticity.

As the name suggests, speed sorts build speed. Because building automaticity is such a crucial goal at the transitional stage, speed sorts are another core activity we use with children at this stage (Bear et al., 2012). We usually do not introduce speed sorts until the third day that students have been working with a set of words and patterns. This allows our students time to solidify the accuracy of their word knowledge before working directly on their automaticity, thus preventing the possibility of becoming overwhelmed or frustrated from the beginning.

1. Pair students in partner teams. The student sorting the words is in the "hot seat." The second student times the first student and checks for accuracy.
2. The student in the hot seat begins sorting. The timer begins timing (handheld or digital timers work well).
3. When the student in the hot seat is done sorting, the second student stops the timer and records the time as Sort 1 (e.g., Mark's Sort 1—45 seconds).
4. Students reverse roles, so that Student 2 sorts the words and receives a time (e.g., Natalie's Sort 1—38 seconds).
5. Students reverse roles again. Student 1 tries to lower his or her first time (e.g., Mark's Sort 2—35 seconds. Mark improved his time by 10 seconds!).

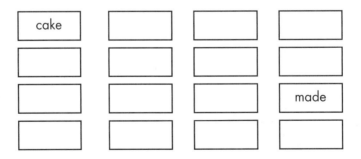

FIGURE 8.5. Concentration game (all cards face down except *cake* and *made*).

Date: *10/15*	
Name: *Mark*	Name: *Natalie*
Time 1: *45 seconds*	Time 1: *38 seconds*
Time 2: *35 seconds*	Time 2:
Time 3:	Time 3:

FIGURE 8.6. Speed Sort Record for Pairs chart (Mark and Natalie).

Figure 8.6 illustrates a partially completed Speed Sort Record for Pairs chart. A printable version of this chart "Speed Sort Record for Pairs" can be found in online Appendix B: Toolkit Activities.

As you can imagine, speed sorts are often our students' favorite activity because they are so motivating! And because students are competing against themselves, and not against one another, they are more motivated to improve.

Modifications

• Teach students to graph their improvements in sorting times. Graphing provides a concrete record of growth and integrates an important math skill.

• Some teachers like to time the entire class at once. All students start sorting at their desks at the same time. As soon as a student finishes, he/she says "Done!" and the teacher states the time, which the student immediately records.

• A final variation of speed sorts that our students always ask for is "Beat the Teach!" In this activity, the teacher sorts the words from each sort in front of the class and then posts the "teacher time" for each sort. Students practice in pairs until they can beat the teacher time. A few students are selected to challenge the teacher time in front of the class.

Instructional Strategy: Hot Seat

• Purpose: to build word-level automaticity.

Like speed sorts, this activity promotes word recognition automaticity and works well when done later in the week. Hot Seat is a modification of the excellent randomized check activity from Morris (2005).

1. Spread the deck of word cards randomly in a grid as in Figure 8.7.
2. Student 1 is in the hot seat. Student 2 is the pointer.

toy	round	town	noise
couch	spoil	boy	scout
brown	howl	sound	ploy
coin	frown	point	clown

FIGURE 8.7. Randomly organized grid for Hot Seat.

3. Student 2 starts the timer and points to a word. As soon as Student 1 recognizes the word correctly, Student 2 points to another word in the grid.
4. Student 2 continues pointing, moving as fast as possible between words immediately after each word is recognized by Student 1.
5. Once Student 1 incorrectly recognizes a word, Student 2 stops the timer and writes down the time (e.g., Mikah's first time is 23 seconds without making a miscue).
6. Roles are switched. Student 2 is in the hot seat and Student 1 is the pointer.
7. The goal is for each student to beat his or her initial time and go as long as possible without incorrectly recognizing a word. Thus, as opposed to a speed sort, the goal is to *increase your time* (e.g., Mikah's second time is 38 seconds without making a mistake).

Modification

As a vocabulary modification, the student in the hot seat must not only correctly recognize the word but additionally provide a correct definition before moving on to the next word. This modification works particularly well during homophone and homograph study.

Recognizing Multisyllabic Words: Decoding by Syllables

Transitional readers will be encountering increasingly sophisticated multisyllabic words in the texts they are reading. While these words should not be the main focus of their spelling instruction until they have a solid control of the single-syllable vowel patterns at this stage, they should be part of their decoding and word recognition instruction. The following reading strategy focuses on teaching students to decode multisyllabic words using the syllable as the unit of analysis.

Instructional Strategy: Reading and Decoding Multisyllabic Words by Syllable

- Purpose: to promote word recognition, decoding, and storage of multisyllabic words and word patterns.

In addition to working with spelling patterns found in single-syllable words, children in the transitional stage need to transfer this pattern knowledge to the multisyllabic words that they encounter in contextual reading. Specifically, transitional readers should be equipped with a basic understanding of how to decode and remember multisyllabic words. As we discussed in Chapter 1, reading knowledge usually precedes spelling knowledge. Put another way, children can usually read many words that they can't yet spell. We refer to this phenomenon as the reading–spelling slant (Frith, 1980; Helman et al., 2012). Therefore, the multisyllabic words and strategies we discuss in this section should be applied to the reading and decoding of these words. These multisyllabic words should not be used as spelling words until students have shown a solid knowledge in the base words and patterns that are the foundation of these words.

There are a number of different approaches to teaching students how to decode words of more than one syllable. Many involve teaching students a number of different syllable patterns along with a set of procedures for breaking words down by syllable or word parts. For most students we have worked with, we use the following four-step streamlined approach that teaches readers how to apply their knowledge of single-syllable patterns learned in this stage to decoding multisyllabic words (see Figure 8.8; a printable version of Figure 8.8 can be found in online Appendix B: Toolkit Activities). (*TIP*: We teach our students that along the way at any step in the process, they should read and decode by analogy. They should always be on the lookout for words and word parts/patterns that look familiar.)

Following are some examples of how this four-step decoding process might look in practice.

1. *Look for smaller words or word parts you already know.* Often, this first step is enough to help the student decode the whole word, or to decode enough of it to figure the word out with contextual clues. Obviously, this strategy works well for compound words like *outsmart, firefighter,* and *flapjack.* However, it also works well for decoding words with familiar word parts like *pushing* (*push* plus the *-ing* ending) and *remain* (the common prefix *re-* plus the word *main,* which could be read by analogy using the *-ain* key word, *rain*).

2. *Scan the word to look for the vowel or vowel patterns.* If the first step isn't enough, then we go to Plan B, looking for syllable parts. In order to identify where syllables start and end, we teach our students to quickly scan the word and look for the vowel or vowel patterns, and then to count the number of consonants between the first two vowel patterns in a word.

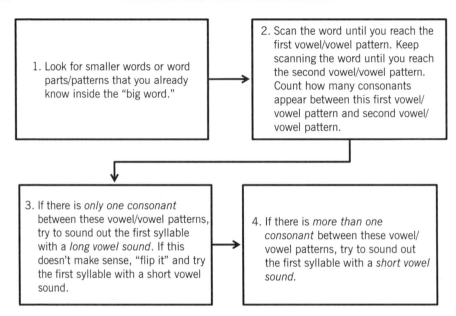

FIGURE 8.8. A four-step streamlined strategy for decoding multisyllabic words.

3. *If there is only one consonant between these vowel/vowel patterns, try to sound out the first syllable with a long vowel sound. If this doesn't make sense, "flip it" and try the first syllable with a short vowel sound.* For example, in the word *pilot*, the student identifies that there is only one consonant, the *l* between the first two vowels (the *i* and the *o*). So, the student would try out the *pi* in *pilot* with a long *i* sound and find out that it was a real word that made sense. With a word like *cavern*, the student might try the *a* with a long *a* sound, decide that it doesn't sound like a real word, and then try it out as a short vowel sound.

4. If there is *more than one consonant* between these two vowel/vowel patterns, try to sound out the first syllable with a *short vowel sound*. In the word *ballot*, the student would identify the two *l*'s between the first two vowels (the *a* and the *o*), and thus try out the *bal* with a short *a* vowel sound, resulting in a real word that would make sense. This would also work for words like *cactus*, in which the two consonants at the syllable break *CT* are not the same letter.

Recognizing Multisyllabic Words: Decoding by High-Frequency Prefixes and Suffixes

When decoding more sophisticated multisyllabic words, decoding by syllable is not always enough. Transitional readers also need to be able to break words down by frequently occurring morphemes, or meaning units. As we discussed in Chapter 1, morphemes are the basic building blocks of meaning in our language, such as the suffix -*ed* signaling the past tense in words like *kicked* and *stacked*.

Introducing high-frequency prefixes and suffixes is helpful not only as a decoding tool, but even more important, it prepares students for the study of morphemes and vocabulary work in the later grades. The good news is that in terms of morphology, a little goes a long way. For example, the four most common prefixes in English (*un-, in-,* and *dis-* all meaning "not," and *re-* meaning "again") were found in 58% of the words in a corpus representing printed American-school English (White, Sowell, & Yanagihara, 1989). High-frequency suffixes that can also be examined at this stage include -*ful*, -*ly*, -*y*, and the comparatives *er/est.*

Instructional Strategy: Building Words—Focus on Prefixes and Suffixes

● Purpose: to build whole words from base words and prefixes and/or suffixes, with a focus on the changes in spelling, meaning, and part of speech.

When discussing prefixes and suffixes at this stage, it is helpful to start with a base word, add a prefix or suffix, and discuss how the *spelling* and *meaning* of the word have changed (Bear et al., 2012). For example, a teacher could write the words *law* and *peace* on the board, discussing their meanings. Next, the teacher could add the suffix -*ful* to both words and discuss how a *lawful person* is literally *full of the law* (and will follow rules) and how a *peaceful person* is literally *full of peace* (and will probably not argue or get in fights). In both words, the noun has been changed to an adjective. A visual like the one below often makes this spelling/meaning change explicit for students.

law + ful = lawful

peace + ful = peaceful

To modify the above activity, you can ask students to create their own words by adding word parts from a prefix/suffix bank and a base word bank. Then, the students can discuss the spelling and meaning of the new words they created (both real words and coined words!). Because students are creating both actual words and coined words that are not actually found in the dictionary, this activity is highly motivating and can lead to rich and humorous discussions (imagine asking students to *rehandle* a pencil in the classroom, again and again and again). A printable version of the activity shown in Figure 8.9, "Building Words Form," can be found in online Appendix B: Toolkit Activities.

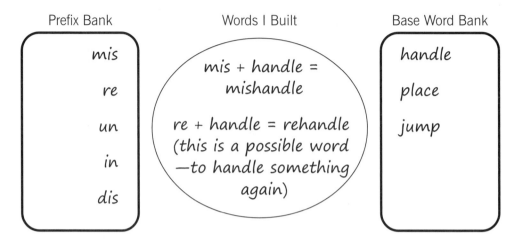

FIGURE 8.9. Building Words—focus on prefixes.

Instructional Strategy: Breaking Words Apart—
Focus on Prefixes and Suffixes

● Purpose: to break whole words apart into base words
  and prefixes and/or suffixes, with a focus on the spelling
  and meaning of the words and morphemes.

This instructional strategy is the opposite of Building Words. We often refer to it as "break it down" with our students (Flanigan et al., 2011). Instead of starting with a base word and adding affixes to build words, you begin with the entire word and ask your students to break the word apart by base words and affixes. For example, you might start with the word *rewrite* and ask your students to find the words or word parts they know, drawing a line between each part as in *re/write*. Then after discussing the meaning of each part, you could ask the class to put the meanings together as follows:

re (again) + *write* = to write something again

A sequence of high-utility prefixes and suffixes that can be examined at this stage is presented in Figure 8.10. When introducing these affixes to your students, start with base words that your students already know (e.g., *make, play*) and then add the affixes (*remake, replay*), discussing how the word meanings have changed. When you encounter base words that students are less likely to know, make sure you have first established their meaning (e.g., "Something that is *visible* is able to be seen") before adding the affix ("So therefore, something that is *invisible* is <u>not</u> able to be seen").

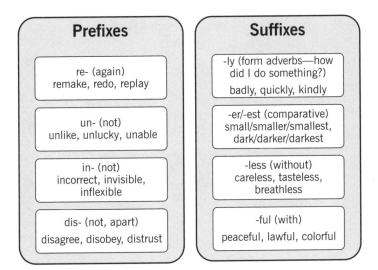

Prefixes	Suffixes
re- (again) remake, redo, replay	-ly (form adverbs—how did I do something?) badly, quickly, kindly
un- (not) unlike, unlucky, unable	-er/-est (comparative) small/smaller/smallest, dark/darker/darkest
in- (not) incorrect, invisible, inflexible	-less (without) careless, tasteless, breathless
dis- (not, apart) disagree, disobey, distrust	-ful (with) peaceful, lawful, colorful

FIGURE 8.10. High-utility prefixes and suffixes.

Word Knowledge Toolkit Part II: Writing Words

As we discussed in Chapter 1, spelling words is more difficult than reading words. Therefore, it is critically important that, in addition to reading words, our students have multiple opportunities to practice writing the words during the week. The following activities provide students opportunities to spell their words in supported, motivating contexts.

Instructional Strategy: Blind Writing Sort

- Purpose: to spell words correctly while simultaneously categorizing them by common spelling patterns.

In a writing sort (Bear et al., 2012), we ask students to accomplish two tasks: (1) spell words correctly and (2) categorize words by pattern. This ensures that students not only are memorizing *how* to spell words but are thinking about *why* the words are spelled that way. Writing sorts are also one of our bread-and-butter assessments, often serving double duty as both an instructional activity and a Friday end-of-week assessment.

1. Students create a chart with their header words for the week at the top of each column (see Figure 8.11; header words are *toy, boil, town, sound*).
2. The teacher calls out a word, a sentence containing the word, and then the word again.

to**y** (oy)	to**w**n (ow)
boy *ploy*	*howl* *brown* *clown*
b**oi**l (oi)	s**ou**nd (ou)
coin *spoil* *point*	*scout* *round* *couch*

FIGURE 8.11. Partially completed writing sort.

3. Students attempt to spell the word correctly while simultaneously placing the word in the correct column.
4. If a teacher wishes to grade this activity as a test or assessment, each word can be awarded two possible points—1 point for correct spelling and 1 point for placing the word in the correct column. This communicates to your students that it is important not only to spell words correctly but to think about the patterns that organize our spelling system.

Modifications

• Writing sorts can also be done in pairs, with one student calling out the words first (playing the teacher) and the other student spelling the words. After 10 words, roles are reversed.

• Writing sorts can be used as an in-class activity, an assessment, and a homework assignment (a parent or sibling can call out the words).

• If the child has no partner to work with (doing homework alone), the student can do an individual writing sort. The student places all the word cards in a pile. The student picks a card, looks at the word and studies it, places the card face down so he/she can't see the word, and then spells the word in the correct column. The student continues in this way until all the words have been spelled and categorized. At the end, the student can check their spelled words against the word cards.

Instructional Strategy: Give Me a Clue!

• Purpose: to improve students' ability to (1) spell words and (2) dig deeper into the meanings of words.

Give Me a Clue! is a writing sort with a vocabulary twist. Students are not only expected to spell and categorize the words but additionally need to be able to articulate word definitions in their own words (as the clue giver), and know the word meanings (as the clue detective). The steps are exactly the same as the writing sort steps above except for two slight modifications:

- The teacher or student calling out the words is called the clue giver. Instead of calling out the word (*toil*) as he pulls the cards from the deck as he would in a blind writing sort, the teacher or student provides the definition as a clue ("This word means really hard work.").

- The clue detective must identify the correct word from the definition and spell it correctly under the appropriate category (*toil* under the *oi* category).

For known words such as *coin*, this will be "easy" for the clue detective, but excellent practice for the clue giver, who will learn how to create a definition in his/her own words ("a round, metal object used as money"). However, even at this stage, there will be more sophisticated words of study whose meanings are not as likely to be known such as *ploy* and *toil*.

Instructional Strategy: SOP—The Sound/Other Word/ Pattern Strategy

- Purpose: to equip children with a simple, three-step mental "game plan" for thinking about how to spell unfamiliar words through the use of analogy.

Students in classrooms we have worked in or observed often need help becoming more strategic spellers. With this in mind, we created the SOP "game plan" to assist them in spelling. This plan of attack will equip your students with a strategy that will enable them to be more strategic as well as more accurate. Figure 8.12 can be used to guide this instruction and can be displayed in your room as a quick reference for your students (see online Appendix B: Toolkit Activities for a printable version of SOP Quick Reference).

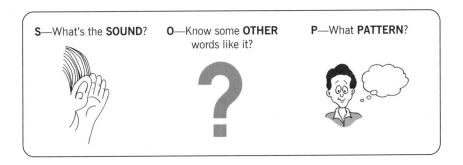

FIGURE 8.12. Sound/other word/pattern (SOP) strategy.

1. <u>S</u>ound. Ask yourself, what is the target *sound* that I'm trying to spell? ("I'm having trouble figuring out how to spell the /ch/ sound in *patch*.")

2. <u>O</u>ther words. Ask yourself, what *other words* do I already know that contain that same target sound? ("I know that *teach* and *catch* both make the /ch/ sound at the end.")

3. <u>P</u>atterns. What *pattern(s)* do these words use to spell that sound? If there is more than one pattern, is there a rule to help you decide between the two? If not, pick one. ("There is the *ch* in *teach* and the *tch* in *catch*. Which one should I use? I think I remember the rule being that if there is a short vowel before the /ch/ sound, you use *tch*. That makes sense, because we use the *tch* in *catch*, a short vowel word I already know. So, I'm going to also use *tch* in *patch*, the word I'm trying to spell.")

Word Knowledge Toolkit Part III: Manipulating Words

In addition to reading and writing words, students need to explicitly focus on the patterns "inside" the words. This is the focus of the third part of your instructional Word Study Toolkit—manipulating words. Specifically, by manipulating words, children will be better equipped to (1) analyze whole words into their constituent word parts and (2) use word parts to build whole words. Our instructional shorthand for this is "building words up," and the reverse process, "breaking words down." By manipulating parts of words, children not only deepen their knowledge of *specific words*, they develop a broader, more flexible knowledge about *how words work* that they can apply to the many less familiar words they will encounter as they begin to read widely.

Instructional Strategy: Building Words— Focus on Spelling

- Purpose: given a target word, to manipulate the parts of that word in order to spell a new target word.

In addition to the comparing, contrasting, and generalizing across words that children do in a word sort, you want to provide your students opportunities to build words from their constituent parts. While word sorting enables students to get at the word from the "outside in," *building words* enables students to get at the word from the "inside out." We often think of Building Words as a first-grade activity focused on spelling for sounds. However, we have had success, particularly with struggling readers, using Building Words with transitional readers in the

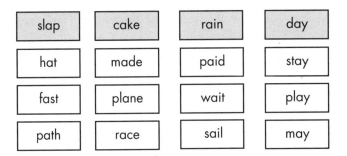

FIGURE 8.13. Completed sort (short *a*, *aCe*, *ai*, *ay*).

within-word pattern stage. We have adapted the procedures of other word-building guidelines during our work with transitional readers and offer our adaptation here (Cunningham & Hall, 1994; Johnston et al., 2009; Morris, 2005).

The following word-building example is based on the short *a*, *aCe*, *ai*, *ay* sort shown in Figure 8.13.

1. Provide each student with a whiteboard, marker, and eraser. After each step, ask students to show you their words.
2. Ask students to spell the word *mad* (see Figure 8.14).
3. Ask students to change *mad* to *made*. Ask them what letters they added/deleted/changed/kept the same and why.
4. Ask students to change *made* to *plane* ("The plane flew in the sky."). Ask them what letters they added/deleted/changed/kept the same and why.
5. Ask students to change a *plane* in the sky to *plain* bread without any butter or jelly. Ask them what letters they added/deleted/changed/kept the same

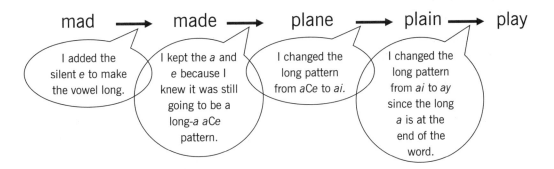

FIGURE 8.14. Manipulating with focus on long *a*.

and why. Discuss the difference in spellings and meanings of these homophones.

6. Ask students to change *plain* to *play*. Ask them what letters they added/deleted/changed/kept the same and why.

As you can see from this example above, Building Words allows students multiple rich opportunities to deeply process individual words and common high-utility orthographic patterns. In addition, this activity also generates rich discussions about how words work across categories.

Modifications

Instead of erasing the parts of each target word to create a new word, ask the student to write each new target word *below* the previous target word as Rasinski (2011) suggests in his word ladders activity. In this way, the student can see the visual *word path* from top to bottom on the page, noting how the word changed from step to step as in the following:

mad

made

plane

plain

play

Instructional Strategy: Building Words—Focus on Reading

- Purpose: to build whole words from smaller word parts and common word patterns, or "chunks."

The Building Words–Focus on Spelling activity described above is essentially an encoding activity—we provide words to our students and ask that they spell them. It is just as important to provide students opportunities to read and decode words. As noted word knowledge researcher Linnea Ehri observed, "Reading and spelling are flip sides of the same instructional coin" (2000, p. 19). We often follow up a building words spelling activity like the one above immediately with a building words reading activity like the one described below.

1. Write the word *plane* on the board. Ask students to read the word and identify the pattern ("*plane*, it's the *aCe* pattern").

2. Erase the *e*. Ask students what this new word is ("It's *plan*—a short-*a* word because you don't have the silent *e* marker any more.").

3. Add an *i* between the *a* and *n*. Ask students what this new word is ("It's *plain*"). Ask students if it is a long or short *a*. ("Why? How is it different from the other *plane*?")
4. Erase the *pl* and insert an *r*. Ask students what the new word and pattern is ("*rain*—the *ai* pattern").

Instructional Strategy: What's Missing?

● Purpose: to focus students' attention on the target features of a given word by erasing a word part and asking them to replace the missing letter or letter pattern.

The What's Missing? game is a simple, quick game-like activity that can help focus students' attention on certain parts of a word (Richardson, 2009). It can be played by the teacher with a group of students or between student pairs as an away-from-teacher activity. Be certain that you focus on erasing the letter or letter patterns that are the focus of instruction for the children you are working with (see Figure 8.15).

1. Teacher writes a word on the whiteboard.
2. Students are given 3–5 seconds to closely "study" the word, trying to remember every letter.
3. Teacher turns the board around so the group can't see the word, "secretly" erases one letter, shows the word again, and asks, "What letter is missing?"

Teacher shows word.

    chain

Teacher shows word with missing letter.

    ch___n

Student writes word with missing letter circled and underlined.

    chain

FIGURE 8.15. What's Missing?

4. On their own whiteboards, students spell the word correctly, circling or underlining the missing letter, and show the teacher.
5. Teacher provides feedback and discusses words and word patterns.

Instructional Strategy: Mix and Fix

● Purpose: to focus students' attention on specific parts of a given word by mixing up the letters and asking them to spell the word again.

Similar to "What's Missing?" the "Mix and Fix" game is a fast-paced, game-like activity that helps focus children's attention on the target features of a word (Richardson, 2009).

- Each student is provided with a set of letter tiles on a magnetic board.
- Teacher asks students to spell a word with the tiles (e.g., "Use your tiles to spell the word *through*.").
- Teacher asks students to study the word carefully for about 5–10 seconds, pointing out and/or discussing important patterns, parts, or distinct features of the word (e.g., "Notice how the *-ough* pattern in *through* looks similar to *rough* and *tough*, but sounds very different. *Through* is an oddball.")
- Students mix up the letters.
- Teacher says, "Ready, set, spell!"
- Students try and reorder the letters as accurately and quickly as possible. When they are ready for the teacher to check them, they show the magnetic board to the teacher and state, "Done!"
- Teacher and students discuss the word again, with the teacher correcting any student mistakes. The same word can be repeated two to three times if extra practice is needed.

Word Knowledge Toolkit Part IV:
Transferring Word Knowledge to Context

The ultimate goal of word study is not more word study; the ultimate goal of word study is to help our students become better readers, writers, and thinkers. This is why we need to explicitly support our children's attempts to transfer their word knowledge into contextual reading and writing. Unfortunately, as we discussed in Chapter 1, this type of knowledge transfer is often the "missing link" in word study instruction. The following activities, within the context of the principles of word study transfer discussed in Chapter 1, will support your students' attempts to apply word knowledge into their reading and writing.

Instructional Strategy: Word Hunts in Writing

● Purpose: to promote the transfer of word knowledge to students' contextual writing (an alternative to traditional editing).

How can we help our students apply their newly learned spelling skills in contextual writing? How can we prevent our students from groaning when we say, "It's time to edit your writing piece"? Word Hunts in Writing is one of the most powerful activities we have found for supporting our students' transfer of spelling skills to their writing (Flanigan et al., 2011). In addition, word hunts separate the editing process—which can often be overwhelming, particularly for struggling writers—into manageable pieces. This activity works best when your students are ready to edit a piece of written work or when your students are given the opportunity to look back in their writing portfolio across multiple pieces of written work.

1. With your students, decide on a piece or pieces of written work that are ready to be edited. Generally, these pieces should have gone through the steps of the writing process.

2. Based on the spelling features that your students have examined so far this year, create an editing chart with the features and key words across the top (see a partially completed chart in Figure 8.16 and a printable version "Word Hunt in Writing Chart" in online Appendix B: Toolkit Activities). Tell your students that while editing for spelling, they are only responsible for finding words that follow the patterns on this editing chart.

3. While editing their written work, if a student finds a *misspelled* word that follows one of the patterns on the chart, they circle it, correct it, and write it in the chart under the "Words I Corrected" category.

4. While editing their written work, if a student finds a *correctly spelled* word that follows one of the patterns on the chart, they circle it and write it in the chart under the "Words I Spelled Correctly" category.

Target Features (Write two to four target features across the columns.)	OI BOIL	OY BOY	OW HOW	OU SOUND
Words I Spelled Correctly	spoil toil noise	toy	clown how	ground
Words I Corrected	tinfoil		drown drowsy	sound

FIGURE 8.16. Word hunt/editing chart.

5. Students receive an "extra credit" point for (1) words that they spelled correctly and (2) words that they misspelled but corrected. In this way, students are provided positive feedback regardless of *when* they correctly spelled the word (during the initial draft writing or during the editing process), as long as they eventually got it right.

As teachers, we often say, "We need to hold students accountable." But when we ask students to edit for spelling, we are sometimes holding them accountable for words and patterns that we haven't yet taught. In addition, the editing process can be particularly overwhelming for struggling writers, for whom sometimes half of the words in their piece are misspelled. Word Hunts in Writing solve both of these dilemmas by holding the students accountable only for the patterns we have taught and by making the editing process much more manageable through its focus on only a few key features at a time.

Modifications

• To make this process even less overwhelming and more supportive, scan the child's paper beforehand, note one spelling feature the student spelled correctly and one spelling feature the student needs to work on. Write these two target features as categories at the top of the editing chart. In this way, you are setting the student up for success.

• Ask students to work in pairs, scanning each other's papers to "double-check" their editing work. Often, our students like to edit for spelling backward, from the end of the paper to the beginning. This helps them focus on the misspellings so they don't confuse reading for revision with reading for editing.

Instructional Strategy: See the "Big Picture" and Using Key Words

• Purpose: to promote the transfer of word knowledge to students' contextual reading and writing.

As educators, we regularly use graphic organizers in science and social studies to help students visually see how all of the information they are learning fits into a "big picture" when studying major concepts or topics in these subjects. We use a specific type of graphic organizer, a story map, to help our students see how all the events, characters, problems, and solutions in a story fit together in a narrative story structure. So, why don't we use graphic organizers when teaching students about spelling patterns? This is where the "big-picture" graphic organizer comes into play. See Figure 8.17 for a big-picture graphic organizer for the sounds of *o*.

We believe that one of the best ways to help students transfer their word knowledge skills to contextual reading and writing is through the use of a big-picture

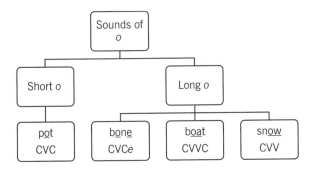

FIGURE 8.17. Big-picture graphic organizer for sounds of *o*.

graphic organizer (1) prominently displayed in the room; (2) included in the students' word study notebooks; and (3) referred to during word study, supported reading and writing, and coaching interactions. When students see how the patterns they are studying fit into a coherent picture, they are much more likely to use these spelling patterns in reading and writing because they make sense. A few teaching tips when using the big picture:

• Introduce the big-picture graphic organizer on a chart paper when you introduce a sort. This allows students to see how the patterns fit together right from the start of instruction, in addition to seeing how the patterns fit with previous word patterns studied.

• Use consistent key words for each feature (*pot, bone, boat, snow* in Figure 8.17) to help students when reading and spelling by analogy. These key words should be *known* words to the students so that they can refer to them when trying to read and spell *new* words that follow these same patterns.

• Refer to the big-picture graphic organizer during contextual reading and writing. For example, if a student is trying to spell the word *clone* during writing workshop, refer him or her to the big picture and ask what the possibilities for a long-*o* sound might be ("How many possible patterns do we know for the long-*o* sound? Could it be *ow* as in *snow*? Why not? That's right, because *o* is usually at the end of the word. So which two possibilities are left? Can the key words help us here?").

Focus on Decoding: Word Knowledge Instruction at the Front End of the Zone

In Chapter 7, we discussed the specific orthographic features that you should directly teach your transitional stage readers for decoding (not spelling) to help them read the more sophisticated multisyllabic words they are encountering in the texts they are reading. The Tiered Spelling Inventory (TSI) is designed to help you identify your students' needs at the back end of the zone—meeting their spelling needs. You also need to be cognizant of your students' needs at the front end of the zone—meeting their decoding needs. The texts your students are reading warrant this attention at both ends of the word knowledge zone. This work fits within a balanced framework where you provide instruction for reading *and* writing words, as well as encouraging transfer of these skills. To this end, this approach will help your students become more strategic readers and writers, moving them forward and out of the transitional reader stage. Remember the following guidelines/tips/rules of thumb for decoding instruction at the front end of the zone:

- Tie this decoding instruction to the texts your students are reading as best you can.
- Build on the key features you are studying at the back end of the zone when moving to the front end of the zone (e.g., teach how the *ai* pattern in words like *rain* is also found in multisyllabic words like *contain*).
- Remember that this instruction is focused on decoding and reading the words, and students should not be tested in their spelling of these words.

How to Respond When a Child Struggles to Read a Word

What should you do when a child you are reading with struggles to read a word? We end this chapter with this question because it is perhaps the key moment when "the rubber meets the road," when you, as the teacher, are able to provide coaching as the child is attempting to apply his or her word knowledge skills during real reading. As we have mentioned in previous chapters, there are no simple answers to this question. Much depends on the child's word knowledge and the type of miscue the child has produced, among other factors. Based on work by Johnston et al. (2009), Morris (2005), and Clark (2004) we offer the following recommendations for your responses when a child is struggling to read a word in text:

• First, don't do anything. Allow the child time to try and work through the word, using context and decoding ability. If you always correct the child immediately, he or she will be less likely to try and develop independent word-learning strategies and will become overreliant on you.

• If the child's miscue changes the meaning of the passage or does not make sense, allow the child time to read to the end of the sentence to see if he or she realizes this. If the child goes back and self-corrects, provide specific praise such as "I liked the way you went back to self-correct when you realized it didn't make sense. That's what good readers do."

• If, however, the child does *not* go back to self-correct an error that changes the meaning of the text and begins to read the next sentence, you have the option to stop him or her and say, "This is what you read . . . does that make sense?"

• If the child's error does *not* change the meaning of the passage, you can allow the child to read on and, if you want, revisit the miscue after the reading.

If, after giving the child time, he or she is still struggling with the word, you can provide support by asking questions or with prompting, such as:

• What do good readers do when they are trying to figure out a word?
• What could you do here?
• Do you see any word parts or patterns you already know?
• What part of the word are you having trouble with?
• Does this word look like another word you already know?
• Let's reread the sentence and see if that helps us.
• [Cover up part of the word to highlight a known part.] You know this word/pattern/part. What does it say?
• Decode the part you know; I'll help you with the rest.
• Do you see a vowel team/vowel pattern/consonant you know?
• Let's skip the word, read on, and come back to see if that helps us.
• Scan the word and look for the syllable breaks.

Of course, there are times when it is appropriate to simply give a child the word, particularly in the following three situations: (1) with difficult words containing patterns the child has not yet studied, (2) with phonetically irregular words that are not decodable, and (3) when the teacher simply wants the child to gain some momentum in his or her reading. This last situation may occur if the child stumbled on a previous sentence, and the teacher wants to help the child "build up a head of steam." If you find yourself having to give a lot of words to the child or provide scaffolding again and again, then the child is probably reading a text that is too difficult. A quick reference for how to respond to students when they struggle is "What to Do When a Reader Needs Help with Words," which can be found in online Appendix B: Toolkit Activities.

Conclusion

We firmly believe that when we teach our students in a developmentally responsive way, we provide them with the appropriate level of challenge for optimal growth in their word knowledge. Of course, the Word Knowledge Toolkit described in this chapter is intended to be only one essential component of an overall approach to literacy instruction in which students are also provided direct and explicit word knowledge instruction along with large blocks of time to apply their developing word knowledge skills in contextual reading and writing. In this way, we will be able to help all of our children reach their literacy potential.

As your transitional-stage students move on to more advanced stages of literacy development, you will have given them a firm foundation in word knowledge that will enable them to access the increasingly complex texts and concepts they will encounter in the upper-elementary, middle, and high school grades. Just as important, your students will leave with a positive disposition about words so that they continue to be engaged in their own word learning throughout their school careers and beyond. When we teach this way, teaching students how to think critically about words while modeling our own enthusiasm, students develop into independent word learners who have the knowledge, skills, and dispositions necessary for future success.

References

Adams, M. J. (1990). *Beginning to read: Thinking and learning about print.* Cambridge, MA: MIT Press.

Adams, M. J., Foorman, B. R., Lundberg, I., & Beeler, T. (1998). *Phonemic awareness activities for young children.* Baltimore: Brookes.

Adler, D. A. (2004). *Cam Jansen and the mystery of the Babe Ruth baseball.* New York: Puffin Books.

Allington, R. L. (2011). *What really matters for struggling readers: Designing research-based programs.* New York: Longman.

Arnold, R. (2006). *Hi! Fly guy.* Singapore: Scholastic.

Badian, N. A. (1994). Preschool prediction: Orthographic and phonological skills and reading. *Annals of Dyslexia, 51,* 179–202.

Ball, E. W., & Blachman, B. A. (1991). Does phoneme awareness training in kindergarten make a difference in early word recognition and developmental spelling? *Reading Research Quarterly, 26,* 49–66.

Bancroft, H. (1997). *Animals in winter.* New York: Harper Collins.

Barchas, S. (1987). *I was walking down the road.* New York: Scholastic.

Bear, D. R. (1992). The prosody of oral reading and stage of word knowledge. In S. Templeton & D. Bear (Eds.), *Development of orthographic knowledge and the foundations of literacy: A memorial Festschrift for Edmund H. Henderson* (pp. 137–186). Hillsdale, NJ: Erlbaum.

Bear, D. R., Invernizzi, M., Templeton, S., & Johnston, F. (2012). *Words their way: Word study for phonics, vocabulary, and spelling instruction* (5th ed.). Boston: Pearson.

Bear, D. R., Templeton, S., & Warner, M. (1991). The development of a qualitative inventory of higher levels of orthographic knowledge. In J. Zutell & S. McCormick (Eds.), *Learner factors/teacher factors: Issues in literacy research and instruction: Fortieth yearbook of the National Reading Conference* (pp. 105–110). Chicago: National Reading Conference.

Bear, D. R., Truex, P., & Barone, D. (1989). In search of meaningful diagnoses: Spelling-by-stage assessment of literacy proficiency. *Adult Literacy and Basic Education, 13,* 165–185.

Beaver, J., & Carter, M. (2005). *Developmental reading assessment* (2nd ed.). New York: Pearson.

Berninger, V. W. (1999). Coordinating transcription and text generation in working memory during composting: Automatic and constructive processes. *Learning Disabilities Quarterly, 22,* 99–112.

Berninger, V. W., & Graham, S. (1998). Language by hand: A synthesis of a decade of research on handwriting. *Handwriting Review, 12,* 11–25.

Berninger, V. W., Vaughan, K. B., Abbott, R. D., Abbott, S. P., Rogan, L. W., Brooks, A., et al. (1997). Treatment of handwriting problems in beginning writers: Transfer from handwriting to composition. *Journal of Educational Psychology, 89,* 652–666.

Blachman, B. A. (1994). What we have learned from longitudinal studies of phonological processing and reading, and some unanswered questions. *Journal of Learning Disabilities, 27,* 287–291.

Bradley, L., & Bryant, P. E. (1985). *Rhyme and reason in reading and spelling.* Ann Arbor: University of Michigan Press.

Brown, J. (2009). *Flat Stanley: His original adventure!* New York: Harper Collins.

Byrne, B., & Fielding-Barnsley, R. F. (1991). Evaluation of a program to teach phonemic awareness to young children. *Journal of Educational Psychology, 82,* 805–812.

Capucilli, A. S. (1996). *Biscuit.* New York: Harper Collins.

Capucilli, A. S. (2002). *Biscuit goes to school.* New York: Harper Collins.

Chall, J. S. (1983). *Stages of reading development.* New York: McGraw-Hill.

Clark, C. (1996). *The lucky duck.* Parsippany, NJ: Modern Curriculum Press.

Clark, K. F. (2004). What can I say besides "sound it out"? Coaching word recognition in beginning reading. *The Reading Teacher, 57,* 440–449.

Clay, M. M. (2006). *An observation survey of early literacy achievement.* Portsmouth, NH: Heinemann.

Common Core State Standards (CCSS). (2010). Common Core State Standards. Retrieved from *www.corestandards.org.*

Coxe, M. (1997). *Big egg.* New York: Random House.

Cunningham, A. E., Nathan, R. G., & Schmidt Raher, K. (2011). Orthographic processing in models of word recognition. In M. L. Kamil, P. D. Pearson, E. Birr Moje, & P. Afflerbach (Eds.), *Handbook of reading research* (Vol. 4, pp. 259–285). New York: Routledge.

Cunningham, A. E., Perry, K. E., Stanovich, K. E., & Share, D. L. (2002). Orthographic learning during reading: Examining the role of self-teaching. *Journal of Experimental Child Psychology, 82,* 185–199.

Cunningham, P. M., & Hall, D. P. (1994). *Making words, grades 1–3: Multilevel hands-on phonics and spelling activities.* New York: Good Apple.

Dictionary.com. *Toolkit.* Retrieved March 15, 2013, from *http://dictionary.reference.com.*

Dolch, E. W. (1936). A basic sight vocabulary. *Elementary School Journal, 36,* 456–460.

Duke, N., & Carlisle, J. (2011). The development of comprehension. In M. L. Kamil, P. D. Pearson, E. Birr Moje, & P. Afflerbach (Eds.), *Handbook of reading research* (Vol. 4, pp. 199–228). New York: Routledge.

Edwards, P. D. (1995). *Four famished foxes and Fosdyke.* New York: Harper Trophy.

Edwards, P. D. (1996). *Some smug slug.* New York: Harper Trophy.

Edwards, S. L. (2003). Writing instruction in kindergarten examining an emerging area of research for children with writing and reading difficulties. *Journal of Learning Disabilities, 36,* 136–148.

Ehri, L. C. (1997). Learning to read and learning to spell are one and the same, almost. In C. A. Perfetti, L. Rieben, & M. Fayol (Eds.), *Learning to spell: Research, theory, and practice across languages* (pp. 237–269). Mahwah, NJ: Erlbaum.

Ehri, L. C. (2000). Learning to read and learning to spell: Two sides of the same coin. *Topics in Language Disorders, 20,* 19–36.

Elkonin, D. (1971). Development of speech. In A. V. Zaporozhets & D. B. Elkonin (Eds.), *The psychology of preschool children* (pp. 111–182). Cambridge, MA: MIT Press.

Ellis, N., & Cataldo, S. (1992). Spelling is integral to learning to read. In C. M. Sterling & C. Robson (Eds.), *Psychology, spelling, and education* (pp. 112–142). Clevedon, UK: Multilingual Matters.

Engles, D. (1996). *Rush, rush, rush*. Parsippany, NJ: Modern Curriculum Press.

Flanigan, K. (2007). A concept of word in text: A pivotal event in early reading acquisition. *Journal of Literacy Research, 39*, 37–70.

Flanigan, K., Hayes, L., Templeton, S., Bear, D. R., Invernizzi, M., & Johnston, F. (2011). *Words their way with struggling readers: Word study for reading, vocabulary, and spelling instruction, grades 4–12*. Boston: Pearson.

Flanigan, K., & Lanzetti, K. (2005/2006). Shop-a-word at word mart. *Virginia Journal of Reading, 29*, 60–61.

Fountas, I. C., & Pinnell, G. S. (1996). *Guided reading: Good first teaching for all children*. Portsmouth, NH: Heinemann.

Frith, U. (1980). *Cognitive processes in spelling*. London: Harcourt, Brace, Jovanovich.

Frith, U. (1985). Beneath the surface of developmental dyslexia. In K. Patterson, J. Marshall, & M. Coltheart (Eds.), *Surface dyslexia: Neuropsychological and cognitive studies of phonological reading* (pp. 301–330). London: Erlbaum.

Fry, E. B. (2004). *1000 instant words: The most common words for teaching reading, writing, and spelling*. Westminster, CA: Teacher Created Resources.

Fry, E. B., & Kress, J. E. (2006). *The reading teacher's book of lists* (5th ed.). San Francisco: Jossey-Bass.

Ganske, K. (2014). *Word journeys: Assessment-guided phonics, spelling, and vocabulary instruction* (2nd ed.). New York: Guilford Press.

Gaskins, I. W. (2005). *Success with struggling readers: The Benchmark School approach*. New York: Guilford Press.

Gehsmann, K. M., & Templeton, S. (2011/2012). Stages and standards in literacy: Teaching developmentally in the age of accountability. *Journal of Education, 191*(1), 5–16.

Gelman, R. G. (1993). *More spaghetti, I say!* New York: Scholastic.

Gibbons, G. (1996). *The reason for the seasons*. New York: Holiday House.

Gill, T. (1992). Focus on research: Development of word knowledge as it relates to reading, spelling, and instruction. *Language Arts, 69*, 444–453.

Gillet, J. W., & Kita, M. J. (1979). Words, kids, and categories. *The Reading Teacher, 32*, 538–542.

Goswami, U., & Bryant, P. E. (1990). *Phonological skills and learning to read*. Hillsdale, NJ: Erlbaum.

Graham, S. (1983). The effects of self-instructional procedures on LD students' handwriting performance. *Learning Disabilities Quarterly, 6*, 231–234.

Graham, S. (2009–2010, winter). Want to improve children's writing? *American Educator*, 20–40.

Graham, S., & Harris, K. R. (2000). The role of self regulation and transcription skills in writing and writing development. *Educational Psychologist, 35*, 3–12.

Graham, S., Harris, K. R., & Fink, B. (2000). Is handwriting causally related to learning to write? Treatment of handwriting problems in beginning writers. *Journal of Educational Psychology, 92*, 620–633.

Helman, L., Bear, D. R., Templeton, S., Invernizzi, M., & Johnston, F. (2012). *Words their way with English learners: Word study for phonics, vocabulary, and spelling instruction* (2nd ed.). Boston: Pearson.

Henderson, E. H. (1990). *Teaching spelling* (2nd ed.). Boston: Houghton Mifflin.

Henkes, K. (1991). *Chrysanthemum*. New York: Harper Collins.

Herman, G. (1995). *My dog talks*. New York: Scholastic.

Hiebert, F. H. (1999). Text matters when learning to read. *The Reading Teacher, 52*, 552–566.

Invernizzi, M., Meier, J., & Juel, C. (1996). *PALS 1–3: Phonological awareness literacy screening* (4th ed.). Charlottesville, VA: University Printing Services.

Johnston, F. R., Invernizzi, M., Juel, C., & Lewis-Wagner, D. (2009). *Book buddies: A tutoring framework for struggling readers* (2nd ed.). New York: Guilford Press.

Justice, L. M., Skibbe, L., Canning, A., & Lankford, C. (2005). Preschoolers, print and storybooks: An observational study using eye movement analysis. *Journal of Research in Reading, 28,* 229–243.

Justice, L. M., & Sofka, S. E. (2010). *Engaging children with print: Building early literacy skills through quality read-alouds.* New York: Guilford Press.

LaBerge, D., & Samuels, S. J. (1974). Toward a theory of automatic information processing in reading. *Cognitive Psychology, 6*(2), 293–323.

Leslie, L., & Caldwell, J. S. (2011). *Qualitative Reading Inventory–5.* Boston: Pearson.

Lewison, W. (1992). *Buzz said the bee.* New York: Scholastic.

Lonigan, C. J., Burgess, S. R., & Anthony, J. L. (2000). Development of emergent literacy and early reading skills in preschool children: Evidence from a latent-variable longitudinal study. *Developmental Psychology, 36,* 596–613.

MCP Authors. (1996). *My monster and me.* Boston: Modern Curriculum Press.

McPhail, D. (1998). *A bug, a bear, and a boy.* New York: Scholastic.

McPhail, D. (2000). *Big pig and little pig.* New York: Scholastic.

Menon, S., & Hiebert, E. H. (2005). A comparison of first graders' reading with little books or literature-based basal anthologies. *Reading Research Quarterly, 40*(1), 12–38.

Morris, D. (2005). *The Howard Street tutoring manual: Teaching at-risk readers in the primary grades* (2nd ed.). New York: Guilford Press.

Morris, D., Blanton, L., Blanton, W. E., Nowacek, J., & Perney, J. (1995). Teaching low achieving spellers at their "instructional" level. *Elementary School Journal, 92,* 163–177.

Morris, D., Bloodgood, J. W., Lomax, R. G., & Perney, J. (2003). Developmental steps in learning to read: A longitudinal study in kindergarten and first grade. *Reading Research Quarterly, 38,* 302–328.

Morris, D., Nelson, L., & Perney, J. (1986). Exploring the concept of "spelling instructional level" through the analysis of error-types. *Elementary School Journal, 87,* 181–200.

Nunn, C. (1990). *A buzz is part of a bee.* New York: Children's Press.

O'Connor, R. E. (2007). *Teaching word recognition: Effective strategies for students with learning difficulties.* New York: Guilford Press.

Olsen, J. (2013). *Printing power.* Gaithersburg, MD: Handwriting Without Tears.

Osborne, M. P. (2012). *Magic tree house #48: A perfect time for pandas.* New York: Random House Children's Books.

Perfetti, C. (2007). Reading ability: Lexical quality to comprehension. *Scientific Studies of Reading, 11*(4), 357–383.

Pernick, G. (1996). *Ted's red sled.* Parsippany, NJ: Modern Curriculum Press.

Pinnell, G. S., & Fountas, I. G. (1998). *Word matters: Teaching phonics and spelling in the reading/writing classroom.* Portsmouth, NH: Heinemann.

Rasinski, T. V. (2011). *Daily word ladders: 80+ word study activities that target key phonics skills to boost young learners' reading, writing, and spelling confidence.* New York: Scholastic.

Read, C. (1971). Preschool children's knowledge of English phonology. *Harvard Educational Review, 41,* 1–34.

Richardson, J. (2009). *The next step in guided reading: Focused assessments and targeted lessons for helping every student become a better reader.* New York: Scholastic.

Rockwell, T. (1973). *How to eat fried worms.* New York: Random House.

Roop, C. (2001). *Octopus under the sea.* New York: Scholastic.

Roy, R. (2006). *A to Z mysteries: Detective camp.* New York: Random House.

Rylant, C. (2003). *Henry and Mudge and the wild goose chase.* New York: Simon & Schuster.

Rylant, C. (2007). *Henry and Mudge and the big sleepover.* New York: Simon & Schuster.

Scanlon, D. M., Anderson, K. L., & Sweeney, J. M. (2010). *Early intervention for reading difficulties: The interactive strategies approach.* New York: Guilford Press.

Scieszka, J. (1996). *The true story of the three little pigs.* New York: Puffin Books.

Share, D. L. (1995). Phonological recoding and self-teaching: *Sine qua non* of reading acquisition. *Cognition, 55,* 151–218.

Stanovich, K. E. (2000). *Progress in understanding reading: Scientific foundations and new frontiers.* New York: Guilford Press.

Stilton, G. (2011). *Geronimo Stilton: Rumble in the jungle.* New York: Scholastic.

Storch, S. A., & Whitehurst, G. J. (2002). Oral language and doce-related precursors to reading: Evidence from a longitudinal model. *Developmental Psychology, 38,* 934–947.

Sulzby, E. (1986). Writing and reading: Signs of oral and written language organization in the young child. In W. H. Teale & E. Sulzby (Eds.), *Emergent literacy: Writing and reading* (pp. 50–89). Westport, CT: Ablex.

Templeton, S. (2007). *Revolutionizing vocabulary instruction, K–12: What does the developmental model tell us?* 22nd George Graham Lecture, University of Virginia, Charlottesville, VA.

Templeton, S., & Bear, D. (Eds.). (1992). *Development of orthographic knowledge and the foundations of literacy: A memorial Festschrift for Edmund H. Henderson.* Hillsdale, NJ: Erlbaum.

Templeton, S., & Morris, D. (2000). Spelling. In M. L. Kamil, P. B. Mosenthal, P. D. Pearson, & R. Barr (Eds.), *Handbook of reading research* (Vol. III, pp. 525–543). Mahwah, NJ: Erlbaum.

Torgesen, J. K., Wagner, R. K., & Rashotte, C. A. (1994). Longitudinal studies of phonological processing and reading. *Journal of Learning Disabilities, 27,* 276–286.

Treiman, R., Pennington, B. F., Shriberg, L. D., & Boada, R. (2008). Which children benefit from letter names in learning letter sounds? *Cognition, 106*(3), 1322–1338.

Walpole, S., & McKenna, M. C. (2007). *Differentiated reading instruction: Strategies for the primary classroom.* New York: Guilford Press.

Walpole, S., & McKenna, M. C. (2009). *How to plan differentiated reading instruction: Resources for grades K–3.* New York: Guilford Press.

Walpole, S., McKenna, M. C., & Philippakos, Z. A. (2011). *Differentiated reading instruction in grades 4 and 5: Strategies and resources.* New York: Guilford Press.

Walton, P. D. (1995). Rhyming ability, phoneme identity, letter–sound knowledge, and the use of orthographic analogy by prereaders. *Journal of Educational Psychology, 87,* 587–597.

White, T. G., Sowell, J., & Yanagihara, A. (1989). Teaching elementary students to use word part clues. *The Reading Teacher, 42,* 302–308.

Wylie, R. E., & Durrell, D. D. (1970). Teaching vowels through phonograms. *Elementary English, 47,* 787–791.

Index

Page numbers followed by *f* indicate figures.

Abstract vowel patterns, 183*f*, 184
Alphabet knowledge
    emergent readers and writers and, 62–63, 66–67
    Font Sort strategy and, 87–90, 89*f*, 90*f*
Alphabetic principle, 37
Analogy. *See also* Decoding skills
    overview, 4–5, 4*f*
    Sound/Other Word/Pattern (SOP) strategy and, 211–212, 211*f*
    Words I Know strategy and, 158–159, 159*f*, 160*f*
Assessment. *See also* Informal Decoding Inventory (IDI); Progress monitoring; Tiered Spelling Inventory (TSI)
    beginning readers and writers, 28–29, 30*f*, 37–42, 40*f*–41*f*, 72–73, 73*f*, 74*f*, 126–128, 127*f*, 129*f*
    Concept of Print strategy and, 78
    Concept of Word assessment, 79-81
    decoding and, 219–220
    emergent readers and writers and, 69
    Initial Sound Sort strategy and, 84–85
    knowing when students are ready to move to the next stage and, 72–73, 73*f*, 74*f*, 126–128, 127*f*, 128*f*
    overview, 25–26, 54–55
    Personal Word Wall strategy and, 153–155, 154*f*
    progress monitoring and, 50–54, 50*f*, 52*f*, 53*f*, 54*f*
    transitional readers and writers and, 192–195, 192*f*, 194*f*
    word knowledge instructional zone and, 13–14
    Word Knowledge Toolkit for Beginning Readers, 137
Automatic word recognition (sight words). *See also* Sight words
    beginning readers and writers and, 109, 121*f*, 123, 127, 127*f*, 156
    emergent readers and writers and, 12, 12*f*, 68*f*, 72–73, 75
    Fast Reads strategy and, 144–145, 145*f*
    Hot Seat strategy and, 203–204, 204*f*
    overview, 4*f*
    Speed Sort strategy and, 202–203, 203*f*
    transitional readers and writers and, 190, 197

Balanced literacy diet. *See* Instruction
Be the Word strategy, 77*f*, 82, 98
Beginner stage of word knowledge. *See also* Beginner tier of the TSI
    characteristics of beginning readers and writers, 107–112, 107*f*, 108*f*, 110*f*, 111*f*, 180*f*
    Common Core State Standards (CCSS, 2010), 121, 121*f*
    daily and weekly schedules, 123–126, 124*f*, 126*f*
    instruction, 122–123, 122*f*
    knowing when students are ready to move to, 72–73, 73*f*, 74*f*
    knowing when students are ready to move to the next stage and, 126–128, 127*f*, 129*f*
    literacy standards in CCSS and, 22*f*–23*f*
    milestones of, 123
    overview, 12*f*, 104–107, 105*f*, 106*f*, 128
    word knowledge instructional zone and, 112–121, 114*f*–115*f*, 116*f*, 118*f*, 119*f*
Beginner tier of the TSI. *See also* Beginner stage of word knowledge; Tiered Spelling Inventory (TSI)
    interpreting the results from, 45–47, 46*f*, 47*f*
    overview, 28, 30*f*, 37–42, 40*f*–41*f*
    scoring, 39, 40*f*–41*f*
    when to stop and when to continue, 39, 41–42, 41*f*
Big Picture/Key Words strategy, 131*f*, 174–175, 175*f*, 197*f*, 218–219, 219*f*
Blending sounds, 161–163, 162*f*, 164*f*, 165*f*
Blind Writing Sorts strategy, 197*f*, 209–210, 210*f*
Board games, 149–150, 150*f*, 160
Book organization, 78*f*. *See also* Concept of Print strategy
Breaking Words Apart strategy, 208, 209*f*
Building Words-Reading strategy, 197*f*, 207, 208*f*, 214–215
Building Words-Spelling strategy, 197*f*, 212–214, 213*f*

Chunking skills, 7–8, 9*f*, 190, 197
Class record, 45–47, 46*f*

Clay's Observational Survey, 78
Common Core State Standards (CCSS, 2010)
    beginning readers and writers and, 108, 108*f*, 121, 121*f*
    emergent readers and writers and, 67, 68*f*
    literacy standards in, 20–24, 22*f*–23*f*
    transitional readers and writers and, 187–188, 188*f*
    Word Knowledge Toolkit and, 18
Common long vowel patterns. *See* Long vowel patterns
Complex consonant patterns, 183*f*, 184–185, 185*f*
Concentration strategy, 148, 148*f*, 197*f*, 201–202, 202*f*
Concept of Print strategy, 77–79, 77*f*, 78*f*. *See also* Print concepts
Concept of word assessment, 79–81
Consonant patterns, 183*f*
Consonant-vowel-consonant (CVC) short vowel patterns, 182
Contextual reading and writing, 19–20, 127–128, 217–219, 217*f*, 219*f*
Conventional spellings, 181*f*

Daily schedules. *See* Schedules
Decoding skills. *See also* Analogy
    beginning readers and writers and, 119–121, 119*f*, 122–123
    Informal Decoding Inventory (IDI), 50–54, 52*f*, 53*f*, 54*f*
    multisyllabic words and, 204–208, 206*f*, 208*f*, 209*f*
    overview, 4–5, 4*f*
    transitional readers and writers and, 179–182, 180*f*, 181*f*, 186, 187*f*, 190, 197
    Word Knowledge Toolkit for Transitional Readers, 219–221
Developmental factors
    beginning readers and writers and, 8–13, 10*f*, 12*f*, 112–121, 114*f*–115*f*, 116*f*, 118*f*, 119*f*
    developmental model of word knowledge for grades K-2, 12–13, 12*f*
    emergent readers and writers and, 8–13, 10*f*, 12*f*, 58–67, 59*f*, 60*f*, 61*f*, 62*f*, 63*f*, 64*f*, 65*f*
    literacy standards in CCSS and, 21, 24
    model of word knowledge for grades K-2, 12–13, 12*f*
    overview, 8–13, 10*f*, 12*f*
    transferring word knowledge to context and, 19–20
    transitional stage of word knowledge and, 179–182, 180*f*, 181*f*
    word knowledge instructional zone and, 13–14, 14*f*, 15*f*
Dictated Sentences strategy, 131*f*, 169–170, 172–174
Double-Duty Sorts strategy, 131*f*, 132–136, 134*f*, 135*f*

Elkonin boxes, 165, 165*f*
Emergent stage of word knowledge. *See also* Emergent tier of the TSI; Word Knowledge Toolkit for Emergent Readers
    characteristics of emergent readers and writers, 58–67, 59*f*, 60*f*, 61*f*, 62*f*, 63*f*, 64*f*, 65*f*, 180*f*
    daily and weekly schedules, 69–71, 71*f*

instruction, 66–68, 69*f*
    knowing when students are ready to move to the next stage and, 72–73, 73*f*, 74*f*
    literacy standards in CCSS and, 22*f*
    milestones of, 69
    overview, 12*f*, 56–58, 57*f*, 75, 76–77, 77*f*
Emergent tier of the TSI. *See also* Emergent stage of word knowledge; Tiered Spelling Inventory (TSI)
    interpreting the results from, 45–47, 46*f*, 47*f*
    overview, 28, 30–37, 30*f*, 31*f*, 33*f*, 34*f*, 35*f*, 36*f*, 75
    scoring, 32–35, 33*f*, 34*f*
    when to stop and when to continue, 35–37, 35*f*, 36*f*

Fast Reads strategy, 131*f*, 144–145, 145*f*
Final blends and diagraphs, 114*f*–115*f*, 117, 118*f*
Fingerpoint reading, 79, 81
Fluency, 178–182, 180*f*, 181*f*, 190
Font Sort strategy, 77*f*, 87–90, 89*f*, 90*f*

Games
    Initial Sound Sort strategy and, 86
    Rhyme Work strategy and, 93–95
    Word Knowledge Toolkit for Beginning Readers, 131*f*, 146–150, 146*f*, 147*f*, 148*f*, 149*f*, 150*f*, 160–161
Get to the Word strategy, 77*f*, 82–83
Give Me a Clue! strategy, 197*f*, 210–211
Graphic organizers, 174–175, 175*f*, 218–219, 219*f*
Guess My Category sort strategy, 197*f*, 198–199, 199*f*, 200*f*
Guess My Word activity, 96, 100
Guided Reading, 108, 108*f*, 180*f*

Handwriting instruction, 66–67. *See also* Instruction
Head, Shoulders, Knees, and Toes activity, 98
High-frequency prefixes or suffixes. *See* Prefixes; Suffixes
High-Frequency Word Assessment, 153, 155
High-frequency words. *See also* Automatic word recognition (sight words); Sight words
    beginning readers and writers and, 123
    Fast Reads strategy and, 144–145, 145*f*
    Parking Lot activity, 148–149, 149*f*
    Personal Word Wall strategy and, 152–158, 154*f*, 156*f*, 158*f*, 159*f*, 160*f*
    Sentence Building Strategy and, 143
Homophones/homographs, 185
Hot Potato activity, 94–95
Hot Seat strategy, 197*f*, 203–204, 204*f*
How Many Words? activity, 99, 99*f*

I Spy Sound Blending activity, 162–163, 162*f*
Informal Decoding Inventory (IDI). *See also* Assessment; Progress monitoring
    overview, 50–55, 52*f*, 53*f*, 54*f*
    transitional readers and writers and, 192–195, 192*f*, 194*f*
    Word Knowledge Toolkit for Beginning Readers, 137
Initial blends and digraphs, 113, 114*f*–115*f*, 116
Initial Sound Sort strategy, 77*f*, 83–86, 87*f*, 88*f*

Instruction. *See also* Word Knowledge Toolkit for
        Beginning Readers; Word Knowledge Toolkit
        for Emergent Readers; Word Knowledge Toolkit
        for Transitional Readers; Word Knowledge
        Toolkits
    beginning readers and writers and, 122–123, 122*f*
    comprehensive approach to, 15–16, 16*f*
    emergent readers and writers and, 63–64, 66–68,
        69*f*
    handwriting instruction, 66–67
    one-size-fits-all approach to, 8–13, 10*f*, 12*f*
    transferring word knowledge to context and,
        19–20
    transitional readers and writers and, 182–186,
        183*f*, 184*f*, 185*f*, 187*f*, 188–189, 189*f*
    word knowledge instructional zone, 13–15, 14*f*,
        15*f*
    Word Knowledge Toolkit and, 16–19, 17*f*

Knowledge maintenance, 49–50, 50*f*

Letter Hunts strategy, 77*f*
Letter sounds
    beginning readers and writers and, 123
    Double-Duty Sorts strategy and, 132–136, 134*f*,
        135*f*
    emergent readers and writers and, 62–63, 62*f*, 63*f*
    Initial Sound Sort strategy and, 83–86, 87*f*
    knowing when students are ready to move to the
        next stage and, 73
    Sentence Frames strategy and, 102–103, 103*f*
    transferring word knowledge to context and,
        100–103, 102*f*
Letter-name spelling, 111–112, 181*f*
Letters, 4*f*, 5, 5*f*, 78*f*
Lexile levels, 108, 108*f*, 180*f*
Literacy diet. *See* Instruction
Literacy standards, 20–24, 22*f*–23*f*. *See also*
        Common Core State Standards (CCSS, 2010)
Long vowel patterns, 182–184, 183*f*, 184*f*, 187*f*

Make a Match activity, 94
Manipulating words
    transitional readers and writers and, 191
    Word Knowledge Toolkit for Beginning Readers,
        126, 131–132, 131*f*, 161–169, 162*f*, 164*f*, 165*f*,
        166*f*, 168*f*
    Word Knowledge Toolkit for Emergent Readers,
        77*f*, 92–100, 95*f*, 97*f*, 99*f*
    Word Knowledge Toolkit for Transitional Readers,
        196, 197*f*, 212–216, 213*f*, 215*f*
    Word Knowledge Toolkits and, 17, 17*f*, 18
Memory reading, 58–60, 59*f*, 60*f*, 61*f*, 79–81
Mix and Fix strategy, 197*f*, 216
Mix It Up! strategy, 131*f*, 167–169, 168*f*
Monitoring student progress. *See* Progress monitoring
Morphemes, 4*f*, 5, 5*f*
Move It and Say It strategy, 131*f*, 163–165, 164*f*, 165*f*
Multisyllabic words
    transitional readers and writers and, 186, 187*f*
    Two-Step Sort strategy and, 200, 201*f*
    Word Knowledge Toolkit for Transitional Readers
        and, 204–208, 206*f*, 208*f*, 209*f*
Mystery Bag activity, 96–97, 100

Nonsense word spelling, 7–8, 9*f*

Observational assessment, 78, 129, 128*f*. *See also*
        Assessment
Onset-Rime Work strategy, 77*f*, 99–100
Oral language
    beginning readers and writers and, 122*f*
    emergent readers and writers and, 69*f*
    transitional readers and writers and, 177, 185,
        188–189, 189*f*
Orthographic Features of Study chart, 183*f*
Orthography
    Double-Duty Sorts strategy and, 132–136, 134*f*,
        135*f*
    overview, 6, 6*f*
    Word Sorts (Guess My Category) strategy and,
        198–199, 199*f*, 200*f*

Parking Lot activity, 148–149, 149*f*
Personal Word Wall strategy, 131*f*, 152–158, 154*f*,
        156*f*, 158*f*, 159*f*, 160*f*
Phonemic awareness, 64–65, 163–165, 164*f*, 165*f*
Phonics
    beginning readers and writers and, 121*f*
    emergent readers and writers and, 68*f*
    literacy standards in CCSS and, 22*f*–23*f*
    transferring word knowledge to context and, 102*f*
    transitional readers and writers and, 188*f*
Phonological awareness
    beginning readers and writers and, 121*f*
    emergent readers and writers and, 63–66, 64*f*, 65*f*,
        68*f*
    literacy standards in CCSS and, 22*f*–23*f*
Picture Captions strategy, 77*f*, 91–92, 102
Preconsonantal nasals, 117–118, 118*f*
Prefixes, 206–208, 206*f*, 208*f*, 209*f*
Pretend reading, 58–60, 59*f*, 60*f*, 61*f*
Print concepts
    Concept of Print strategy and, 77–79, 77*f*, 78*f*
    emergent readers and writers and, 58–60, 59*f*, 60*f*,
        61*f*, 68*f*
    literacy standards in CCSS and, 22*f*–23*f*
Print meaning, 78*f*
Print organizations, 78*f*
Print-referencing categories, 78–79
Progress monitoring
    beginning readers and writers and, 54*f*, 126–128,
        126*f*, 127*f*
    emergent readers and writers and, 49, 54*f*, 69
    knowing when students are ready to move to the
        next stage and, 72–73, 73*f*, 74*f*
    overview, 47–54, 48*f*, 50*f*, 52*f*, 53*f*, 54*f*
    transitional readers and writers and, 54*f*, 192–193,
        192*f*
Puppet Sound Blending activity, 163

Quick Write strategy, 77*f*, 90–91

Racetrack Game activity, 97, 97*f*
R-controlled vowels, 119*f*, 120
Read-alouds
    beginning readers and writers and, 124, 125
    emergent readers and writers and, 69*f*, 70, 71
    transitional readers and writers and, 190

Reading words
    beginning readers and writers and, 110–112, 110*f*,
        111*f*
    emergent readers and writers and, 76–83, 78*f*
    transitional readers and writers and, 191
    Word Knowledge Toolkit and, 17, 17*f*, 18
    Word Knowledge Toolkit for Beginning Readers,
        126, 131–150, 134*f*, 135*f*, 138*f*, 142*f*, 143*f*, 145*f*,
        146*f*, 147*f*, 148*f*, 150*f*
    Word Knowledge Toolkit for Emergent Readers,
        77–83, 77*f*, 78*f*
    Word Knowledge Toolkit for Transitional Readers,
        196, 197*f*, 198–208, 199*f*, 200*f*, 201*f*, 202*f*,
        203*f*, 204*f*, 206*f*, 208*f*, 209*f*
Recognizing Multisyllabic Words strategy, 197*f*,
    204–208, 206*f*, 208*f*, 209*f*
Retelling of stories, 58–60, 59*f*, 60*f*, 61*f*
Rhyme, 65, 79
Rhyme Work strategy, 77*f*, 92–95, 95*f*
Rhyming Go Fish activity, 94
Rhyming Head, Shoulders, Knees, and Toes activity,
    95
Rhyming Picture Sorts activity, 93

Schedules
    beginning readers and writers and, 123–126, 124*f*,
        126*f*
    emergent readers and writers and, 69–71, 71*f*
    transitional readers and writers and, 190–192, 191*f*
See You Later, Alligator activity, 93–94
Segmenting words, 103, 163–165, 164*f*, 165*f*
Sentence Bingo activity, 147, 147*f*, 160
Sentence Building strategy, 131*f*, 141–143, 142*f*, 143*f*
Sentence Frames strategy, 77*f*, 102–103, 103*f*
Sentence writing, 102–103, 103*f*, 131*f*, 169–170
Short vowels, 113, 114*f*–115*f*, 116–117
Show Me! strategy, 131*f*, 166–167, 166*f*
Sight words. *See also* Automatic word recognition;
        Automatic word recognition (sight words)
    beginning readers and writers and, 109, 123, 127, 127*f*
    Fast Reads strategy and, 144–145, 145*f*
    overview, 4, 4*f*
    Personal Word Wall strategy and, 152–158, 154*f*,
        156*f*, 158*f*, 159*f*, 160*f*
    Sentence Building Strategy and, 143
Small-group reading instruction
    beginning readers and writers and, 122*f*, 123,
        125–126
    emergent readers and writers and, 69*f*, 70
    transitional readers and writers and, 190, 191
Sorting for Reading activity, 134–136, 135*f*
Sorting for Sound activity, 133–134
Sound Blending strategy, 131*f*, 161–163, 162*f*, 164*f*,
    165*f*
Sound cards, 86, 87*f*, 88*f*
Sound Hunts strategy, 77*f*
Sound/Other Word/Pattern (SOP) strategy, 197*f*,
    211–212, 211*f*
Speed Sort strategy, 197*f*, 202–203, 203*f*
Spelling. *See also* Spelling patterns; Tiered Spelling
        Inventory (TSI)
    beginning readers and writers and, 110–112, 110*f*,
        111*f*, 113–118, 114*f*–115*f*, 116*f*, 118*f*, 121*f*, 122
    emergent readers and writers and, 62–63, 68*f*

literacy standards in CCSS and, 22*f*–23*f*
transferring word knowledge to context and, 102*f*
transitional readers and writers and, 179–182,
    180*f*, 181*f*, 188*f*
word knowledge instructional zone and, 13–15,
    14*f*, 15*f*
Writing Sorts strategy and, 151–152, 152*f*
Spelling patterns. *See also* Spelling
    Blind Writing Sorts strategy and, 209–210, 210*f*
    characteristics of transitional readers and writers
        and, 181–182, 181*f*
    Double-Duty Sorts strategy and, 134–136, 135*f*
    overview, 4*f*, 5, 5*f*, 7–8, 9*f*
    Writing Sorts strategy and, 151–152, 152*f*
Standards, 20–24, 22*f*–23*f*. *See also* Common Core
        State Standards (CCSS, 2010)
Story structure, 58–60, 59*f*, 60*f*, 61*f*
Strategic Readers strategy, 131*f*, 136–141, 138*f*
Student progress, monitoring. *See* Progress
        monitoring
Suffixes, 206–208, 206*f*, 208*f*, 209*f*
Syllable Work strategy, 77*f*, 95–97, 96, 97*f*

Targeted Word Hunts strategy, 77*f*, 101–102, 102*f*
Text selection, 80, 109, 179
Tic-tac-toe activity, 146, 146*f*
Tiered Spelling Inventory (TSI). *See also* Assessment;
        Beginner tier of the TSI; Emergent tier of the
        TSI; Spelling; Transitional tier of the TSI
    beginning readers and writers and, 122
    decoding and, 219–220
    interpreting the results from, 43, 45–47, 46*f*, 47*f*
    knowing when students are ready to move to the
        next stage and, 72–73, 73*f*, 74*f*, 127–128, 127*f*
    overview, 25–29, 27*f*, 28–29, 30*f*, 54–55
    Tracking Text strategy and, 80
    transitional readers and writers and, 189, 192–195,
        192*f*, 194*f*
    Word Knowledge Toolkit for Beginning Readers,
        137
    Word Knowledge Toolkit for Emergent Readers
        and, 103
Toolkit, word knowledge. *See* Word Knowledge
        Toolkits
Tracking Text strategy, 77*f*, 79–82
Transferring word knowledge to context
    demonstrating and maintaining, 127–128, 127*f*
    knowing when students are ready to move to the
        next stage and, 72–73
    progress monitoring and, 50–54, 52*f*, 53*f*, 54*f*
    Word Knowledge Toolkit and, 17, 17*f*, 19
    Word Knowledge Toolkit for Beginning Readers,
        126, 131–132, 131*f*, 169–175, 172*f*, 173*f*, 175*f*
    Word Knowledge Toolkit for Emergent Readers,
        77*f*, 100–103, 102*f*
    Word Knowledge Toolkit for Transitional Readers,
        196, 197*f*, 216–219, 217*f*, 219*f*
Transitional stage of word knowledge. *See also* Word
        Knowledge Toolkit for Transitional Readers
    characteristics of transitional readers and writers,
        178–182, 180*f*, 181*f*
    Common Core State Standards (CCSS, 2010),
        187–188, 188*f*
    daily and weekly schedules, 190–192, 191*f*

Transitional stage of word knowledge *(cont.)*
  decoding and, 219–221
  instruction, 182–186, 183*f*, 184*f*, 185*f*, 187*f*,
      188–189, 189*f*
  knowing when students are ready to move to,
      126–128, 127*f*, 129*f*
  knowing when students are ready to move to the
      next stage and, 192–195, 192*f*, 194*f*
  literacy standards in CCSS and, 23*f*
  milestones of, 189–190
  overview, 12*f*, 176–178, 195
Transitional tier of the TSI. *See also* Tiered Spelling
      Inventory (TSI)
  interpreting the results from, 45–47, 46*f*, 47*f*
  overview, 28, 30*f*, 42–43, 42*f*, 44*f*–45*f*
  scoring, 43, 44*f*–45*f*
Two-Step Sort strategy, 197*f*, 200, 201*f*

Vocabulary development, 70, 210–211
Vowel digraphs, 119*f*, 120–121
Vowel diphthongs, 119*f*, 120–121
Vowel-consonant-*e*, 119*f*, 120, 123

Weekly schedules. *See* Schedules
What's Missing? strategy, 197*f*, 215–216, 215*f*
Within-word spelling pattern, 181*f*
Word Hunts in Reading strategy, 131*f*, 171–172,
      172*f*
Word Hunts in Writing strategy, 131*f*, 172–174, 173*f*,
      197*f*, 217–218, 217*f*
Word knowledge, 69*f*, 70, 122*f*, 127–128
Word knowledge instructional zone. *See also*
      Instruction; Word recognition
  beginning readers and writers and, 112–121,
      114*f*–115*f*, 116*f*, 118*f*, 119*f*
  emergent readers and writers and, 63–64, 66–68,
      69*f*
  overview, 13–15, 14*f*, 15*f*
  transitional readers and writers, 182–186, 183*f*,
      184*f*, 185*f*, 187*f*
  transitional readers and writers and, 197
Word Knowledge Toolkit for Beginning Readers.
      See also Beginner stage of word knowledge;
      Instruction; Word Knowledge Toolkits
  daily and weekly schedules, 124–125, 124*f*
  manipulating words, 131–132, 131*f*, 161–169,
      162*f*, 164*f*, 165*f*, 166*f*, 168*f*
  overview, 130–132, 131*f*, 175
  reading words, 131–150, 134*f*, 135*f*, 138*f*, 142*f*,
      143*f*, 145*f*, 146*f*, 147*f*, 148*f*, 150*f*
  transferring word knowledge to context and,
      131–132, 131*f*, 169–175, 172*f*, 173*f*, 175*f*
  writing words, 131–132, 131*f*, 150–161, 152*f*,
      154*f*, 156*f*, 158*f*, 159*f*, 160*f*
Word Knowledge Toolkit for Emergent Readers.
      See also Emergent stage of word knowledge;
      Instruction; Word Knowledge Toolkits
  manipulating words, 92–100, 95*f*, 97*f*, 99*f*
  overview, 76–77, 77*f*, 103
  reading words, 77–83, 78*f*
  transferring word knowledge to context and,
      100–103, 102*f*
  writing words, 83–92, 87*f*, 88*f*, 89*f*, 90*f*

Word Knowledge Toolkit for Transitional Readers.
      See also Instruction; Transitional stage of word
      knowledge; Word Knowledge Toolkits
  decoding and, 219–221
  manipulating words, 212–216, 213*f*, 215*f*
  overview, 196–198, 197*f*, 221–222
  reading words, 198–208, 199*f*, 200*f*, 201*f*, 202*f*,
      203*f*, 204*f*, 206*f*, 208*f*, 209*f*
  transferring word knowledge to context and,
      216–219, 217*f*, 219*f*
  writing words, 209–212, 210*f*, 211*f*
Word Knowledge Toolkits, 16–19, 17*f*, 72–73. *See
      also* Instruction; Word Knowledge Toolkit for
      Beginning Readers; Word Knowledge Toolkit
      for Emergent Readers; Word Knowledge Toolkit
      for Transitional Readers
Word manipulating. *See* Manipulating words
Word reading. *See* Reading words
Word recognition. *See also* Automatic word
      recognition; Decoding skills
  beginning readers and writers and, 121*f*
  emergent readers and writers and, 68*f*
  literacy standards in CCSS and, 22*f*–23*f*
  overview, 1–2, 4*f*, 5–6, 6*f*, 24
  reasons to focus on, 2–4, 3*f*
  transferring word knowledge to context and,
      19–20
  transitional readers and writers and, 188*f*
Word study, 70–71, 71*f*, 124, 126, 190, 197–198
Word walls, 131*f*, 152–158, 154*f*, 156*f*, 158*f*, 159*f*,
      160*f*
Word Work strategy, 77*f*, 97–99
Word writing. *See* Writing words
Word-by-word reading, 110–112, 110*f*, 111*f*
Words, transferring. *See* Transferring word
      knowledge to context
Words I Know strategy, 131*f*, 158–159, 159*f*, 160*f*
Writing, 179–182, 180*f*, 181*f*
Writing instruction, 69*f*. *See also* Instruction
Writing Observation Guide, 74*f*, 129, 128*f*, 194*f*
Writing Sorts strategy, 131*f*, 151–152, 152*f*
Writing words
  beginning readers and writers and, 110–112, 110*f*,
      111*f*
  emergent readers and writers and, 62–63, 62*f*, 63*f*,
      64*f*
  transitional readers and writers and, 191
  Word Knowledge Toolkit for Beginning Readers,
      126, 131–132, 131*f*, 150–161, 152*f*, 154*f*, 156*f*,
      158*f*, 159*f*, 160*f*
  Word Knowledge Toolkit for Emergent Readers,
      77*f*, 83–92, 87*f*, 88*f*, 89*f*, 90*f*
  Word Knowledge Toolkit for Transitional Readers,
      196, 197*f*, 209–212, 210*f*, 211*f*
  Word Knowledge Toolkits and, 17, 17*f*, 18
Writing workshop
  beginning readers and writers and, 122*f*, 124, 125,
      126
  emergent readers and writers and, 70, 71
  transitional readers and writers and, 190, 191
Written language, 69*f*, 122*f*

Your Pile–My Pile activity, 157